My Favourite Restaurants

in Calgary & Banff

6th Edition

John Gilchrist

Edited by Catherine Caldwell

Escurial Incorporated
Calgary, Alberta

Published by
Escurial Incorporated
9519 Assiniboine Road SE
Calgary, Alberta
Canada T2J 0Z5
Phone: 403•255•7560
Email: escurial@telus.net

Library and Archives Canada Cataloguing in Publication

Gilchrist, John, 1953–
My favourite restaurants in Calgary & Banff / John Gilchrist ;
edited by Catherine Caldwell. – 6th ed.

Includes index.
ISBN 10: 0-9693106-5-X
ISBN 13: 978-0-9693106-5-5

1. Restaurants—Alberta—Calgary—Guidebooks. 2. Restaurants—Alberta—Banff—Guidebooks. 3. Calgary (Alta.)—Guidebooks. 4. Banff (Alta.)—Guidebooks. I. Caldwell, Catherine, 1956 – II. Title.

TX910.C2G54 2006   647.957123'38   C2006-904510-0

CREDITS:
Interior & Cover Production: Jeremy Drought, Last Impression Publishing Service,
    Calgary, Alberta
Cover Illustration: Jon Sawyer, Calgary, Alberta
Printing: Friesens Corporation, Altona, Manitoba

Printed and bound in Canada

Table of Contents

Acknowledgements iv
Foreword v
Introduction vii

Big Eats I
Little Eats 139
Dining in Downtown Calgary (Map) 158

The Lists: Add Ons 160
            Baked Goods/Sweets 160
            Banff/Lake Louise 160
            Breakfast/Brunch 161
            Canadian 161
            Canmore 161
            Chinese 162
            Coffee Bars 162
            Contemporary 162
            Diners 162
            Drinks 162
            Food Markets 163
            French/Continental 163
            German/Austrian 163
            Greek 163
            Hamburgers/Hot Dogs 163
            High Tone 163
            Historic Setting 163
            Indian 164
            Interesting Ambience 164
            Italian/Pizza 164
            Japanese 164
            Latin American 165
            Middle Eastern 165
            Most Obscure 165
            Okotoks/Foothills 165
            One of a Kind (Almost) 165
            Red Meat 165
            Romantic 166
            Seafood/Sushi 166
            Thai 166
            Vegetarian 166
            Vietnamese 166

The Best of the Best 167

Acknowledgements

WE wanted to try something different with the cover of this edition. We mulled around various ideas involving dinner plates and finally decided what needed to be done. We needed to call Richard and Brenda White, two people with more ideas than any couple should have. We met them over coffee, and before I could knock back a double espresso, an idea had sprouted. It revolved around a finger-smear of the number six (for the sixth edition—get it?) left in raspberry sauce on a used dessert plate. Bingo!

The Whites are but two of the key friends who have supported this—and all—of our books. I say "our" because I acknowledge the true power behind the words, my wife and editor, the charming Catherine Caldwell. Although the reviews are my opinions, I (almost) always bow to Catherine's judgment. Above that, both her ability to smooth out my writing and her sense of punctuation are beyond compare. She is truly Queen of the Comma (and a fine dinner companion).

As well, we jointly thank Barb and Bob Gerst, Silvia and Leo Perry, Lynn and Cam Hodgson, Elizabeth Haigh, and Christine and Graham Chambers for their unwavering support during the process. And although they say you can choose your friends but not your family, we'll happily throw Catherine's two sisters—Barb and Jayni—along with their respective husbands Roy Kaufman and Pat Young, into that friend mix. They all figure in various parts of these reviews, sometimes by being dragged along to restaurants, other times by scouting out new joints to hit. It's a good team.

And speaking of family, where would Catherine and I be without our parents? A big, happy thanks to Sally and Keith Caldwell and Marion and Dawne Gilchrist.

We also want to acknowledge the partnership with the Calgary Downtown Association for the third time around. Their participation is invaluable.

Let's not forget stalwart designer Jeremy Drought who once again prettied-up our pages and did so in record time. Thanks also to cover artist Jon Sawyer for patiently adapting all our whims and making our finger-smear a reality. Good work guys.

And how about that James Martin, eh? Can that kid write or what? It's his fourth Foreword for us. A few more, and we may compile them into a book by themselves.

Then there are the restaurateurs who continue to put out the food. Just think how skinny I'd be without all of you! Thanks!

Foreword

by James Martin

L AST Thursday, I chased a plate of General Tso's chicken with a fortune cookie: *You are one of the people who "goes places in life."* Truer words were never wrote—assuming those quotation marks weren't meant to "imply" that I'm "actually" a hopeless "charity case."

Yep, I'm a chap who has gone places. Here? Indeed. There? Check. Everywhere? No, but I've gotten within three bus stops and liked what I saw. North/south, up/left, there's always one constant (two, counting dandruff). *Food.*

(I'm writing this sentence while two-fisting a smoked meat on rye. Hot fat trickling down both forearms, my typing prowess nonetheless remains tbuonowswsm sib;r tiy rgubj>)

Wherever I go, there I eat. The gentle click of a temporomandibular joint, the rhythmic grind of molars, the high-pitched giggle of salivary enzymes as they set about their business: chewing is the soundtrack of my life. All it takes is a nip of cardamom, or a waft of turducken, to jimmy the floodgates of memory.

I'm blessed with perfect culinary recall, give/take some embroidery. When in Rome, I've eaten tuna-topped pizza, using the crusts to incite a symphony of cooing and pecking amongst the pigeons swarming Campo de Fiori. I've stood next to a roadside shack in the Himalayan foothills of N. India, scarfing down heaven-sent aloo tikki with one hand, nursing a bouquet of toy helicopters in the other. (Think a mitfull of plastic mini-choppers would render one immune from the relentless patter of itinerant toy salesmen? Negatory. But that aloo tikki made up for the hassle. Must've been the tamarind.) Then there was the time I found myself two klicks over Iceland, simultaneously savouring my second sunset in six hours (can't explain it, so don't ask) and a tender turkey-cheddar wrap, while my fellow passengers quietly slumbered.

Perfection, all.

Oh sure, there have been missteps. Rural Wyoming does great T-bone, lousy stout. There are better things to eat in Denver than sautéed rattlesnake. (The problem wasn't the rattler. The problem was the unconscionable act of death-by-drowning-in-cream-cheese.) And don't get me started on Lisbon, where I mashed three unripe bananas into a mickey of absinthe, resulting in: emetic rumblings, mistaken bidets, and unhappy landladies. Stupid bananas.

Enough travel talk. Regardless of how far/wide I wander, Calgary will always be home. And this toddling town has given me oodles of delightful food memories.

I still dream about the steak and Guinness pie at a certain Mission pub. (Hint: it's "The ___ & ___.") Something about flaky pastry soaking up thick, delicately spiced tomato sauce got me every time—with "every time" loosely translating as "twice weekly." I even squirreled away a yellowing newspaper clipping of the chef's secret recipe, minus (I suspect) a key ingredient or two. (Probably something deviously obvious, perhaps a single Kopi Luwak coffee bean finely ground by elves using a platinum-rimmed mortar.) Then, like a phantom, the pie vanished from the menu. When I finally mustered the gumption to quiz a waitress, she played dumb. "Nope. Never had that here." A little mystery keeps romance fresh.

Then there are the perennials, like that fixture of the Stampede midway, Those Tiny Donuts. Oh, how I used to beg for a bag of that miniaturized, deep-fried goodness! I whined! (Tempers flared.) I kicked! (Strangers glared.) I cried! (Security guards circled, trigger fingers a-itch.) My jiggery-pokery always paid glorious dividends. Sweet, sweet sugar! Thine crystalline touch haunts me still. Forgive my maudlin outburst, but nostalgia warms the ice cap that is my heart. [Cue the trumpet-honk of nose blowing.] Ah, the summer of 2004. *Sniff.* Good times.

Since we're talking Stampede, allow me to brag about once infiltrating the *ne plus ultra* of cowboy dining: ranahans. Secreted away on the third level of the Grandstand, ranahans is so exclusive that it doesn't stoop to: (a) taking reservations, (b) opening more than ten days/year, or (c) using capital letters. Yet there I was, rubbing shoulders with captains of industry, royal blue-bloods, and Hollywood glitterati. (None of whom, I dare suggest, compare to the exquisitely roasted AAA Alberta beef tenderloin drizzled with sage au jus. Darn fine sushi, too.) And I did so without impersonating a waiter or hiding in the endive delivery.

I'd love to chalk up my coup to sparkling personality and a thick head of hair, but the truth is: I know a guy, and this guy is *connected.* Modesty prevents me from using his name (once, over backyard burgers, Winston Churchill suggested namedropping as the pinnacle of tackiness–Gandhi & I nodded vigorously, then pushed Elvis into the pool), so let me just say that this guy knows his way around the Calgary dining scene. Whether you're out to impress Important Clients Who Like French Reductions, or simply looking for a quick pizza after escorting third cousins on a rousing evening of community theatre, this guy knows *just the perfect place.* His brain is an indispensable storehouse of eatin' info. (Without tipping my hand, let's say that *maybe* he's been reviewing Calgary and area restaurants on CBC Radio for, like, over twenty-five years. He *may* also write a weekly *Herald* column, but that's all you'll get out of me.)

Hey, you know what would be crackerjack? If you could somehow download all this guy's know-how into a single, easy-to-use compendium. Something portable that fits into a purse or glove compartment, so you could take him with you, every place you went. Why, you'd never go hungry again!

Nobody steal my idea, okay?

James Martin will write for food.
His craftsmanship can be seen in The Penguin Anthology of Canadian Humour *and on the freshly painted exterior of his mom's house.*

Introduction

ANYBODY notice a boom going on around these parts? This "economy" thing has not been easy on the restaurant business. On the one hand, we're seeing a record number of new—and good—restaurants opening around Calgary and the Bow Corridor. On the other, though, we're anticipating the imminent demolition of a number of buildings that house good eateries (think Penny Lane Mall, the Aberdeen Block, and more.) So, like many things, it's a fluid market.

The boom has also impacted restaurant staffing. There just aren't enough cooks, servers, managers, bartenders, and so on to go around. That means service in the local hospitality industry isn't always where it should be and inconsistencies in the kitchens will come as no surprise.

That's where this book comes in. Calgary has hit a million people, many of whom want to eat out. And has anyone counted how many people live in Canmore and the Bow Corridor lately? There are also loads of visitors who want to try our fare. No matter which group you're from, I'm hoping that this compendium will steer you to the primo places, food establishments to which you are happy to give your (or someone else's) hard-earned dollars.

This book is all about my favourites in the local food scene. The reviews are compiled from research and writing I have done for CBC Radio One's *Calgary Eyeopener*, the *Calgary Herald*, *Avenue* or *Where Calgary* magazines, and the food and travel programs I do for the University of Calgary.

There is no advertising in this book—no one paid to be here. I've included all sorts of multicultural cuisines from establishments that do things as close as possible to the way they are done "back home." No short cuts. No cheaping out. That doesn't necessarily mean expensive. I look for value in a meal or the food I buy. Most of the establishments reviewed in this book are owner-operated, usually a good indicator of a decent place. There are no chains: Not that I don't like them; they just don't need my help. There are few places that have more than three locations—I have to cut it off somewhere. And I've tried to balance the book in terms of cultures included, prices, dining styles, and geographic locations.

There are over 230 recommended spots for food on these pages, about half of which are new since my last book in 2003. There's a new Tibetan café, a Belgian-inspired brasserie, a Serbian creperie, a vegan/vegetarian spot, and lots of new bistros and sushi bars. There are even places in Carstairs and Airdrie.

There are two main sections to this book—"Big Eats" and "Little Eats." There's sometimes a fine line between these two categories, but generally, Big Eats is about restaurants that offer a full sit-down meal and are a page in length. Little Eats are shorter and are about places that either specialize in one aspect of food (say chocolate or baked goods), are food markets, or serve snacks or fast meals (like burgers or takeout sandwiches).

Here are more nuts and bolts:

- The "Big Eats" and "Little Eats" sections are each arranged alphabetically.

- In order to include as many food establishments as possible, I've created what I refer to as "Add Ons." In some of the reviews, there is information on additional, related establishments—these are the Add Ons. But the thing is, you won't find these Add Ons as you flip alphabetically through the book. For the full lineup, you'll need to check out "The Lists" and "The Best of the Best," starting on page 160 and 167 respectively.

- All phone numbers begin with the area code 403 unless otherwise noted.

- Each downtown restaurant or food outlet is indicated by a "Downtown That's the Spot" logo. The map on page 158 shows all the downtown locations. (Handy, eh?)

- Credit Card abbreviations are as follows: **V** for Visa, **MC** for MasterCard, and **AE** for American Express.

- Cost categories are based on dinner for two with appetizers, main courses, and desserts (or equivalent) and include tax but not drinks or gratuity: **$** means under $40, **$$** ranges from $40 to $70, and **$$$** pushes over $70. (The way prices are going, I think I'll include a **$$$$** category next time.)

- New to this book is "corkage." It's now possible in some places to bring your own wine (store-bought that is, not homemade hooch) to an eatery. There is often a charge for glassware and handling. That's known as "corkage," and if a restaurant is licensed to do this, I've included that information, and the price, in the paragraph preceding each Big Eats review.

- I wish we could have some consistency on smoking. This book covers four different jurisdictions from Calgary and the area west, plus a few more to the north and south. Each seems to have a slightly different spin on smoking. I can't figure it all out, so good luck. We're thankfully edging toward a totally non-smoking environment, but this book indicates the status of things in the summer of 2006.

Whether you're new to town or you're an old-timer, I hope you enjoy this book. There's a lot of good eating in here. I should know. I ate the whole thing.

John Gilchrist
Calgary, Alberta
August, 2006

Aida's

Lebanese

2208–4 Street SW
Phone: 541•1189
Monday 11 am–9 pm, Tuesday–Thursday 11 am–10 pm
Friday & Saturday 11 am–11 pm
Reservations recommended, especially on weekends — Fully licensed — Non-smoking
V, MC, AE, Debit — $–$$

S HORTLY after the turn of the last millennium, a new restaurant popped up on 4th Street SW. For an area with many restaurants, a number of which have come and gone over the years, this wasn't a notable event in itself. An L-shaped room that would seat about fifty, Aida's (pronounced eye-duhz) was small and unassuming. And charmingly, the owner named it after herself.

Her choice of name was hardly ego driven. Aida is one of the more humble restaurateurs I've met. But she's a known commodity, having had Café Med just a few doors away in the 1990s, and she wanted people to know that she was still around.

It didn't take long before crowds were forming for her lentil soup, crunchy fattoush salad, and creamy, garlicky hummus. The food is good here, in part because the Lebanese food culture offers so much variety and freshness and flavour. It has both intensity and simplicity at the same time. And the rich, zippy tastes of Lebanese cuisine satisfy everyone, from the most assiduous vegan to the most carnivorous carnivore. I've seen tabbouleh lovers and lamb-kebab aficionados dine peacefully at Aida's. And then there is Aida. Her food just tastes better. She's one of those people who imbues goodness into it. Why? Who knows? Best not to question that which works.

Suffice it to say that Aida's fattoush is the best I've had anywhere. Lots of greens, crisp pita, tasty dressing, and a sprinkling of sumac come together to elevate this dish beyond boring salad-dom. And her dips—especially the hummus and the red-pepper-based mouhammara—are exceptional. I like her kebabs, her soups, and her kibbeh. I can't really think of anything I don't like about Aida's food. She also tries to keep Lebanese wine and beer on the menu for those who want the full cultural experience.

I can't complain about the prices either. Aida's is one of the best-value restaurants in this book. The falafel (chickpea patties) platter, for example, includes fattoush or tabbouleh and a dip of either hummus or baba ghannouj (made with eggplant) for $9.50. And service-wise, you won't go wrong either. Aida has a faithful staff, some of whom have been there for years, though admittedly, it hasn't been that long since Aida's opened. (I named Aida's the Best New Restaurant of 2000 in one of my CBC Radio broadcasts.)

I just hope it's many years before Aida decides to retire. (This building may be scheduled for demolition in the future, but I'm keeping my fingers crossed that doesn't happen either.)

Alexis Bistro

French

4824 – 16 Street SW
Phone: 214 • 3616
Monday – Friday 11:45 am – 3 pm, Monday – Thursday 5 pm – 10 pm
Friday & Saturday 5 pm – 11 pm
Reservations recommended, especially on weekends — Fully licensed — Corkage $20
Patio — Non-smoking
V, MC, AE, Debit — $$–$$$

ALEXIS is one of the hot crop of bistros to pop up recently. And it's one of the boldest restaurant concepts I've seen. Not that the food and experience are that outrageous. No, Alexis is the kind of good contemporary French bistro that you'll find in most major cities right now. The difference here—and the boldness—is its location in the heart of Altadore, at an address that will have most people asking, "Where?"

Over the years, various restaurants have come and gone in this strip-mall location; it's a residential spot that has had difficulty attracting customers from across town. To put a high-end, contemporary bistro in this location is bold, but it seems to be working.

Alexis is a top-notch place. The room itself is lovely, done in the current whites and browns and highlighted with an interesting broken-plate chandelier and a polished concrete floor. It's very chic and "in." It's also loud with all those hard surfaces, but it's energizing too.

One of the owners, Brett Johnson, was an original partner in Muse (a restaurant in the Kensington area), and he has put together a strong restaurant team. An appetizer of seared ahi tuna with sautéed wild mushrooms and a veal reduction is simply outstanding, elevated beyond the norm by a richness in the veal reduction that brings out elements of chocolate and licorice. That's one dish that haunts me. A dish of mussels with roasted tomatoes and chorizo is rich and smoky, with velvety smooth mussels. And the scallops in a Riesling cream are excellent. The food at Alexis is good, especially the seafood.

The wine list is short but well conceived and food friendly, and the service is good too. The introduction of lunch service has broadened its appeal. But be warned—Alexis does not have neighbourhood mom-and-pop pricing. Dinner for two, with a couple of glasses of wine, is upwards of $100. The real question is, does the quality and value match the price? And as well as any other upscale place around town, yes it does.

Alexis does have two other ace cards. When it's warm out, it has one of the few patios not pushed right up against a major thoroughfare. And it's got loads of free parking right out front. Great any time, but especially fabulous when it's cold out.

Anpurna

Indian (Vegetarian)

175B–52 Street SE
Phone: 235 • 6028
Tuesday–Friday 11 am–2:30 pm, 5 pm–8:30 pm, Saturday & Sunday 11 am–8:30 pm
Reservations recommended — No alcoholic beverages — Non-smoking
V, Debit — $

As far as obscure restaurants go, Anpurna has it all: an oddball location, an interesting decor, unique food, unusual hours, and great prices. Anpurna features vegetarian Gujarati cuisine, meaning the vegetarian food of Gujarat, a western state of India. Not all of the food of this state is vegetarian, but Anpurna focuses on that side of it, as well as on a few vegetarian dishes from other regions. And it's good food.

First, though, you have to find Anpurna. It's in a little strip mall on the southwest corner of Memorial Drive and 52nd Street SE. You can only enter the parking lot if you're heading east or south, so if you miss it, be prepared for an elaborate turnaround process.

Once found, Anpurna exudes a rough-hewn charm that is partly leftover from the fish and chip shop that used to inhabit the place and partly applied by owners Bena and Heimat Raiyarella. The chairs are vinyl and chrome, a map of India adorns one wall, a pop cooler hums in front of another wall, and a bunch of Bollywood videos sits in a rack awaiting rental. They've perked up the spot over the past few years with new carpets and new wall hangings, but it still retains a casual, family tone.

There are about thirty items on the Anpurna's menu, none of which contain meat, fish, or eggs. Some do have dairy products though.

We almost always have a masala dossa each, simply because it's the best in town. (Not that you can get a lot of dossas locally, but still, it's excellent.) This is a kind of crispy crepe made from lentil-flour batter. It is fried on a large, flat grill and then folded around cooked, spiced potatoes. It's served with a small bowl of dal, which you can either pour over the dossa or use for dipping. Any way you do it, it's a great dish.

And we always have the kachori too, a dish locally unique to Anpurna. These are little dough balls filled with lentils. Doesn't sound terribly exciting does it? But dip them in a sprite mint sauce and you've got one lively appetizer. We usually get a couple of extras to take home. They reheat nicely for a snack.

Now I do have to caution you that prices have skyrocketed over the past few years. Some are edging perilously close to the $11 mark! Which means Anpurna not only offers great food, but exceptional value.

3

Atlas

Persian

#100, 1000 – 9 Avenue SW
Phone: 230 • 0990
Tuesday – Sunday 11 am – 9 pm
Reservations recommended, especially on weekends — No alcoholic beverages
Non-smoking
V, MC, AE, Debit — $ – $$

AMIR and Satyar Khezri are good boys. That's what their mother, Pari Khezri, says. And she ought to know. She spends her working hours with them at Atlas Specialty Supermarket & Persian Cuisine. Amir manages the kitchen, Satyar handles the front end, and Pari oversees the whole operation with a smile. Her gentle demeanour sets the tone for Atlas—a friendly, family-owned restaurant in the burgeoning west end of downtown Calgary.

Atlas has gained a loyal following for its kebabs; for its Persian stews of walnuts, pomegranate paste, and chicken or of eggplant and beef sirloin; and for its Persian dry goods. There's a nice selection of Persian pickles, dried fruits, salted almonds, and pomegranate juice beside the sixty-seat dining room. Sand-coloured tiles cover the floor, and a desert-dune motif adorns the walls. A silver samovar sits in one corner showing that, as in all good Persian restaurants, hot tea is always available.

The food is at once traditional and contemporary. Spiked on huge flat skewers, the beef strip loin (barg), the chicken (joojeh), and the ground-beef (koobideh) kebabs sizzle on the grill. Next to the skewers, fillets of salmon may be cooking under a slather of Persian spices. Amir sometimes uses one of his mother's herb mixes to create a new dish, substituting salmon for a traditional Iranian white fish. North American ingredients have allowed him to think more globally about the cuisine.

The global thinking adds a fresh attitude to the menu too, showing a little Calgary sass from the twenty-something brothers. The Kia Combo is "named after the guy who invented it," and the Atlas Special is "so good we named it after ourselves." And although the platter for two is obviously for sharing, customers are encouraged to "tackle it alone for the king-sized appetite." There's nothing hidebound about these folks.

Although the Khezris have adapted to their new community, they remain on the outside in one aspect: They do not serve alcohol. Since it is contrary to their Shia beliefs, they leave that to other restaurants. Instead, they'll cheerfully pour another glass cup of tea for their customers. And in a nod to tradition, Amir and Satyar will teach newcomers the true Persian way of drinking it (pop a sugar cube into your mouth and strain the tea through it). Sometimes tradition can't be improved upon.

They're good boys, Amir and Satyar. Just ask Pari.

Avenue Diner

Contemporary Comfort Food

105 Stephen Avenue Walk SW
Phone: 263•2673
Monday to Friday 7 am–3 pm, Saturday & Sunday 8 am–3 pm
Reservations not accepted — Fully licensed — Patio — Non-smoking
V, MC, AE, Debit — $–$$

S o you're strolling Stephen Avenue, admiring all the restaurants, wondering which one to choose for lunch. You salivate over a few menus and your stomach starts to growl. But so does your wallet. Look at those prices! Just fine if someone else's expense account is footing the bill, but today you're dining on your own dime. You want something stylish, but with enough substance to fill the hole that's been gaping since you missed breakfast. If you don't want to break the bank, where do you go?

Avenue Diner is a good bet. They label their cuisine as Contemporary Comfort Food. They serve breakfast all day, plus they do big sandwiches and soups and turkey pot pie and mac and cheese. And they do it with panache. You can get a salmon club sandwich with both grilled and smoked salmon plus capicollo ham, roasted red-pepper cream cheese, and fresh basil. For $13. Not bad at all. Or how about a grilled cheese sandwich with brie, gruyère, and cheddar for $10? Or lemon-ricotta pancakes with blueberry sauce for $10?

They have an eye for style at Avenue Diner. Owner Heather Chell is one of the most stylish restaurateurs in the city, and she serves both style and substance on her plates too. Want half a grapefruit? She'll have it grilled and topped with pomegranate syrup. How about an omelette? She'll get you one with wild mushrooms, spinach, and aged cheddar. The place may be called a diner, but don't expect to find any greasy spoons here.

Just hope to find a table. Avenue is a long, narrow room with a lunch counter out front and a raised table area in the back. The walls have been taken down to the original sandstone, and a long banquette in the back eases the cramped seating. But it's still tight, even tighter when you've pounded back one of Avenue's lunches. You may need help extricating yourself if you've eaten an appetizer, a main course, and a dessert.

My recommendation to those with an average-sized appetite? Delete one of the first two courses to save room for dessert. The brownie with vanilla ice cream, the rice pudding, the apple-berry crumble, or whatever they've whipped up that day will need some serious space in your innards. But it's well worth the self-control. And no matter how many courses you indulge in, Avenue Diner will be a relief to your wallet.

Baker Creek Bistro

Casual Gourmet

Bow Valley Parkway, 13 kilometres east of Lake Louise
Phone: 522•2182
June–Thanksgiving: Daily 8 am–2 pm, 5 pm–10 pm — Call for fall & winter hours
Reservations recommended — Fully licensed — Corkage $19 — Deck — Non-smoking
V, MC, Debit — $–$$$

ARRIVING at Baker Creek Chalets is akin to stumbling on a collection of fairy tale cottages in the middle of the woods. Which, come to think of it, is pretty much what the chalets and Baker Creek Bistro are—rustic log cabins nestled in tall pines, topped with shiny red roofs, lush with overflowing flower baskets, in the summer at least. In the winter, change that last one to cabins settled in meringue-like snow drifts peaked against smoking chimneys. Baker Creek Chalets and the accompanying bistro are idyllic.

They are almost exactly halfway between Castle Junction and Lake Louise on the Bow Valley Parkway (Highway 1A), the only collection of buildings on that twenty-kilometre stretch. Baker Creek makes a quiet, refreshing stop when motoring in this region.

But Baker Creek Bistro is much more than a rest stop. With John Udell, former chef of Bonterra, at the bistro's helm, the food achieves a level that would be well received anywhere.

I had a crepe filled with cured salmon and rolled in lemon aioli a couple of years ago and can still taste it. That clean, distinct, tantalizing flavour is crisp in my mind. These days, Udell has a crepe-less menu, at least he did when I wrote this. But he's always changing things. Who knows—they may be back on by now.

Udell does, however, have a dinner appetizer of lobster and sesame cannoli with cucumber salsa and sweet-pepper sauce ($14). Sounds like a fair replacement. If a lunch sandwich is in order, there's venison and onion rings on baguette with a salad ($16). Or if you're up for breakfast, there's a Baker Creek BLT with hash browns ($10). And if you brought the kids along, there's a grilled cheddar sandwich with curly fries ($6). I could handle one of those myself.

And there's always dessert. Bread pudding with vanilla gelato and poached pears; apple cobbler with maple-walnut gelato; pineapple upside-down cake with crème fraîche and rum sauce. It's all good stuff.

This is high-quality food without the sky-high mountain prices. The top price at dinner is $36 for a venison chop with prosciutto, elk involtini, and corn cake. Not bad, considering. And considering the setting, the log cabin dining room, the big view, the carved bears that peak into the dining room through the windows, it's well worth it.

Note: Baker Creek Bistro's hours shorten in the non-summer months. Make sure to call ahead and check exact opening times.

www.bakercreek.com

Bali

Indonesian

611–6 Street SW
Phone: 261•9888
Monday–Friday 11 am–2 pm, Monday–Thursday 5 pm–9 pm
Friday & Saturday 5 pm–10 pm
Reservations recommended — Fully licensed — Non-smoking
V, MC, AE, Debit — $–$$

I N spite of the numerous oil connections between Alberta and Indonesia, we've never seen much for Indonesian cuisine around Calgary. Fortunately, the Bali opened in 2005 and helps fill that gap.

It's a cheerful place with a Southeast Asian look. It was previously an Asian-fusion restaurant called Passion, and the Bali owners kept the waterfall wall near the door and the contemporary Asian chairs and wall sconces. And they have added carvings and decorations from Indonesia.

There are options on how to approach the Bali's menu. They serve three versions of rijsttafels, the Dutch-Indonesian hybrid of small dishes served for sharing. The Royal rijsttafel has nineteen dishes and serves up to four people for $120. The simpler Deluxe at $80 has thirteen dishes. That's not a bad deal, and it's an interesting way to eat Indonesian. But we decided to choose off the menu.

We ordered five dishes for four of us (each one in the $12 to $14 range), plus an individual bowl of coconut rice each. We started with gado-gado, the salad of vegetables, egg, noodles, and peanut sauce. It was a great gado-gado with a seriously spiced peanut sauce. We also had the shrimp curry, the coconut chicken, the Bali spicy beef, and the sweet pork dish known as babi kecap. We liked them all, but the faves were the shrimp curry and the sweet pork, thanks to their distinctive, forceful sauces. Each dish was sided with some greens and some diced carrots—not much for variety in that area. The variety comes in the sauces on the meats.

On a cautionary note, this is not the place for delicate palates or those who don't like "different" flavours. It's also not the place if you have peanut allergies. It's almost impossible to remove peanuts from this cuisine, so it's just best to avoid the Bali if you are one of the unfortunates.

We also had a dessert of shaved ice with a brown-sugar syrup poured over top and small green-bean noodles floating about in it. If you like Chinese bubble teas and tapioca desserts, this is okay. But if you don't, it has a texture you may find off-putting.

We found service at the Bali to be charming and pleasant. They have both Indonesian and Dutch staff who can explain the dishes and offer cultural insights. And given the sparseness of Indonesian restaurants around here, that's a good thing.

Bangkoknoi

Thai

1324 Centre Street N
Phone: 277•8424
Monday–Friday 11:30 am–2:30 pm, Monday–Thursday 5 pm–9:30 pm
Friday & Saturday 5 pm–10 pm, Sunday 5 pm–9 pm
Reservations accepted — Fully licensed — Corkage $25 — Non-smoking
V, MC, Debit — $$

S OME Thai restaurants are more visible than others. Partly that's because some restaurateurs are good at marketing and being noticed. Others tend to sit back and let the food do the talking. Bangkoknoi falls into the latter category.

Bangkoknoi's Centre Street location is the former Scooza-Mi and, before that, the Ercole's spot. It's a visually active room that has been done in sumptuous blues and golds and overlain with Thai decorations. The restaurant may be demure in its marketing, but once inside, there is no subtlety about the Thai look. That extends to the plates and cutlery: bronze forks and spoons, beautiful gold-filigreed plates and rice bowls, and a colourful assortment of hand-painted dishes. Perfect for the elegant, colourful food served on them.

If we had only one cuisine to eat for the rest of our lives, Thai would likely be it. Catherine says that good Thai food makes her hungrier as she eats. And I can tell that Bangkoknoi's food works its wonders on her because, when we're there, she eats faster than I do and concentrates more on eating than on conversation. She hardly ever talks at Bangkoknoi.

We both love a dish called shu shee salmon, big chunks of grilled salmon served in a thick red-curry sauce. The fish and the curry complement each other perfectly, the creaminess of the curry highlighting the grilled salmon taste (I want to run out and get some just by writing about it). We also like the larb, a northeastern Thai dish of spiced chicken tossed with red onion, scallions, and cilantro. And the panang curry, although with a similar sauce to that of the shu shee salmon, is heightened by pineapple. Even the coconut rice is creamy and luscious.

This is skilful cooking, rich and aromatic, lovely on the plate, and satisfying on the palate. And light on the pocketbook. Most dishes hover around $10; the seafoods roll up to $12 or $13. Great value. All nicely served by family members.

And the restaurant name? Bangkoknoi refers to one of the owners (his name is Noi) and his hometown. It's as if I moved to Thailand and opened a restaurant called "Calgaryjohn." Now wouldn't that be an interesting thing to do?

But until then, I'll have to content myself with the food of great Thai restaurants like Bangkoknoi and a few quiet moments with the charming Catherine.

The Bavarian Inn

Bavarian & Austrian with a Rocky Mountain Twist

75 White Avenue, Bragg Creek
Phone: 949·3611
Wednesday–Friday 5 pm–close, Saturday & Sunday 11:30 am–close
June–August: Also open Tuesday 5 pm–close
Reservations recommended — Fully licensed — Deck — Non-smoking
V, MC, Debit — $$–$$$

THE Bavarian Inn has the woody, spotless look of a Black Forest inn and a menu of Bavarian and Austrian dishes to match. It's divided into two sections, a dining room with booths and tables focused around a fireplace and a lounge with more casual seating. Outside there's a deck surrounded by big spruce trees. It's the kind of place where the beer steins are chilled and the welcome is warm, whether you're in hiking boots or a jacket and tie.

And when spargel is in season, it is totally packed. Spargel is white asparagus grown under a straw cover so that the chlorophyll doesn't develop. During the May to June season, the folks at The Bavarian Inn fly it in regularly from Holland and Germany. Good white asparagus has a delicate, almost sparkly taste. I think much of the appeal is that it is one of the first spring vegetables to hit the plate, and it tastes so fresh and clean. And during the season, they do it justice at The Bavarian Inn with weekly menus of soups, salads, and main courses to satisfy their regulars' passion for the spears.

We started our spargel dinner with a plate of the white asparagus in a sun-dried tomato vinaigrette and fresh spinach in a smoked-bacon and garlic dressing. The flavours offered a tart, forceful backdrop to the asparagus. We also had a bowl of puréed white-asparagus soup that was creamy and delightful. For the main course, I tried the white asparagus with Wiener schnitzel, steamed potatoes, and dollops of three different hollandaise sauces—tomato, tarragon, and regular. I liked it a lot. The schnitzel, a thin slice of breaded veal, was well prepared and leaned toward saltiness, but the sauces and the almost neutral quality of the asparagus worked well with it.

Spargel-season dishes vary in pricing from year to year, but are usually in line with the regular menu. And regular main plates are in the $19 to $34 range.

Service is provided by a team who are obviously proud of their food and familiar with the many regulars who come to The Bavarian Inn. They do an excellent job of bringing hot food and cold drinks promptly to their hungry fans.

The Bavarian Inn has a lot of good things going for it—good food, nice room, excellent service, and a lovely setting. And, of course, the spargel.

www.thebavarianinn.com

Belgo

Belgian-Inspired Brasserie

501–8 Avenue SW
Phone: 265•6555
Monday–Wednesday 11 am–11 pm, Thursday & Friday 11 am–midnight
Saturday noon–midnight
Reservations recommended — Fully licensed — Corkage $15 — Patio — Non-smoking
V, MC, AE, Debit — $$$

BELGO opened in early 2006 to great fanfare. It was to be a serious restaurant from the folks who brought us the Cowboys and Ceili's night spots. The owners chose an ambitious Belgian brasserie theme and put a full remake on the old Mr. Big 'n' Tall shop.

They did a nice job on the building. It's got some great art-deco bones, lots of windows, and a ceiling high enough to incorporate a mezzanine level. It's done mostly in black and white, with wood floors, red highlights, and art-deco lamps. There are many discreet areas for private discussions, but also ample perches for checking out others in the room. Let's not forget, there's more than just dinner on the menu here.

If you're looking for quiet and calm, this is not the place. Belgo is loud. I think it's too loud, but they say they have embraced a brasserie liveliness. So the music is pumped up and it bounces off all those hard surfaces. Be forewarned.

Belgo's food is neither really brasserie style nor really Belgian, aside from some good moules frites, done with lemon-grass and coconut milk, sorrel and Chardonnay, or chorizo and tomato-fennel broth, that is. It is more of a high-end tavern or a global-contemporary restaurant. Regardless, it's good, probably better than it needs to be.

The croque monsieur is an elegantly huge spin on the traditional French sandwich. The roasted lamb, brie, and caramelized onion sandwich is slippery but really well prepared. And the soups I've had here—including a pea soup poured from a French press coffee pot at the table—have all been excellent. Certainly not cheap though.

The quality of the food is due to the smartest move the Belgo owners made when they opened this place. They needed a really good chef to make Belgo a serious restaurant, and they found him in Shaun Desaulniers. Previously executive chef at The Fairmont Palliser, Desaulniers is one of the new breed of young, talented Canadian chefs who understands food and the restaurant industry.

And I don't want to forget the beer. They have twenty-five kinds of Belgian beer, each of which comes with its own glass. It's darned fine beer too. Expensive, though, rolling up to $12 for a Trappist ale.

Belgo has all come together into a lively, energetic package. And it's so popular that the owners expanded, doubling the space, after only a few months.

www.belgo.ca

Bella Italia

Italian

91 East Lake Crescent NE, Airdrie
Phone: 948•0039
Monday–Friday 11:30 am–2 pm, Monday–Saturday 5 pm–10 pm
Reservations recommended — Fully licensed — Non-smoking
V, MC, Debit — $$

WE Calgarians like to slip out of town for dinner once in a while. So how about a trip to Airdrie and a visit to Bella Italia? It's owned by Sal and Anna Maria Monna, the couple who used to own Sal's Deli & Italian Market on Macleod Trail. The Monnas got out of the food biz for a while, but when a restaurant space became available in Airdrie, they dove right back in.

To get to Bella Italia, you go to the most northerly Airdrie exit off the QE2 Highway, head east about fifty metres, then take the first right back south so you are paralleling the highway. It's a short distance down that road.

It's not a terribly scenic neighbourhood unless you're into farm equipment. But inside, Bella Italia has the look and feel of a comfortable Italian trattoria. They've got the red-and-white checkered tablecloths, the wrought iron, and the faux arches. It's casual and roomy enough to allow both for couples who want a quiet meal and for family groups.

The food fits the tone. It's traditional Italian—minestrone soup, fettuccine alfredo, lasagna, and chicken cacciatore. Nothing wrong with that as long as it's done well. And Anna Maria Monna is one good cook, light on the creams and oils, forceful on the hearty flavours of Italian cooking.

The homemade sausage has a perfect meaty presence along with some sautéed peppers and onions, and the Caesar salad is a crunchy, zippy rendition. The pastas exhibit the best of robust Italian cooking. The spaghetti carbonara is simple and luscious, and the spaghetti and meatballs are likewise simple, rich, and full-bodied—well-seasoned meatballs with perfectly cooked pasta in a great tomato sauce with some parmesan. What else do you need?

Dinner prices are reasonable. That sausage appetizer is $8.50. The carbonara is $14.50, as are the meatballs—and these are not meek portions. Chicken and veal dishes are about $17 to $19—super value for what you get. Lunch prices are a bit lower still.

The Monnas are running a family operation that appeals to other families and the diverse crowd in the Airdrie area. And it's working. They are packed all the time. Bella Italia is just an all round pleasant place with good food, prices, and service. Not much of a view, but what can you do?

The Belvedere

Global Contemporary

107 Stephen Avenue Walk SW
Phone: 265•9595
Monday–Friday 11:30 am–close, Saturday 5 pm–close
Reservations recommended — Fully licensed — Corkage $25 — Patio
Non-smoking dining room, smoking in lounge
V, MC, AE — $$$

ABOUT halfway through my plate of roasted caribou, I realized I had to slow down. I'd been picking up speed ever since diving into the silky-tender slices of game, powering down on the beluga-lentil and wild-mushroom cassoulet, and sliding it all quickly through the saskatoon-port reduction. Not that I was in a hurry. I was just compelled by animalistic urges to cram as much of this gorgeous food into my gullet as quickly as possible.

But then it struck me. I am not an animal! I am a restaurant critic! (A fine line, to be sure.) I must slow down and savour this food. How often do I get to enjoy caribou anyway? How often do lentils and mushrooms taste this good? How often are saskatoons put to such good use?

Under the skilled hands of Chef Alain Chabot, every night it would seem. The current Belvedere chef—the fourth in a stellar line of cooks—is in full command of his kitchen and his culinary faculties.

For this book's meal, we ate a flawlessly prepared dinner at The Belvedere. I'm thinking there must have been some small piece out of place. I'm thinking ... oh yeah—the tables are a little small if you're dining as a foursome.

The mussels and sausage in Chardonnay-saffron sauce were exquisite. Chabot's take on this Iberian classic elevated it beyond any I've had. Often the sausage is too fatty or too much oil is used or the mussels just don't make it. This version had me scooping up the broth long after the mussels were gone.

Catherine's organic tomato gazpacho with niçoise olive coulis was declared to be better than the one I make. A cruel blow, but true nonetheless. Her halibut, with new potatoes, a leek-and-bacon rissole, and a saffron-corn nage, was a *Gourmet* magazine cover in-waiting and a blast to the palate.

This is some good cooking. Beautiful ingredients, intelligent concepts, precise execution. Even the sticky toffee pudding was the best I'd ever had.

So The Belvedere still excels and deserves its place in the top handful of Calgary's finer dining restaurants. The room is great, the service is capital "P" Professional, and the wine list and wine-pairing advice are outstanding.

Not cheap, no. The mussels were $14 (actually, a bargain for the quality and quantity), the halibut, $31 (likewise, good value), and the caribou, $42. With a couple of glasses of wine and desserts, a $200 price tag for two is common.

So slow down!

www.thebelvedere.ca

Big Fish

Seafood

1112 Edmonton Trail NE
Phone: 277•3403
Monday–Friday 11:30 am–11 pm, Saturday & Sunday 10 am–11 pm
Reservations accepted for 5 pm–6:30 pm only
Fully licensed — Corkage $15, Free corkage Wednesdays — Patio — Non-smoking
V, MC, AE, Debit — $–$$

D WAYNE and Alberta Ennest—the owners of Diner Deluxe, Urban Baker, and Vue Cafe—know a dead parrot when they see one. So when the Blue Parrot, located next to their Piato restaurant, expired, they quickly moved in and opened Big Fish.

The conversion from smoky bar to smoke-free fish house was quick. The Ennests cleaned up, repainted, installed a new bar/fish-bar and a mismatched swack of furniture, added some nautical lights and a blues soundtrack, and opened in mere days. It looks great. It's casual and mostly comfortable, depending at which table you're sitting. You'll notice in the information paragraph above that there are few reservations taken, but it has still become a popular neighbourhood hangout.

And then there's the menu. Seafood focused, of course—steamed mussels with green curry, seafood pot-au-feu, cedar-planked Arctic char, grilled tuna with wasabi-lime yogurt, and so on. Nice ideas that also range from soups and salads to sandwiches and even surf-and-turf choices.

I like the roasted corn and lobster bisque, which is filled with the roasted flavours of both ingredients. And the sandwiches aren't bad. They have a soft-shell crab one with wild-boar bacon. And a fried oyster po' boy. And even a grilled buffalo burger with balsamic-onion relish for the unrelenting carnivore. The sandwiches are served with greens and sauces on bread from the Urban Baker down the street—they can be slippery, messy, and just plain difficult to eat. Be prepared. Big Fish is that kind of place.

Plus, they have an outstanding oyster bar. The oysters are as fresh and well handled as I've seen in Calgary. You can get them straight up or with a lime-black-pepper granita or a warm caper and chive mignonette.

Big Fish is loud, hot, crowded, and fun. It's a bit irreverent and pleasantly casual. But the food is good, so don't miss out.

Having established Big Fish, the Ennests closed Piato—their contemporary Greek concept next door—in the summer of 2006 and converted the space to a Southwest-influenced steak house called **Open Range** (*1114 Edmonton Trail NE, 277•3408*). With Big Fish on one side and Open Range on the other, we now have an intriguing surf-and-turf option. The Open Range menu is as creative as that of Big Fish, with elk and black-bean chili, lamb T-bones with sage-pancetta-pecan relish, and a beef rib-eye in a molasses-peppercorn crust.

Piato is hopefully moving to a new, higher-traffic location in the near future.

Big Rock Grill

Contemporary Grill

5555 – 76 Avenue SE
Phone: 236•1606
Monday – Friday 11:30 am – 2 pm
Reservations recommended — Fully licensed — Corkage $15 — Patio — Non-smoking
V, MC, AE, Debit — $$

MANY wineries in the Okanagan and Niagara Peninsula have nice restaurants attached to their facilities. Visitors love the winery tours, the bucolic settings, and the trendy wine country menus that round out the experience.

But in Alberta we don't have much of a wine industry; we have a beer industry. So when Ed McNally and the creative thinkers at Big Rock built a spiffy new brewery in 1996, they included a restaurant that was to be their own interpretation of the winery diner. The location was in a field off Glenmore Trail in an area where lunch out meant getting fries and a burger from a bus parked nearby. The idea of a 120-seat eatery with a big patio and a fireplace and a top-notch chef seemed, well, a little odd.

But Big Rock has always been known for odd, market-bucking ideas that somehow work: commissioned art on beer labels, no big marketing campaigns, beer without pasteurization. Those ideas have paid off in the past for Big Rock, and likewise, the Big Rock Grill has become a huge success. Now surrounded by other large buildings, the Grill has a built-in market that packs the place on a daily basis. Arriving without a reservation on most weekdays is risky business. And if it's sunny, you'd better get there early to procure one of the sought-after patio seats. Fully ensconced in greenery, it is an oasis in the Southeast.

The top-notch chef is Klaus Wöckinger, once the head chef at La Chaumière and former owner of Dante's (now La Tavola) in the soon-to-be-demolished Penny Lane Mall. Working with another Klaus, his son, Klaus senior has assembled a menu that satisfies the predominantly male lunch crowd and adds a depth of sophistication to the area.

Among the sirloin burgers and chicken wings (marinated in Grasshopper ale), you'll find salmon steak en papillote, seafood ragout, and Wiener schnitzel. It's robust cuisine with an elegant touch, yet not overworked or pretentious. With the salmon being the most expensive item at $16, it's a menu that surprises first-timers.

The food is always well prepared and is served swiftly by attentive staff. Also adding to the pleasure is a long line of draft beer taps flowing with Big Rock, a huge cooler filled with more Big Rock in cans and bottles, and a gift shop featuring—that's right—Big Rock caps and shirts and other required paraphernalia. (You don't order a Miller Lite here.)

www.bigrockbeer.com

Big T's

Wood-Smoked Southern Barbecue

8330 Macleod Trail SE (Heritage Plaza)
Phone: 252•5550

2138 Crowchild Trail NW
Phone: 284•5959

Daily 11 am–11 pm
Reservations not accepted — Fully licensed — Non-smoking
V, MC, AE, Debit — $ – $$

I N these days of non-stop media on healthy food options, it's good to know there are still places for big guys with big appetites. I mean big-belly boys who like to drive trucks, drink beer, and eat. Preferably meat. With a side of meat and maybe a little more meat. One of the best destinations for this checkered-shirt crowd is Big T's BBQ and Smokehouse.

Sure, I'm engaging in gender stereotyping of a certain kind, but first, I count myself as one of the above (okay, I've got a Camry, not a Ford 350). And second, have you been to one of the Big T's? If so, just how many delicate ladies did you see there? And I'm not counting the waitresses.

Big T's is a guy place. Oh, we're happy to bring the missus along. That way we get to eat everything she leaves. And someone has to drive the truck home, right? But when the menu includes a One Meat Meal, a Two Meat Meal, meat loaf, a rack of ribs with any meat, and numerous sides of meat, who does that really appeal to?

Now in fairness, looking deeper into the menu, I see some salads and soups and such, but you can add any meat for $5 and even the salads are served with cornbread. When in Rome …

Big T's slow smokes their pork shoulders, beef briskets, ribs, and chicken for hours and serves them with four house-made sauces. They don't adhere to a specific barbecue style such as Memphis, Kansas City, or West Texas—rather, they include recipes from various areas of the southern US.

And it's decent. Sometimes the pulled pork gets a little dry and occasionally the side dishes are pallid compared to the meat, but overall, it is pretty good. When fresh out of the smoker, the pulled pork is really dynamite. I particularly like the ribs, big and meaty and saucy. The beans are usually okay, and they do a nice slaw. The fries aren't the best in town, but they're serviceable. As are the desserts. Nothing outstanding there. Decent rice pudding, okay butter tart, but no bread pudding. They do a Wild Turkey and chocolate pie, but I find that a serious bread pudding is the best thing for weighing down all that meat.

It's the way us big-belly boys like our barbecue.

The Bison Mountain Bistro

Rocky Mountain Comfort Food

#213, 211 Bear Street (The Bison Courtyard), Banff
Phone: 762 • 5550
Monday–Friday 9 am–midnight, Saturday & Sunday 10 am–midnight
Reservations recommended — Fully licensed — Patio — Non-smoking
V, MC, AE, Debit — $$–$$$

FOLKS in and around Banff heralded the completion of The Bison Courtyard in early 2006. It's one of the larger projects to pop up in downtown Banff in years—it's an environmentally friendly building that holds both retail and housing.

Through The Bison General Store at street level, you head upstairs to the restaurant. Here, The Bison Mountain Bistro showcases the classic Banff wraparound view: windows on three sides and a big deck looking onto Rundle, Sulphur, and Tunnel Mountains. The interior complements the surroundings—it's simple and open and cleanly decorated to give almost everyone some kind of view.

The food is mountain contemporary: a lot of bison, plus birch-glazed salmon, wild-mushroom tagliatelle, duck carpaccio, and thyme-roasted chicken. There are interesting ingredients and combinations—apple-cheddar mashed potatoes, tuna niçoise with smoked tomatoes and quail eggs, saskatoon-berry chutney, preserved lemons, and so on.

I went for an all-bison dinner, appropriate I suppose, for The Bison Mountain Bistro. The bison onion soup was rich and deep in flavour, with a cap of thick bread and comte cheese. (There's a lot of great cheese on this menu—one of the owners used to be a partner in Janice Beaton Fine Cheese in Calgary, so that explains that.) The soup leaned just a touch too far on the sweet side for my palate, but still, it was extremely good. Then came my braised bison cheeks, beautifully done with a base of taleggio-laden polenta, smoked tomatoes, and stewed fennel. A big plate of food for $25, and a nice dish all around.

There is a less elaborate menu for lunch with burgers and wood-fired pizzas and a breakfast entree until 5 p.m. Plus there are separate breakfast, brunch, and lounge menus. They mean for this to be a well-used restaurant.

Now to the bathrooms where you'll find composting toilets with no water and no flushing required. The toilets cleanse themselves with a foam that automatically coats the bowl with every use. If you go, you have to go. These are quite unique, at least these days. When I was a kid on the farm, we had a composting toilet too, with no water and no flushing either. We called it an outhouse.

Anyway, The Bison Mountain Bistro fills a gap in the Banff market. It is elegantly rustic, the food is hearty and satisfying, and it's the kind of place I expect to find in Banff. I like it. Even without the view and the toilets, I'd still go.

www.thebison.ca

Bistro Provence

French (Provençal)

52 North Railway Street, Okotoks
Phone: 938·2224
Tuesday–Friday 11 am–1:30 pm, Tuesday–Saturday 5:30 pm–10 pm
Reservations recommended — Fully licensed — Corkage $15 — Patio — Non-smoking
V, MC, Debit — $$–$$$

'M going out on a limb here. I'm including a restaurant in this book to which I have not been. Well, sort of. Let me explain this departure from my usually irrevocable rules.

From 1996 to 2005, La P'tite Table was a landmark in Okotoks. It was one of the area's premier French restaurants. And since it was situated in the 1882–built Post Office, it had an historic cachet much appreciated in the rapidly growing town.

But after nine years, Owner Thierry Meret wanted a change and less kitchen stress. He decided to embrace the currently popular bistro style of French restaurant and started cooking comparatively simple fare, where the elements on the plate were few in number but high in intensity. The service remained efficient and friendly, but the price tag was lower. It was casual dining with quality. The name was different too. It became Bistro Provence.

But then, just before this book went to the printers, I heard that Meret was selling the place. "Scrap the page," I thought. "Grab the car keys, Catherine. We need to go find another good place to eat."

But before heading out, I called Meret. He explained that he was selling Bistro Provence to Nicolas Desinai, then executive chef at Priddis Greens as well as owner of the Simple Gourmet in Bridlewood. And that his fellow Frenchman would be taking over Bistro Provence in the fall of 2006. I called Desinai and confirmed the information and found out that he and *his* wife Catherine would be moving into the residence above the Okotoks restaurant. And that he would be keeping Bistro Provence in much the same tone that Meret was leaving it.

So there you have it. I've had Desinai's cuisine at both Simple Gourmet and Priddis Greens. It's good. And I believe him when he says Bistro Provence will remain much the same. So, let's hope.

For reference, here are a few dishes that were on the final Meret-developed menu: tapas ranging from house-smoked salmon with lemon and cilantro cream cheese on baguette to sautéed frog legs (most tapas are under $10); and main courses of salmon on braised lentils and a bacon-Merlot cream ($18), braised duck legs in red-wine sauce with pesto-mashed potatoes ($24), and grilled strip loin on juniper-scented red cabbage with roasted shallots ($26). The latter dish was the most expensive on the menu.

So, come out on the limb with me. I think it's a safe bet.

www.bistro-provence.ca

Bistro Twenty Two Ten

Canadian

2210–4 Street SW
Phone: 228 • 4528
Tuesday–Friday 11:30 am–2 pm, Tuesday–Saturday 5:30–close
Reservations recommended — Fully licensed — Corkage $15 — Non-smoking
V, MC, AE, Debit — $$

Two young chefs, Jason Armstrong and Alexandra Chan, took over the space at 2210–4 Street SW in 2005, and with skills that complement each other's, they created Bistro Twenty Two Ten. Their first task was to put a fresh beige-and-brown look on the place. The dining room is quite pleasant: Big windows look out onto 4th Street, a banquette lines one wall, interesting glass chandeliers light the room, and an elevated area creates some privacy. It's not big, but it's surprisingly comfortable.

The same can be said about the lunch or dinner menus. There are sixteen or seventeen items on each, and they are a collection of modern Canadian bistro fare—a braised short-rib sandwich with caramelized onions and blue-cheese mayonnaise, seared salmon with vegetables in a citrus cream, a chicken and pine-nut flatbread, that sort of thing. They are tight, manageable menus that focus on fresh flavours and simple, pleasant combinations.

So a soup of peas with crisp pancetta is a lovely bowl of contrasts with the fresh taste of peas and the salty crunch of pancetta. The soup is not overworked or too processed; rather, the natural flavours come forward. The grilled chicken sandwich on sourdough is, likewise, just a good sandwich, with moist chicken, smoky bacon, a little tomato and spinach, and a red-pepper aioli. It's straight-ahead, simple, and good and comes with frites and a salad. The salad is a little too simple with just a pile of greens and a vinaigrette. It could use a little more zip in the dressing or another ingredient to increase the interest. And the frites have a good taste, but are fiddly small and difficult to eat politely either with cutlery or fingers.

Desserts at Bistro Twenty Two Ten are always good. Chef Chan specializes in them, so you'll find a flourless almond-chocolate cake with chocolate mousse and caramelized banana (that's just one dessert!) and profiteroles with a fudge sauce and dulce de leche gelato. Not bad at all.

Desserts are $7 to $9, sandwiches are $10 or $11, and dinner entrees run up to the mid- and high $20s. Not nearly as expensive as some of the other new bistro-ish places.

Bistro Twenty Two Ten is a strong newcomer in the neighbourhood-bistro category. It's a great place for folks in the Mission area to walk to, and it's comfortable, affordable, and varied enough to make a regular place. It's maturing nicely with its two talented young chefs.

Note: This building may be scheduled for demolition in the future. That would be a shame.

www.bistro2210.com

Bow Valley Grill

Seasonal Canadian

405 Spray Avenue (Fairmont Banff Springs), Banff
Phone: 762•6860
Monday–Saturday 6:30 am–11 am, Monday–Friday 11:30 am–2 pm
Saturday 11:30 am–4 pm, Sunday 11 am–2:30 pm
Sunday–Thursday 6 pm–9 pm, Friday & Saturday 6 pm–9:30 pm
Reservations recommended — Fully licensed — Non-smoking
V, MC, AE — $$–$$$

I am in constant awe of the Bow Valley Grill. For that matter, I'm pretty much in constant awe of the rest of the Fairmont Banff Springs too.

The Bow Valley Grill is the hotel's catch-all restaurant, the place that serves breakfast, lunch, and dinner, handles tour groups and Sunday brunchers, and deals with intimate couples and in-a-hurry skiers, all with equal skill. And although I always love the food at the Springs high-end **Banffshire Club** and their German-tinged **Waldhaus** (*see phone number above for both*), I've decided to focus this book's review on the Bow Valley Grill.

The Grill has been around since the Springs' big reno a few years back. They opened up an underused space and expanded it back into the kitchen, creating a serpentine dining area with a superb view. You look down the Bow River to the Fairholme Range—it's almost enough to make you miss the food. With its curved dining areas, spaces have been created for dining groups small and large. I've seen big bus tours come in for lunch and go totally unnoticed by romantic couples having a quiet meal. The staff are quick to reset and realign the room to meet the needs of the next visitors. It's one of the most flexible dining rooms I've seen.

And it's also one of the best attended by staff. When Catherine and I popped in for breakfast, they noticed she was wearing black pants and immediately exchanged her white napkin for a black one. Nice touch.

Apart from the staff and the view, the big star of the Bow Valley Grill is the buffet, a curving, fifty-foot showcase of foods open to the kitchen behind. They put out a beautiful breakfast selection—breads, cheeses, desserts, salads, hot entrees, more cold choices—as well as a separate Japanese breakfast buffet. The brilliance is that the customers slide along one side while the cooks add on dishes from the other. So when a duck and cambozola pizza is needed, it arrives hot from the oven in seconds. Same with the eggs Benedict, the lamb sausages, the scalloped potatoes, and on and on. I like to just stand there and watch how well it all works.

Now it's not cheap. There are various prices for the breakfast, lunch, dinner, and brunch buffets. And there are separate menus for lunch and dinner if a buffet isn't your thing.

But food-wise, service-wise, and view-wise, the Bow Valley Grill has it all.

www.fairmont.com/banffsprings

Boyd's

Seafood

#100, 5211 Macleod Trail S
Phone: 253•7575
Sunday–Thursday 11 am–9 pm, Friday & Saturday 11 am–10 pm
Reservations accepted — Fully licensed — Non-smoking
V, MC, Debit — $–$$

SOMETIMES I just feel like fish and chips. And when that gotta-have grabs me, it's off to Boyd's I go.

Boyd's is suitably nautical for a seafood joint. There are model boats and fishing paraphernalia, plastic tablecloths and squeeze bottles of ketchup, tartar sauce and bottles of malt vinegar. The place looks so seafaring, customers start talking about sailing and fishing while waiting in line for a table.

It's around lunchtime some days that there is that wait. In spite of Boyd's large size, it can pack up midday with folks after their fish and chip fix. And the combos keep flying out of the kitchen: cod and chips, haddock and chips, sole and chips, halibut and chips.

Now that's not all Boyd's does. You can get seafood by the bucket here: breaded oysters, shrimp-and-crab Louie, king crab legs at $37 a pound, and on and on. And then there are daily specials of jambalaya and ahi tuna and balsamic-glazed salmon. I suppose some people actually order them, but what I always see is plate after plate of fish and chips.

Which, of course, I had. The two-piece Atlantic cod meal with chips and coleslaw was on for $11 that day instead of the usual $13.50. A big pile of freshly cut fries were cooked to that slightly bendable, oily texture. Fish and chips are about bendable fries—not too crisp. And decent coleslaw—this one was in a ceramic cup, not one of those plastic ones. Classy. The fish came in two long, breaded strips, not too thick, not too thin. Good cod, steaming hot, but the batter could have been crisper. Considering how hot the fish came from the fryer, it was overly soft on the outside.

I also had a small bowl of seafood chowder that was packed with scallops, shrimp, haddock, and halibut. For $3.50 a cup, a heck of a deal. But the fish had fallen apart and had turned into a kind of stringy mush. Not good—nice flavour, poor texture.

On the service side, I'm always impressed with Boyd's. They're pleasant, helpful, they know their fish, and they keep their customers happy. To the point where the little package of crackers that came with my soup had been pre-crumbled—okay, maybe that wasn't intentional.

Anyway, Boyd's did a pretty good job of satisfying my fish and chips need. Crisper on the fish and a lighter touch on the soup and crackers would be appreciated though.

Brava Bistro

New World Mediterranean

723–17 Avenue SW
Phone: 228•1854
Monday–Saturday 11:30 am–3 pm, Sunday–Wednesday 5 pm–10 pm
Thursday–Saturday 5 pm–midnight
Reservations highly recommended, especially on weekends — Fully licensed — Corkage $25
Patio — Non-smoking
V, MC, AE — $$–$$$

A lot of people like Brava Bistro because of Executive Chef Kevin Turner's inspired turn on Mediterranean cuisine. Others like Brava's see-and-be-seen wine bar or its curved and cozy booths. There are even a few who like the bizarre Red Mile contrast of dining in contemporary elegance while watching the game on big-screen televisions across the street at Melrose (the screens really are that big).

Although we like all the above, our favourite Brava moment is their Sunday Supper. On the first Sunday of each month, Brava does a three-course, limited choice, prix fixe dinner for $29. It's a good deal and the food is primo. Sunday Supper is meant to be hearty and casual, and the food reflects this. There might be big chunks of crispy roast chicken or big plates of braised beef or big bowls of pasta. And robust salads or soups and big-old slabs of pie. Pastry Chef Jennifer Wilhelmsen makes one stellar fruit crisp. It's all good cookin' and good eatin' too—way better than what we do at home on a Sunday evening.

We are also pretty fond of Brava's wine list, as intelligent and food-friendly as they come. Brava's general manager Dewey (yes, just Dewey) has included a good selection by the glass or the half-bottle, so it's possible to pair up courses.

Past the Sunday Supper, Brava puts out a very decent menu, albeit a little pricier. The lobster gnocchi remains my pick for its richness and its sweet combo of peas, baby carrots, lobster, and lots of butter. Healthy and sinful at the same time. How can you beat that? And although duck confit has become the obligatory ingredient on every contemporary menu around, Brava has been making and preserving ducks longer and better than almost anyone else.

There are many good things to say about Brava. In a book of favourites, it truly is one of my most favoured faves. A wash of millennium-inspired taupes and brown with mirror highlights, the decor is pleasantly neutral and comfortable. I wish they had a better outdoor option—17th Avenue does not make for the quietest or most smoke-free patio. And parking in the area has become a pain. But those are small concerns. The skillful service, the comfortable setting, and the food more than make up for it.

And as long as they save us a space for Sunday Supper, we'll keep coming back to Brava. And so will a lot of other people.

www.bravabistro.com

Buchanan's

Chophouse

738–3 Avenue SW
Phone: 261•4646
Monday–Friday 11 am–10 pm, Saturday 5 pm–10 pm, Bar open until 2 am
Reservations recommended — Fully licensed — Patio — Non-smoking
V, MC, AE, Debit — $$–$$$

POSTED at Buchanan's entrance is a plaque that reads, "No cigars, no handguns, no nuclear weapons, no restaurant critics." That last one is bolded. Gotta love that. Not that the sign has ever stopped me from entering and enjoying Calgary's oldest chophouse. I like the cheeky upfrontness of the warning and their desire to cater to their public rather than to the rarified few of us who write about restaurants (sigh…).

Buchanan's has always been like that—a little cheeky, a little bold. When it first opened in 1988, most folks thought the location was a bit, shall we say, wacky. At that time, the area was desolate, a combination of dilapidated houses and up-and-coming construction sites. Since then, it has gained the most urban feel of anywhere in Calgary.

Michael and Carol Buchanan can be called neighbourhood visionaries, but they didn't move into the area to try out a new concept. They decided on a chophouse theme for their eponymous restaurant and went about re-creating a style that has been around for over a century. High-backed wooden booths, stained glass, sports and movie memorabilia, a creaky wood floor, and paper-topped tables highlight the room. Wraparound windows brighten what would otherwise be a dark, woody interior, and a cozy bar is hived-off to one side.

Aside from the look, the thing that most makes Buchanan's a chophouse is the meaty menu of steaks, burgers, pork chops, lamb chops, and prime-rib chops. If they could do a fish chop, they probably would, but they settle for fillets of halibut, snapper, and salmon along with a few pastas and chicken dishes.

One cannot mention Buchanan's without paying homage to their cheeseburger, another retro-visionary piece of culinary lore. Back in the last century, when it seemed that every restaurant was turning to pre-formed, portion-controlled burgers, Buchanan's bucked the trend by grinding their own extra-extra-lean sirloin in-house. The result was—and still is—a meaty burger cooked to order. Like it should be. On a warm summer day, when Buchanan's patio sizzles under the sun, over a hundred pounds of sirloin can meet its fate on the grill inside. This cheeseburger has made Buchanan's a destination for many of us who need to have a meaty fix on a regular basis.

So, defying the prohibition against restaurant critics, I continue to darken Buchanan's door, hoping someday to be better regarded than nuclear weapons.

www.buchanans.ca

Buffalo Mountain Lodge

Rocky Mountain Cuisine

Tunnel Mountain Road, Banff
Phone: 760•4484
Daily 7 am–10 pm
Reservations recommended — Fully licensed — Patio — Non-smoking
V, MC, AE, Debit — $$–$$$

THERE'S an odd juxtaposition to dining in this window-wrapped restaurant owned by Canadian Rocky Mountain Resorts: As you savour your elk tenderloin, you can watch their brethren relax on the grounds outside. The plated elk is from the owners' Canadian Rocky Mountain Ranch, and the outdoor elk are National Park protected. It seems we want it both ways in Banff—we want the game on the plate, and at the same time, we want it in the wild. And preferably without a lot of connection between the two. Buffalo Mountain Lodge offers the best of both worlds.

The dining room is gorgeous. It's dark green and heavily beamed, with vaulted ceilings and a crackling fireplace in the lobby lounge. Most of the tables are parked by huge windows. The lodge is part way up Tunnel Mountain, so it's a tranquil departure from the bustle of Banff Avenue.

Buffalo Mountain serves meals throughout the day. Breakfast rolls out with a mixed grill of eggs, elk sausage, bacon, potatoes, and toast ($11), brioche French toast ($10), and eggs Benedict ($12). Lunch features gazpacho with a crab and scallop cake ($15), a lamb burger ($16), and grilled wild salmon ($18). Dinner pulls out the stops with caribou medallions in a red-currant glaze ($38) and that elk tenderloin ($40). For the gamey gourmand, the platter of smoked buffalo, venison ham, peppered duck breast, game pâté, and elk salami ($24) is good. It's mountain-top pricing, but it's also one of the most unique cuisines and settings in Banff.

Canadian Rocky Mountain Resorts also operates the seasonal and rustic **Cilantro Mountain Café** (*760•4488*) in a former ski rental shop across the parking lot. That menu runs to pizzas and pastas with a contemporary spin and a few loftier items such as Arctic char with saffron risotto ($29) and seared duck breast with a wild-rice cake ($29).

Also in the mountain parks, this group owns **Deer Lodge** at *109 Lake Louise Drive* in Lake Louise (*522•4202*) near the Fairmont Chateau Lake Louise, as well as **Emerald Lake Lodge** (*250•343•6321*) in Yoho National Park just west of Field, BC. Both have good dining rooms with menus similar to Buffalo Mountain. Emerald Lake also offers casual dining at the seasonal **Cilantro on the Lake** (*250•343•6321*).

But back to Banff. Buffalo Mountain and Cilantro also have two of the best and most unheard-of patios there. Just watch out for marauding elk seeking revenge for their comrades.

Buzzards

Cowboy Cuisine

140–10 Avenue SW
Phone: 263•7900
Sunday–Tuesday 11:30 am–9:30 pm, Wednesday & Thursday 11:30 am–10 pm
Friday & Saturday 11:30 am–10:30 pm
Reservations recommended — Fully licensed — Large decks
Non-smoking restaurant, smoking in pub
V, MC, AE — $$

TWENTY-SIX years and counting. Over a quarter-century in the restaurant business. I can't even imagine how many million litres of beer have been consumed at Buzzards, how many sunburns have been acquired on the deck, and how many prairie oysters have been sliced and diced at their annual Testicle Festival.

And yet Buzzards owner Stuart Allan exudes the energy of someone fresh to the business. While many other restaurateurs have come and long gone, and while many restaurant concepts have faded from memory, Allan and Buzzards soldier happily on.

Allan has found the right mix of tried-and-true and innovation. His was the first place to offer an outside deck, a novelty in the early 1980s that seems laughably simple today. And the Buzzards of 2006 has new flooring, new plasma televisions, new deck tables, new bathrooms, new kitchen equipment, and on and on. Buzzards keeps up with the trends.

But it never forgets from whence it came. The bar side has the feel of an English pub—complete with the haze of smoke. The deck (or decks, since they now wrap around the whole establishment) looks ready for a Stampede party any time of the year. And on almost any day, you can find some hardy soul out there quaffing a Buzzard Breath Ale, custom-made by Big Rock Brewery.

The dining room straddles tourist-friendly Cowboy Cuisine and business-lunch comfort food. From the bacon-wrapped meat loaf and the trout with roasted almonds to the macaroni with three cheeses and the ten-ounce rib-eye, it's good eating. Not delicate, not overly fussed-up, just good food prepared well. And priced accordingly. The rib-eye tops out the menu at $24, the macaroni is $11, and the meat loaf is $15. And there's always Buzzards Burger, a twenty-six-year tradition, handcrafted on site. But again, Buzzards is not hide-bound. There is also a chicken burger, a lamb burger, a free-range buffalo burger, and even a garden burger. They learned long ago that vegetarians like Buzzards too.

And then there is the Testicle Festival, *the* thing to bring out-of-town visitors to. Prairie oysters do exist, they are prepared in many ways, and some people actually eat them. They're not all that bad, a little chewy and lacking in flavour by themselves, but after a couple of Buzzard Breaths, they just slide right down.

At least so says Allan. And after this long, he should know.

www.cowboycuisine.com

Café Soleil

Mediterranean Tapas & Wine Bar

208 Caribou Street, Banff
Phone: 762•2090
Daily 11 am–4 pm, 5 pm–10:30 pm
Reservations accepted — Fully licensed — Non-smoking
V, MC, AE, Debit — $$–$$$

KATE Lane and Stephan Prevost work both sides of the street. Caribou Street in Banff, that is. Their restaurants, Typhoon and Café Soleil, situated on opposite sides of Caribou Street, have become two of the mountain town's favourite eateries over the past few years.

In 2002, they took over a moribund café space on Caribou Street and created **Typhoon** (*211 Caribou Street, 762•2000*), an eclectic Asian restaurant. Prevost drew upon his six years of cooking experience in Japan to create a menu that spanned Asia and introduced his version of Shanghai noodles, green-papaya noodles, and butter chicken to Banff.

Then, in late 2003, a space attached to Brewster's Mountain Lodge became available. Café Soleil was thus born. Bigger than Typhoon, Café Soleil seats about sixty people in a cheerful, eclectic space. A fireplace occupies one area, while small Christmas lights dangle overhead. Lane's paintings splash colour onto the walls, and an open kitchen allows Prevost room to create his Mediterranean tapas and wine bar menu.

Café Soleil has a menu that fits the Banff crowd perfectly: lamb keftas in balsamic tomato sauce, garlic prawns sautéed in pastis, grilled chicken and fig skewers in piri piri sauce, and lamb lollipops with harissa sauce over chickpea-potato purée. That last dish gained Café Soleil instant notoriety when, after being open only three weeks, Prevost entered it into the prestigious Fetzer Appetizer Challenge. A major competition, the Fetzer was hotly contested by three dozen chefs from across Alberta who were charged with creating an appetizer to pair with a Fetzer wine. Prevost won.

Café Soleil has sold a lot of lamb lollipops since that victory. And a lot of other tapas, pastas, panini, and desserts such as their Catalan-style orange crème brûlée, the pear clafoutis, and the mission figs poached in sherry with chocolate syrup and whipped cream. Nice, very nice. It has become a popular place for locals and visitors alike to indulge in a bite, a glass of wine (all Old World wines here), and a pleasant atmosphere.

The past few years have been a whirlwind for the unique pair. They've maintained their business partnership and grown two successful restaurants while nurturing their own lives (Prevost is married, has two young sons, and is active in Banff's theatre scene; Lane has two adult daughters and is a talented painter). In this balance, they've worn a path across Caribou Street, a path that I expect will only become deeper with time.

www.cafesoleil.ca

Capo

Contemporary Italian

#4, 1420–9 Avenue SE
Phone: 264•2276
Monday–Friday 11:30 am–2 pm, Monday–Saturday 5:30 pm–10 pm
Reservations essential — Fully licensed — Corkage $25 — Non-smoking
V, MC, AE — $$$

CAPO is about dinner as theatre. The script is a tightly written menu of five antipasti, four pastas, five *secondi* (what we in North America consider a main course), and a handful of desserts. The set is a room that focuses around a large central table and interweaves the kitchen and service staff with the customers. The cast is whomever happens to book in for a meal. This is not a neighbourhood pizzeria, nor is it a place to hide away in a corner and have a private dinner for two. This is a place where the dining experience hinges not only on the quality of the kitchen and the service, but on who else happens to be in the room.

Capo—which means "chief" or "chef" in Italian—is also about showcasing the skills of Chef/Owner Giuseppe Di Gennaro, the former chef at Il Sogno. Di Gennaro likes to be part of the interaction between his customers, his staff, and his food. He's an active participant in the experience, not just from his kitchen perch, but from his presence in the dining room too. He talks with customers, pours their soup from a copper kettle into large white bowls at the tables, and delivers glasses of dessert wine topped with brandy.

This is a small room—thirty-two seats—with big attitude. It's at once stylish and refined, crowded and animated. Designer Sally Healy wrapped the room with a tall, beige, leather banquette and highlighted the ceiling with large, vinyl globe lights, each one lit in light blue. Mirrors expand the room, and a mica-flaked tile wall hives off the kitchen. A large port in the kitchen wall creates a pass-through to where Di Gennaro can be seen finishing plates.

There'll be no sitting on the fence about Capo. People will either love it or hate it. Some will find the food—thyme-marinated grilled prawns with shellfish-saffron cream, micro-mushrooms, and pork belly ($29) or perhaps zucchini carpaccio with roasted grape-tomatoes, goat cheese, cured beef tenderloin, and honey-roasted garlic crostini ($13)—inspired and elegant. Some will find the room energizing, sophisticated, and cosmopolitan. Others will find the place claustrophobic, overly exposed, loud, and expensive. All will be right.

One thing is certain. Few restaurants can thrive these days being safe and complacent. Capo has a huge attitude and some serious ability to back it up. And it will succeed because of that. But it's definitely not for everyone.

www.caporestaurant.ca

Carver's

Steak House

2630–32 Avenue NE (Sheraton Cavalier Hotel)
Phone: 250•6327
Monday–Saturday 5:30 pm–10:30 pm, Sunday 5 pm–9 pm
Reservations recommended — Fully licensed — Non-smoking
V, MC, AE, Debit — $$$

MMMM ... meat! With meat sauce! Mmmmm. That's what I have to say about Carver's, a temple of meat residing in the Sheraton Cavalier. A windowless, time-warped, hotel dining room, Carver's is all about meat. And by meat, I mean beef, AAA Alberta beef done eight different ways and in sizes from a six-ounce fillet ($31) and a ten-ounce New York strip loin ($32) to a twenty-two-ounce porterhouse ($41) and a chateaubriand for two ($74). Mmmmm ... meat!

To be fair, and to round out the menu, there is a rack of lamb, a chicken breast, a grilled salmon, and a sea bass, plus a list of appetizers that includes escargots and lobster bisque. (Escargot and lobster bisque? What decade is this?) But let's get serious. Carver's is about beef.

It's excellent beef. Big, steaming hunks of it, prepared perfectly, served on sizzling cast-iron platters with huge steak knives, a lump of mashed potatoes, and a gravy boat of meat sauce. I suppose I should call the sauce "demi-glace" since that sounds more "culinary," but in truth, it's meat sauce. Mmmmm ... meat!

Forget about the potatoes. Please. Sure, you need something white and starchy to balance out the meat, but Carver's swirl of potatoes has always been a cardboardy afterthought. It hasn't changed. Good potatoes, these are not.

And the appetizers? They're okay, but merely a delaying tactic while you wait for your meat. The "garden fresh salad" that comes with each steak is a pile of greens wrapped in a long slice of cucumber. It's in need of disassembly in order to eat, but it's fresh and the dressings are good—the blue cheese is one of the best I've had.

Side dishes are available for your meat too. There are mushrooms ($9), steak fries ($6), asparagus ($10), and so on ($10 for asparagus? Yikes!). But the garlic toast is free. (What did I say about a time warp?) And then there's the meat. Mmmmm ... meat!

And dessert. Jumbo slabs from giant cakes. Everything is big, including a Texas-sized cheesecake. And you know, the crepes with peppered and flamed strawberries and ice cream are great. Done tableside by the excellent staff (as many things are, including a Caesar salad), the crepes are superb.

So let's do away with any facade. Carver's is about meat and dessert. Mmmmm ... meat! Mmmmm ... dessert!

The Casbah

Moroccan

Downstairs, 720–11 Avenue SW
Phone: 265•9800
Friday 11:30 am–2 pm, Monday–Thursday 5:30 pm–10 pm
Friday & Saturday 5:30 pm–11 pm
Reservations recommended — Fully licensed — Corkage $15 — Non-smoking
V, MC, Debit — $$

Let's slip away to North Africa to a little place I know called The Casbah. It's just down a few steps off 11th Avenue.

The Casbah is Moroccan, and the room has been done from end to end in Moroccan hassocks, ceramics, antiques, tapestries, and lamb-skin lamps. The walls are a rich saffron orange, and a Moroccan soundtrack fills the air. In one corner, a plasma television plays a rolling slide show of Moroccan scenes. The seating is on cushioned benches, with tables mostly for groups of four. It is a beautiful room, and those steps leading down to it add a secretive tone.

We started dinner with one of my favourite Moroccan dishes, the bestilla Fassia. This is a fascinating blend of chicken, eggs, caramelized onions, saffron, ginger, and cinnamon, all baked in phyllo pastry and sprinkled with icing sugar. It's sweet and savoury, smooth yet crunchy. The Casbah's rendition is excellent. Two of us shared it along with the shrimp brioua, shrimp baked in phyllo with saffron, rice, cilantro, and paprika. Very tasty, and for those who like it spicier, it comes with a small bowl of biting-hot harissa sauce.

For the main courses, we shared a tajine and a couscous dish, giving us lots of flavours and textures. The tajine (which is a kind of stew) was made with sweet potatoes, prunes, and almonds. The couscous came with caramelized onions, chickpeas, and raisins. Each was $14, but we added chicken to the tajine and lamb to the couscous for an extra $6 and $7 respectively. (Many of the dishes start off vegetarian and then can be enhanced with various meats. Smart idea and very flexible.) Both entrees were served with a hot, crusty Moroccan bread.

Beyond all the lovely food at The Casbah, there are the Moroccan dining traditions. The staff rinse your hands with rose-scented water, and cutlery is optional. Eating with the thumb and first two fingers of the right hand is considered elegant dining in Morocco. But The Casbah has cutlery for the finger-averse. And if you're lucky, they may also be stocked with some Moroccan wine from French movie star Gerard Depardieu's winery. It's pricey but tasty.

The food here is excellent, and the experience is comfortable and social. Moroccan is a food culture that goes back many centuries, but hasn't been done a lot in Calgary. So come with me to The Casbah, or maybe take someone you like better.

www.casbahrestaurant.ca

Catch

Seafood

100 Stephen Avenue Walk SE
Phone: 206•0000
Monday–Friday 11 am–10 pm, Saturday 5 pm–10 pm
Reservations recommended — Fully licensed — Patio — Non-smoking
V, MC, AE, Debit — $$–$$$

CATCH was a long time in development, cost a lot of money, and opened with major hoopla. A large, four-storey operation, it was a little uneven in its early days, but it has since matured into a very good restaurant. Or I should say, two very good restaurants.

The upper floor holds an upscale, contemporary dining room, while the main floor has a lively and noisy oyster bar, a place to kick back and relax. The oyster bar is heavy on the wood, with a row of booths on one side, a line of chairs fronting the bar on the other, and tall tables in between. The old sandstone bank setting works perfectly for this style—it's got the high ceilings and deeply coved windows, tin ceilings, and mosaic-tile flooring. I could easily believe that it had been there since 1920 if I didn't look too closely.

The Catch oyster bar is comfortable for those wearing suits or sneakers, and with its attachment to the Hyatt Regency, it's become the casual dining option for hotel guests. Casual fits the menu too, with inclusions of fish and chips, a burger, clam chowder, and a Caesar salad. But this is no pale seafood joint. The food here is serious business and is some of the best seafood I've had anywhere, regardless of proximity to the coast.

Both levels do a crab cake that is almost essential on any visit. A single but dense Dungeness crab cake is laid over a bed of greens, surrounded by a panang curry and topped with a mango chutney. Great flavours, pure food. Darned expensive at $16, but so good. Same with the clam and oyster chowder. You can taste the ocean and that's a positive comment. It's rich and full bodied in a way I always want chowders to be but rarely are. This one is intense, creamy, and packed with mollusks.

On to the main courses. The moules frites, a simple preparation of mussels and french fries, almost redefines the genre. The mussels are huge, fresh, perfectly cooked, not a bad one in the works. And the fries are great, although they are a fish-and-chip fry and not a true crispy frite. Good saffron aioli with them though.

And I have to mention the price again. Catch is expensive. Dinner for two is going to be around $100, even in the oyster bar. But the quality is there.

www.catchrestaurant.ca

Centini

Modern Italian

160 Stephen Avenue Walk SE
Phone: 269•1600
Monday–Thursday 11:30 am–11 pm, Friday 11:30 am–midnight
Saturday 5 pm–midnight
Reservations recommended — Fully licensed — Patio — Non-smoking
V, MC AE, Debit — $$–$$$

THE dye job is looking good. When Centini took over the short-lived Blonde location in 2002, some feared the spot might be cursed. But with an injection of colour and energy, Centini soon proved that the Telus Convention Centre space works just fine.

Fabio Centini's energy is infectious. It fills the room, flows past the Vespa parked in the doorway, and spills into the street. He's garnered a cadre of followers who love his food, his wine, and his charm.

But it hasn't been Centini alone that has made this restaurant the busy place that it is. Although he toils tirelessly, Centini is quick to point out that Chef de Cuisine Stephen Grant does much of the "heavy lifting" in the kitchen. Grant is a talented young chef, and his calm, concentrated demeanor is the perfect foil to Centini's energy. Also coming in for praise is Maître d' Gustavo Yelamo, as professional and gracious a front man as there is in the business. In 2006, Yelamo was honoured at the city's White Hatter Awards as the best restaurant host in Calgary.

The room itself helps the place hop too. The open kitchen remains from the Blonde days and provides a fine view of the chefs. And the dining room layout is as it was. But the colours are much warmer, the decor holds more interest, and the seating is more comfortable and well spaced.

So, the table is set: lovely room, good cooks, great staff. But does it all come together on the table? Yes, it does. Centini's pastas, such as the seafood linguine packed with calamari, prawns, scallops, and more or the gnocchi with gorgonzola cream, are excellent. His soups are always a revelation. And the veal tenderloin with roasted shallots and mustard is heavenly. At $39, it's lofty in price too, but this is not a bargain joint. The ingredients are all high end, from the bison fillet with porcini mushrooms and white-truffle oil ($54!) to the Valrhona chocolate mousse ($14). There's nothing cheap about this stuff.

Centini is the kind of place to be taken to, to let the staff fawn over you, and to be treated like a star. It's like going to a food spa. But it's also a place to have a quick nosh and a glass of wine at the bar, a fine place for a quick—and cheaper—pick-me-up.

It's amazing what a little colour and energy can do.

www.centini.com

Chef's Studio Japan

Japanese

#108, 709 Main Street, Canmore
Phone: 609•8383
Daily 4:30 pm–10:30 pm
Reservations recommended — Fully licensed — Corkage $10 — Non-smoking
V, MC, AE, Debit — $$

MANY people who are familiar with the Canmore dining scene think Chef's Studio is great. But there are others who have never heard of it. The address is a little deceptive. It has to be the most hidden restaurant in Canmore, tucked as it is behind the Bank of Montreal and down a small alley off Main Street. It's not a tiny place though. It seats about sixty at tables and the sushi bar, and it has quite a pleasant, if somewhat dark, decor.

Chef's Studio, as you can tell by the name, is into the look of the food. They explain that in Japan, people eat with the five senses. So the food must look good as well as taste, smell, and feel good. I'm not sure how it's supposed to sound, but I think a lot of that is handled by the ambience of the room, which is tranquil.

And this is about the prettiest sushi I've ever had. The smoked eel roll wrapped around sushi rice and tempura was precisely rolled, cut, and then placed on a banana leaf and ceramic tray. The symmetry was near perfect. The seared and peppered tuna was also lovely, and the blend of textures, so well conceived. I even got a kick out of the Zero Roll, which is deep-fried tofu sliced and shaped into a big zero and arranged around brown rice and sesame seeds. Tofu and brown rice together may not sound all that exciting, and frankly, from a taste perspective, they aren't. But it sure was pretty.

Chef's Studio does a creative array of sushi too—one of the partners spent years training in Japan as a sushi chef. If I have one concern, though, it's the sushi rice itself. I found it a little hard, with too many broken grains, and it didn't hold together all that well. Maybe it was just the day, but it wasn't as good as the rest of the food.

And the rest of the food is beautiful too. They also serve cooked teriyakis, tempuras, and such. Probably the most attractive dish I had was a bowl of nambanzuke salmon, which was marinated, deep-fried, and placed with brine and vegetables in a glass bowl similar to a rose bowl.

I believe Chef's Studio is now the only Japanese restaurant in Canmore. And if you're only going to have one, Chef's Studio is a pretty good option to have.

www.chefsstudiojapan.com

Chez François

French

1604 Bow Valley Trail (Green Gables Inn), Canmore
Phone: 678•6111
Monday–Saturday 7 am–2 pm, Sunday 7 am–3 pm, Daily 5 pm–10 pm
Reservations recommended for lunch & dinner — Fully licensed — Corkage $15–$25
Non-smoking
V, MC, AE, Debit — $$–$$$

I F there is a better soup maker in the Bow Valley than Jean-François Gouin, I don't know who it is. I can still taste the lobster bisque I had at his Chez François restaurant over fifteen years ago. In my mind, it defines how that dish should be prepared. And I was amazed at a consommé he brought to a function a few years ago. It wowed not only me (I had three helpings), but blew away most of the other chefs in attendance. The clarity of the broth and the sharpness of the flavours were superb. Gouin puts the time and effort into doing it right. That simple consommé took days of roasting and simmering and clarifying.

We often underestimate the skill of the soup maker. But to me it signifies the quintessential talent of the chef. Do they have the patience, the ability, the wherewithal to strip food down to its essence in a soup? Or do they hide it under thickeners and boost it with packaged mixes?

At Chez François, they do the real deal. For one lunch, I started with a bowl of carrot-orange soup infused with cilantro. The flavours sang with richness and strength. Even the cilantro, an herb of which I am not particularly fond, added a subtlety to the dish I had not expected. Marvelous.

But enough of soup. A man cannot live on soup alone. Well, I probably could, but that's another story.

For the rest of my lunch, I had a Reuben sandwich made with good smoked meat, sauerkraut, and gruyère, a less greasy version than I've had elsewhere. The remainder of the lunch menu includes salads, more sandwiches, pastas, and some bigger ticket items, along with more soup of course.

Chez François is also known to serve a superb eggs Benedict, making it a popular breakfast place for Calgarians heading west. Its location in the Green Gables Inn makes for a quick pit stop one hour from the city. And unless the tour buses really have the place packed, service is prompt.

But they don't stop at breakfast and lunch. In the evening, Chez François moves upscale with a more classic French menu that includes pork tenderloin in a roquefort sauce, braised duck in a Grand Marnier sauce, and escargots in puff pastry. They also offer a six-course table d'hôte menu for a reasonable $55 and a shorter, three-course version for $34.

Both come with soup.

Chili Club

Thai

1904–36 Street SW
Phone: 217•8862
Monday–Friday 11:30 am–1:30 pm
Sunday–Wednesday 4:30 pm–9 pm
Thursday–Saturday 4:30 pm–10 pm

555–11 Avenue SW
Phone: 237•8828
Monday–Friday 11:30 am–1:30 pm
Sunday, Tuesday & Wednesday 4:30 pm–9 pm
Thursday–Saturday 4:30 pm–10 pm

Reservations recommended — Fully licensed — Non-smoking
V, MC, AE, Debit — $$

THERE have been various iterations of the Chili Club for a couple of decades now. It was one of the first Thai restaurants in town, but it has moved around a lot over the years. Right now, there are two outlets, both of which have the same menu and a similar style.

The 36th Street Chili Club is a small room painted in dark browns and black. The tabletops are black, the napkins are brown, the wood decorations are dark, and even the plates are dark brown. It's very dark for a place that seats just over thirty. But it's not oppressive. Somehow, in spite of the tiny space, the darkness works. Maybe it's just because they have kept the look simple. Or maybe it's because the food is distractingly good. (The 11th Avenue location is also tiny, mostly red, and serves kick-ass food as well.)

The Chili Club has always been known for their forceful preparations. They use a designation of one, two, or three chilies, and three chilies is one serious burn.

But it's not all about heat. The larb gai (that's a salad of toasted chicken, Chiang Mai style) is doused with lime and served on a bed of spinach. It's a two-chili dish, but it's not overpowering about it. The main flavours are the chicken and the lime. Nice salad.

If you do want to stoke it up, the appropriately named Crying Tiger is the way to go. Marinated, lightly cooked beef is drizzled with a soy-ginger sauce. With its rich, robust flavours, the tiger won't be the only one crying. Or you can try one of my favourites—the Evil Jungle Prince mixed vegetables—another three-chili dish. The vegetables are great—nice variety, lightly cooked, perfect with coconut rice. Maybe I should say the coconut rice is actually a necessity, since it helps cool things down. Also cooling is a particularly nice bowl of coconut ice cream.

Heat aside, this is good food. The presentation is lovely, although placing some dishes on brown plates does them a disservice because the food disappears into the plate. But I do like the service at these spots. It's quick and efficient, helpful without being overly cautionary about the food. They have been around long enough not to have to warn people about the heat. Look at the name of the joints for heaven's sake.

Chutney

Indian

112–4 Avenue SW (Sun Life Plaza)
Phone: 263•1400
Monday–Friday & Sunday 11 am–2 pm, Monday–Thursday & Sunday 5 pm–10 pm
Friday & Saturday 5 pm–11 pm
Reservations recommended — Fully licensed — Corkage $10 — Patio — Non-smoking
V, MC, AE, Debit — $$

A social phenomenon takes place every weekday downtown. At about 11:57 a.m., office towers expel hundreds of staff foraging for lunch. Breaking free of their corporate chains, they comingle with others like themselves from similar offices. Lawyers head for Buchanan's, gas marketers pop into Belgo, executive assistants grab a table at Prairie Ink, and IT teams meet at the nearest Asian buffet.

Of course I'm being "corporatist" (spreading corporate stereotypes), but regardless, the Asian buffet is the domain of the IT crowd for various reasons. First and foremost, it's quick. You never know what Windows upgrade you'll miss if you take a long lunch. And buffets are usually cheap, which somehow resonates with this crowd that's making big bucks. Then there's the quantity, the perfect amount for a long afternoon of slogging through code interfaces. And finally, there's that slightly exotic tinge that comes from dining Asian, in hope that the cute gal in Purchasing will notice the cachet of mango chutney you spilled on your Dockers (editor's note: sadly, this will not have the effect intended).

So, in search of the pocket-protector crowd, I put on my best pair of Dockers and headed out for lunch at an IT fave: Chutney. It's a former Pied Pickle that's been redone in warm, foody shades of mango, saffron, and turmeric. It's bright and airy, with high ceilings and seating for up to three hundred people. There are two rooms, and in between them, placed and lit like an altar, is a long, double-sided buffet—you can hear sighs of longing and lust when the IT teams catch first sight of it.

And it's a good buffet. Big trays of salads, paneer pakora, and pappadum. Chafing dishes of tandoori chicken, rogan josh, dals, and the obligatory butter chicken. It's roomy and well spaced, a buffet of buffets if ever there was one.

The food is good. For $14, selection is excellent. The key is that each dish has its own character and flavour. The spice blends are good, and the level of spicing is moderate. Chutney doesn't do nan on the buffet; instead, they bring the breads to your table quite briskly.

Beyond the lunch buffet, Chutney has a long dinner list of mostly Punjabi-style dishes. Lots of goat and lamb and even butter prawns for those who want to get really wild and crazy.

Chutney is also affiliated with another fine Indian restaurant, **Namskar** at *202–16 Avenue NE, 230•4447.*

www.chutney.ca

Clay Oven

Indian (Punjabi)

#349, 3132–26 Street NE (Interpacific Business Park)
Phone: 250•2161
Monday–Friday 11:30 am–2 pm, Monday–Thursday 5 pm–9 pm
Friday & Saturday 5 pm–10 pm
Reservations recommended — Fully licensed — Corkage $9.95 — Non-smoking
V, MC, AE, Debit — $–$$

WITH the wealth of new Indian restaurants in Calgary, it's easy to forget places that have been around for a while. Like the Clay Oven—if you knew about it in the first place, that is. It is in one of the most obscure locations in the city.

The Interpacific Business Park is an oddball strip mall if ever there was one. Located just east of the big Husky truck stop on Barlow Trail, it's filled with a multicultural mix of eateries, from the Shawarma King to Fat Kee Noodle House to Thumbs Up Samosas. There's a lot of good eating here. And back in the farthest corner is the forty-seat Clay Oven, a Punjabi-style Indian restaurant. It's the kind of place you feel self-satisfied at finding, until you open the door and are faced with a filled dining room, that is.

Lunch at the Clay Oven is definitely a reserve-ahead deal. They do a good Indian buffet for a reasonable $10, but the Clay Oven is not just bargain dining. I have said many times that they have the best Indian breads in the city. They just seem to have the touch.

With all the new places, I wanted to be sure that the Clay Oven still held the local bread title. So four of us ordered a selection of breads—a chapati, a roti, a paratha, and a nan. They have various flavoured and stuffed breads too, but I prefer the plain ones. Nan is the fluffy, white-flour bread baked in the tandoor oven, and the other three are whole wheat in various forms. All were really good. They had a nice firm texture without being tough and were perfect for eating on their own as well as for scooping up other dishes.

And we did order some food to go with our bread. We had a prawn masala, a lamb curry, a chickpea curry, some saag paneer with the spinach and Indian cheese, and of course, a butter chicken. Spiced more medium than hot, these were forceful, intense dishes, rich and perfect with the breads.

Most dinner dishes at the Clay Oven run about $12 to $15, with vegetable dishes mostly between $8 and $11. It's all good cooking, made better by great bread. The Clay Oven retains its title as the best Indian bread baker in town—at least by my taste—and it offers some of the best value for Punjabi-style Indian cuisine too.

The Coup

Global Vegetarian & Vegan

924–17 Avenue SW
Phone: 541•1041
Tuesday–Thursday 11:30 am–3 pm, 5 pm–10 pm
Friday & Saturday 8 am–3 pm, 5 pm–10:30 pm
Sunday 8 am–3 pm, 5 pm–9:30 pm
Reservations not accepted — Fully licensed — Small patio — Non-smoking
V, MC, Debit — $–$$

VEGETARIANISM can be a problematic restaurant style. First there's the determination as to which vegetarian style to adhere to. The Coup does both vegan and lacto-ovo. In other words, half the menu has no animal products of any kind, while the other half includes some form of dairy and/or eggs. But there's no meat or seafood at all.

Then there's the problem of just what the food is going to taste like. A lot of food cultures include a variety of good vegetarian dishes. And some, such as Ethiopian, Indian, and Thai, have as many vegetarian dishes as meat dishes, if not more. So, many North American contemporary vegetarian restaurants offer a mixed bag of dishes chosen from Asian, Mediterranean, and Californian cuisines. That's primarily what The Coup does, and they do it quite successfully. They serve bowls of Asian noodles and vegetables, quesadillas of falafel and goat cheese, and soups of lentils combined with fruit. Like an apricot-lentil soup. Odd sounding, but really quite nice.

Where The Coup kicks it up a notch is in serving organic focaccia, organic apple pie, organic coffee, organic wine, and so on. They shop a lot at the Calgary Farmers' Market and support small, local, natural producers. Even though The Coup is not exclusively organic, they're very serious about it.

And unlike many similar places I've been in, the owners don't get preachy about it. They are downright pleasant about the whole vegetarian and organic thing. There may be a lot of natural fibres around and more than a few yoga nerds hanging about, but The Coup is a comfortable, friendly place.

Much of the food is very good. The pear, caramelized onion, and melted brie panini is a darn good sandwich in anyone's book. The salads are usually good too. They would be even nicer with some grilled shrimp, but that's not the style here. And for dessert, you can have cheesecake or chocolate torte or that apple pie—all organic.

The Coup seats about thirty-five inside, and there is a three-table patio out front. It's a cute, minimalist place with polished concrete floors, vertical wooden panelling, kitschy 1950s lamps, and compelling New Age and world beat soundtracks. I like the idea, the space, and the people who run The Coup. I can get my meat fix elsewhere.

www.thecoup.ca

Coyotes

Contemporary Southwestern

206 Caribou Street, Banff
Phone: 762 •3963
Daily 7:30 am–10 pm
Reservations recommended — Fully licensed — Corkage $20 — Non-smoking
V, MC, AE, Debit — $$

WE most often end up at Coyotes for breakfast. Few other Banff eateries outside of the hotels offer breakfast, but that aside, Coyotes has a nice morning tone. The long lunch counter and the menu of buttermilk pancakes, honey-baked granola, and huevos rancheros are always attractive. The food is big and hearty and always served with a smile.

But occasionally we stop in for lunch or dinner, at least when there's a table available or we've thought to call ahead. Reservations are almost always necessary because Coyotes is one of those places that both locals and tourists frequent. It has a constant hum of activity, with closely placed tables filled with hikers and bikers and weekenders from Calgary.

Coyotes' dinner menu conjures up visions of the Southwest—meaning the Southwestern states of New Mexico and California, not the Southwestern Calgary neighbourhoods of Lakeview and Killarney. So you'll find enchiladas, blue corn, and chorizo, but you'll also see pesto, polenta, and penne. Coyotes is one of the few Southwestern restaurants in our area, but it's not slavish to the style. It almost qualifies as Southwestern-Mediterranean-Californian.

We can get pasta in other places, so we order dishes such as the classic sweet-potato and corn chowder garnished with red-chili sauce and sour cream. It's a blend of smoky flavours, as good a soup as any in Santa Fe. The Southwest Sushi Roll is a tortilla filled with smoked salmon and cilantro mayonnaise in a cross-cultural twist that brings the coast and the desert to the mountains. (It's pleasant, but as a sushi addict, give me raw fish or give me, well, a fishing rod.) Another starter, the orange-chipotle prawns, is a dynamite combination.

Main course selections fill the need for Southwestern purism. A blue-corn chicken enchilada ($21) is lacquered with a dark red-chili sauce that turns the dish almost black. Stacked New Mexican-style, it's a forceful enchilada, not for the meek. Slightly less intense is the grilled chicken breast with tomatillo salsa ($23). Shellacked with Coyotes' own barbecue sauce, the chicken is tender and tasty and well balanced by the salsa.

They don't carry an extensive list of different tequilas, but they still make a pretty good margarita, an essential drink for a Southwestern restaurant. And always the pleasant service. It seems no matter how busy they are, they are consistently good to their customers. And that's a big part of Coyotes' continuing popularity.

Crazyweed Kitchen

Global & Seasonal Cuisine

626 Main Street, Canmore   *1600 Railway Avenue, Canmore*
Reservations recommended for dinner,   *Reservations recommended*
not accepted for lunch
Wine & beer only   *Fully licensed*
(closing upon Railway Avenue location opening) *(opening fall/winter of 2006/2007)*
Phone: 609•2530
Daily 11:30 am–3:30 pm, 5:30 pm–close
Patio — Smoking on patio only
V, MC, Debit — $$

B Y the time you read this, I hope that Crazyweed Kitchen will be in their new, bright, slope-roofed restaurant on Railway Avenue. But at the time of this writing, the date of that move was uncertain. Regardless of the location, Crazyweed is an essential part of any visit to Canmore, so what follows is excerpted and updated from the last edition of this book—it applies mostly to the old location, but I am confident that the Crazyweed attitude will prevail in the new site.

There is no more aptly named restaurant in this book than Crazyweed. The creation of Jan and Richard Hrabec, Crazyweed has become a culinary landmark not only in Canmore but in the entire area. The food is so good it can bring tears to your eyes, but eating here is no typical, traditional experience. It's a little off-kilter and, well, a bit crazy.

Jan Hrabec is the calm culinary genius of the couple. She can squeeze more flavour out of ingredients than any chef in our area. And I mean Any Chef In Our Area. This is the place where other chefs go to eat. Her lamb sandwich with eggplant relish has transported me to another plane of consciousness. Her pizzas are among the best we've eaten outside of Italy. Her salads, her desserts, and her salmon and potato pie are all beyond reproach. To be more succinct, if I were looking at a "last meal" situation, I'd ask Jan to cook it.

And I might ask Richard to serve it. Because he'd tell so many bizarre and fascinating stories, I might just forget why I was there. Richard provides the creative, crackling energy to Crazyweed. His ideas push the space to evolve, helping move Crazyweed along at the front of contemporary cuisine. And his personality fills the space. A meal at Crazyweed is not complete without a Richard experience.

Enough with the praise. It should now be abundantly obvious that Crazyweed is one of my absolute rave-faves in this book. And I know that I am far from alone. But is there a downside here? For me, no. For those treading the tried and true, Crazyweed may be a bit too unusual. That's fine. It's not for the drive-through crowd. It's for those who want creativity and that slightly off-kilter attitude.

Da Guido

Italian

2001 Centre Street N
Phone: 276•1365
Monday–Friday 11:30 am–2 pm, Monday–Saturday 5 pm–11 pm
Reservations recommended — Fully licensed — Non-smoking
V, MC, AE — $$–$$$

WHERE can you go for a good, well-served, traditional Italian meal these days? It seems all the Italian places have gone contemporary or market-style or way downscale. So where can you get a decent bowl of pasta, a steamy stracciatella, or a sweet zabaglione without too much hoopla? Try Da Guido.

Guido Panara, a native of Rome, has been cooking in Calgary since 1984. His first restaurant was a small joint on Centre Street that was hugely popular. He built the current Da Guido in 1990 and has been putting out bruschetta and risotto ever since.

Speaking of bruschetta, Guido's is the best I've had in Calgary. (In Rome too, for that matter.) He roasts the tomatoes, bringing out more flavour than they have any right to have.

Guido is good at the flavour thing. One night, Catherine savoured her plate of penne with vodka and prosciutto in a creamy tomato sauce ($16). Savoured it too long, if anyone is asking me, but then, I can be a fast-eater and was anxious for my next course. Anyway, since no one *is* asking me, let me tell you what she said. She said that Guido had squeezed every last smidgeon of flavour out of the ingredients and onto her plate. (I had to agree. In my impatience, I had helped her with the last few mouthfuls.)

What I had wanted to move on to was my gamberoni fradiavola ($24): huge prawns braised in olive oil, garlic, and an herbed tomato sauce. Big Roman flavours here, the prawns still lightly crunchy and the sauce meant for post-meal scooping. Catherine's scallops al Marsala ($24) were packed with equally intense flavours, this time Marsala and mushrooms. I personally couldn't handle the sweetness of the Marsala, but for those who like the taste, this is your dish.

I prefer my Marsala in zabaglione, cut with egg yolks. Guido does a straight-ahead, non-adulterated version that is thick, creamy, and requires that you take a good walk afterwards. As does his wine list. It's not overly long, but it contains great variety, albeit within the Italian realm.

What else? Da Guido's twin dining rooms are comfortable, and the servers are friendly, professional, and helpful. Da Guido is obviously a high-end place, yet the service creates a relaxed, almost casual atmosphere, and some prices are mid-level for these days.

Guido is one smart restaurateur. He knows his business and his customers well, and he treats them both with respect.

Danube Creperie

Crepes

Downstairs, 1131 Kensington Road NW
Phone: 270•9403
Tuesday–Friday 10:30 am–9 pm, Saturday 10 am–10 pm, Sunday 10 am–5 pm
Reservations accepted Tuesday–Friday
Fully licensed — Corkage $5 — Non-smoking
V, MC, AE, Debit — $–$$

THERE are few Eastern European restaurants around Calgary. There have been Hungarians and Czechs and Poles here for a while, and more recently, folks have arrived from Romania, Bulgaria, and the former Yugoslavia. But for all the immigration, we have only one Hungarian and one Russian restaurant. And, for a few years now, a mostly Serbian creperie called the Danube.

Opened by the mother-daughter team of Smilja and Tamara Pejakov, they focus on crepes—also known as palachinkas—filled with the foods of the countries through which the Danube flows; Serbia features most prominently because that's where the Pejakovs are from.

They make over seventy kinds of crepes here. Many are the savoury kind filled with ingredients such as sautéed peppers, mushrooms, onions and feta or chicken and spinach or salami and egg. A number are slathered with ajvar sauce, a spread made from roast peppers, and all come draped with a creamy, mild garlicky sauce. (That includes the breakfast crepes stuffed with scrambled eggs and smoked sausage.)

The dessert crepes are even more abundant and are filled with everything from brown sugar and cinnamon to Nutella and whipping cream. The brown-sugar one falls under the menu's "traditional" category, while crepes with ingredients such as ricotta, apricot jam, and walnuts are classified as "fancy traditional." Then there are whole categories of custard crepes and coconut crepes and fruit crepes with various other ingredients—think ginger-cookie crumbs or caramel or white chocolate or toasted almonds. Finally, there is a list of "double-sin" palachinkas that are described as two crepes layered with the various fillings. This is crepe heaven.

And these are good crepes. They're large, cooked on a crepe grill using a slightly tangy batter. They're reasonably priced, with most sweet ones coming in at $5 to $7. The custard crepes and the double-sin ones are a buck or two more, and the savoury ones are mostly $6 to $10.

I should mention that the Danube is tricky to spot—it's right beside the Plaza Theatre, but it's downstairs. The room itself is done in various purples and yellows, there's a partly open kitchen, and it seats about thirty-five. Service is pleasant with Smilja at the grill and Tamara serving up the crepes. Sometimes Smilja's other two daughters—Melissa and Maria—help out too.

So if you're looking for a hearty meal or just a coffee and a palachinka before a movie, the Danube Creperie makes an interesting stop. Especially if you speak Serbian.

Diner Deluxe

Contemporary Diner

804 Edmonton Trail NE
Phone: 276•5499
Monday–Friday 7:30 am–9:30 pm, Saturday 8 am–3 pm, 5 pm–9:30 pm
Sunday & Holidays 8 am–3 pm
Reservations accepted at dinner for over 5 & for breakfast Monday–Friday
Fully licensed — Corkage $8, Free corkage Wednesday evenings — Patio — Non-smoking
V, MC, AE, Debit — $

IN the realm of diners, there are real mid-twentieth century diners and contemporary retro diners, and then there is Diner Deluxe. In a world unto itself, Diner Deluxe spans the old and the new, and in the process, redefines the genre.

It would almost be enough for Diner Deluxe to coast on its looks. It has more retro-chic panache than any of its cohorts because it was built as a tribute to the diner era rather than as a restaurant (that's a long story). It's fortunate that Dwayne and Alberta Ennest saw the potential of this art project in 2001 and turned it into a restaurant. The pastel cornices, the angular counters, the mirrors strategically placed to reflect natural light, and the collection of 1950s memorabilia are exceptional. On top of that, the kitchen makes outstanding diner fare.

Residents around the Regal Terrace neighbourhood think of Diner Deluxe as their own. But so do the rest of us, which explains the lengthy breakfast lineups on weekends. To avoid that, we go later in the day since breakfast is served whenever Diner Deluxe is open.

You'll find johnnycake with strawberry compote, maple-fried oatmeal with lemon curd and cream, sourdough French toast, buckwheat muesli pancakes, and on and on. Good breakfast. But lunch and dinner are primo too. There's baked macaroni with sun-dried tomatoes, basil, and white cheddar. There's a braised lamb shank with Dijon-mashed potatoes. There's veal meat loaf with red-pepper relish. And they call this a diner? Now I understand the "Deluxe" part of the name.

The food is big and packs big taste, but not a hefty price. The sirloin steak with pork and beans is $14.50, and that's about as high as it gets. Breakfast tops out at $13.50 for steak and eggs, and eggs Benedict is $10.50. Great value.

Service at Diner Deluxe is of the pierced and pleasant variety. They're doing good work and they seem happy about it. The only downside of Diner Deluxe is that it's busy, but hey, it's also a lot of fun.

Diner Deluxe gets most of its baking—including a near-perfect coconut cream pie—from the affiliated **Urban Baker** (266•3763) right next door. If the lineup is too long, you can just slip into the Baker for a butter tart to slake your hunger.

The Ennests also operate **Vue Cafe** (816–11 Avenue SW, 263•4346) in Virginia Christopher Fine Art. It's great for a light lunch and some excellent art.

Divine

Market-Fresh Cuisine

42 McRae Street, Okotoks
Phone: 938 • 0000
Monday–Saturday 11 am–2:30 pm, Thursday–Saturday 5:30 pm–9 pm
Reservations recommended — Fully licensed — Veranda & patio
Non-smoking restaurant & veranda, smoking on patio
V, MC, AE, Debit — $$

IT takes a lot of moxie to name your restaurant Divine. But moxie is what Darren Nixon and Lareina Wayne have in spades. When they opened their Okotoks restaurant a few years back, they softened the name a bit by calling it Café Divine. But they've since shortened it to Divine, and they splash the name in red ink on black business cards. No subtlety here.

Which is appropriate for the food at Divine. At first glance, the Victorian-style building appears to be a quaint tea house or light lunch café. But a look at the dinner menu reveals slow-braised lamb shank in a tomato, red-wine, and garlic ragout ($23.25) and a Portuguese half-chicken ($22.75). These are big plates with big flavours. So there's no subtlety in the food either. The flavours are forceful yet not over the top. But there is sophistication. Creations such as a roasted beet and sun-dried tomato and ginger soup with a blue-cheese cream are inspired. The bite of ginger leaves a distinct tingle on the tongue, a pleasant and lingering memory of the soup. (Caution: Don't wear anything white while eating this though.) For the more delicate diner, there is a fillet of halibut crusted in cornmeal and served with a tasty, organic black-bean salad ($23.25). Actually, in contrast with the many other big flavours on the menu, the crust on the halibut could use a little more depth of flavour.

Divine satisfies the Okotoks' lunch crowd with a great lamb burger topped with chili-mint cucumbers and a spicy mango mayonnaise ($10.50), a free-range turkey salad with roasted hazelnuts and dried cranberries on a croissant ($10.25), salads, noodle bowls, and more. Desserts are likewise big on size and taste, with oven-warmed brownies topped with ice cream and fruit sauce and a sour cherry crème brûlée topped with a perfect caramelized-sugar crust.

Divine showcases local products and growers not only in their dishes, but also on their shelves. You can do a little shopping while here—pick up a few hothouse tomatoes and squeeze-bottles of organic honey or go international with kosher salt and smoked Spanish paprika.

Decor at Divine is homespun, casual, and friendly, as are the staff. They're an earnest bunch, bent on keeping the water glasses filled and ensuring the plates are delivered hot from the kitchen.

So Divine it is. I like the attitude. And I like the food.

www.divinefood.ca

Divino

Western Canadian Bistro

113 Stephen Avenue Walk SW
Phone: 410•5555
Monday–Wednesday 11 am–10 pm, Thursday & Friday 11 am–11 pm
Saturday 5 pm–11 pm, Sunday 5 pm–10 pm
Reservations recommended — Fully licensed — Patio — Non-smoking
V, MC, AE, Debit — $$–$$$

I T was a dark and stormy night ...
Well, it was. It was the kind of winter night where even a half-block walk feels too far. Where the footing alternates between ice and slush and where Calgary seems like a foreboding place to be.

Fortunately, the goal of our walk was Divino, and in short order, everything became right with the world. Warmed by Divino's fine bistro cuisine and comforted by its casual, professional service, we quickly improved our perspective on our home town. The "new" Divino, in its current location since 2003, has become a bit of a standard around our house. "Is the food as good as Divino's?" Catherine sometimes asks about a new restaurant. "Not quite," I might respond. "But the ambience is similar."

Divino defines, for us and many other Calgarians, upscale casual dining. It's comfortable, stylish, a touch opulent, but not pretentious. It's Canadian bistro food, a hybrid of French classics such as onion soup, foie gras, and veal sweetbreads with local ingredients such as elk strip loin, BC salmon, and Alberta lamb.

A favourite is the lamb-confit sandwich, big piles of tender lamb layered into house-baked bread along with fig jam, braised leeks, and cambozola cheese. There isn't much that's healthy about this sandwich and even less that's pretty. It's drippy, messy, and good. Don't order it if you're trying to impress someone—it's for later in the relationship.

Try the braised short ribs or the lobster cannelloni. Or for Divino traditionalists, there's a black-pepper linguine that has been on the menu since the early 1980s. The big Lyonnaise salad—with its croutons, lardons, and poached egg—will make you think you're in Lyon.

Which is where Chef John Donovan spent some time. He was good before he went to France and even better when he returned. A quiet, studious fellow, he's a heck of a cook. You can watch Donovan run the open kitchen from practically anywhere in the long, narrow restaurant. Small dining areas break up the room and add to the intimate mood. Anywhere you sit, you'll be drawn into the warmth and the professionalism of the place.

So on a dark and stormy night, it's worth that half-block walk. Or even more.

Note: Divino is affiliated with **The Ranche**, a beautifully restored, late 1800s home, at the south end of *Bow Bottom Trail SE (225•3939)*. It's also worth a walk in the park (Fish Creek Provincial Park, that is) for more creative food.

www.divinobistro.com

Eden

Fine French Cuisine with New World Influences

Mountain Avenue (The Rimrock Resort Hotel), Banff
Phone: 762•1865
Daily 6 pm–10 pm
Closed Mondays & Tuesdays from January to April
Reservations highly recommended — Fully licensed — Non-smoking
V, MC, AE, Debit — $$$

THE view from Eden is both stunning and surprising. Banff-dazzled tourists and locals alike are often unaware that the "main" floor of the Rimrock Hotel—which includes Eden—is actually the seventh floor. (Driving up to a seventh floor entrance always make me chuckle. I know, I'm easily amused.) The Rimrock clings to the side of Sulphur Mountain, and half the hotel flows down into the valley. Guest rooms and dining rooms all benefit from the architectural uniqueness of the building. At night, lighting illuminates the trees so that you don't miss the view even in the dark.

Eden is the main dining room in the Rimrock. It's a long, narrow space where all tables feature that view. It's similar to a cruise ship dining room: Tables are lined in two long rows with a walkway down the middle. Likewise, service follows the best of cruise ships and hotels: It is impeccable from end to end. Servers know how to present and clear plates, how to suggest appropriate wines, how to make each diner feel comfortable and special.

Once ensconced in Eden, it is difficult to leave. We feel so well taken care of that we want someone to just roll us back to our room and tuck us in. A meal here is not some dashed-off quickie. Allow a good three hours—we were there almost five hours once.

You are offered a choice between four multi-course options. You can order a three-course meal for $90, four courses for $100, or five for $110. Then there's the eight-course degustation for $150. Wine pairings are available for any of the options, and they vary in price according to the quality of the wine.

Roasted sablefish and braised oxtail ravioli with artichoke confit, seared loin and rack of Alberta lamb with tomato-aubergine caviar, almond-mascarpone pannacotta with passion fruit semifreddo. All perfectly prepared and served in portions for savouring, not gluttonizing. As much attention is given to the colour and style of the plate as to the taste. No effort, or price, has been spared in order to collect the finest ingredients for the menus. Executive Chef Yoshi Chubachi is one of the best in the area, and his skill shines at Eden.

Dining at Eden is a memorable event. It takes time and stamina and a healthy bank account, but it is worth it. Even if just for the view.

www.rimrockresort.com

Fireside Place

Prime Rib & Steak House

115 Main Street (Dominion Hotel), Carstairs
Phone: 337•3053
Sunday–Thursday 11 am–9 pm, Friday & Saturday 11 am–close
Reservations recommended — Fully licensed — Corkage $10 — Non-smoking
V, MC, Debit — $$–$$$

A CBC listener emailed me a message that the food and setting at the Fireside Place were good and that the bathrooms were great. Good food and great bathrooms? I'm there! We headed up to Carstairs as quickly as possible.

The Fireside Place is attached to the Dominion Hotel and has been in operation for over five years. It's a beautiful room of old wood floors, brick walls, and four fireplaces, and it seats about seventy-five in three areas. Decorated with antiques, candles, and wood furniture, the Fireside Place has loads of atmosphere.

The staff are decked out in vested uniforms, and the service combines small town hospitality with a high level of restaurant professionalism. They are quick and cheerful and skilled.

The menu crosses over from mainstream Alberta home cooking to contemporary and international stylings. It rambles from French onion soup and teriyaki wings to liver and onions and cedar-planked salmon with a three-onion marmalade.

We've enjoyed everything we've had at the Fireside Place. The house borscht, a Russian Doukhobor recipe, is great: It's beetless and made with cabbage, carrots, celery, onion, peppers, and dill, with puréed potatoes as a thickener. It's served in big bowls for hearty eaters.

But we've come to think of this as the place for prime rib, available in slabs up to fourteen ounces. Every day, they offer a special comprised of seven-ounces of prime rib, a Yorkshire pudding, a spray of vegetables, potato or rice, and all the other fixings: soup or salad, dessert, and a choice of coffee or pop. For $21.95. Now that's a deal. And it's good. I mean real good. The Caesar salad is large and fresh and contains all the right ingredients—homemade croutons, real bacon, good dressing. It's not one of those that burns you with garlic. The beef is superb, cooked to a medium rare in a special prime-rib oven. Every element on the plate is tasty, including the chunks of cooked carrot. I passed on the pop, but did have their rice pudding. Nice pudding with lots of raisins.

The chef at the Fireside Place knows what he's doing. No pretense here. Just good food, lots of it, and at a decent price. And I did like the bathrooms, including the ladies' (which I took a peak at—they've got a little museum theme going on in there). The Fireside Place is worth the drive from Calgary, and it's a good stop too if you're passing through.

www.firesideplace.ca

Fleur de Sel

French Brasserie

2015–4 Street SW
Phone: 228•9764
Tuesday–Friday 11 am–2 pm, Daily 5 pm–last guest
Reservations recommended — Fully licensed
Non-smoking dining room, 4 smoking seats at bar
V, MC, AE, Debit — $$–$$$

FLEUR de Sel is an acquired taste, both the product itself (a natural sea salt) and the tiny 4th Street brasserie. If you're a salt fan, the grainy salt from the coast of France is as good as it gets. If you're not, it can be too intense, too overpowering. Like the restaurant.

Fleur de Sel is as close to a true French brasserie as can be found in Calgary. Tables are shoehorned into a small triangular space, so tight that you often have to walk sideways between them. Walls are covered in black and white photos of France and large mirrors that let you keep an eye on the proceedings from any angle. A long, curving bar still houses—at least in the summer of 2006—one of the last smoking sections in the city. An open kitchen churns out rich, savoury French cuisine.

And then there's Patrice Durandeau, the energetic owner, chef, maitre d', and master of ceremonies for dining. To truly understand and enjoy Fleur de Sel, one must understand Durandeau. He's a fine chef, a true master of sauces. He's committed to his customers, passing out glasses of Pineau des Charentes and Pernod on a regular basis. His personality fills the room with eccentricity and charm. He's a force of nature that is worth the price of admission. If you don't like a restaurant where the owner's personality is front and centre, Fleur de Sel is probably not for you.

But if you do, and you also like good French cuisine, you need to go to Fleur de Sel. The cassoulet ($26) never disappoints. With large white beans, a rich tomatoey sauce, a sausage, a lamb chop, and a ham steak, this is a meaty, filling entree. The Galloway beef tenderloin ($35) is always tasty too, served with pickled ginger or, on request, peppercorn or Bordelaise sauce. Then there are the mussels in a Dijon mustard and crème fraîche sauce ($14). And an excellent version of onion soup ($8).

Fleur de Sel's food is built from the ground up, in the old-school, traditional French way. It's well prepared, attractively plated, and professionally served, all with a well-conceived wine list and a classic dessert menu of tarte Tatin, chocolate mousse, and crème brûlée.

But you have to like that shoehorned, intense feeling of brasserie dining too. And the sense that, as a diner, you are part of the entertainment. Then you'll acquire a taste for Fleur de Sel.

www.fleurdeselbrasserie.com

Fuze Finer Dining

Contemporary Global

Upstairs, 110 Banff Avenue (Clock Tower Mall), Banff
Phone: 760•0853
September–June: Daily 6 pm–10 pm; July & August: Daily 3 pm–10 pm
Reservations recommended — Fully licensed — Small deck — Non-smoking
V, MC, AE, Debit — $$–$$$

UNTIL recently there weren't many contemporary, mid-range places in Banff, places where you could get a nicely served meal with a glass of wine for under a $100 a couple (yes, that's mid-range these days). But the arrival of Café Soleil, Muk-a-Muk, The Bison Mountain Bistro, and Fuze Finer Dining has filled that gap.

Fuze also fills the upper level of the Clock Tower Mall with a large dining room as well as a private one with a display window into the kitchen, a demonstration kitchen, an elaborate wine cellar, and a culinary boutique. And it is called Fuze Finer Dining. Not *Fine* Dining. *Finer* Dining. So be it.

I like a lot of what Fuze has done. The main dining room is open and fairly airy considering the ceiling is not that high. It's been done in blacks and browns, with booths and well-spaced tables. They also have a handful of tables on a narrow deck over Banff Avenue, but Fuze's one physical shortcoming is that it doesn't take much advantage of the view. That, combined with its upstairs, out-of-the-way location, makes it more appealing for dinner than for lunch.

When they first opened, they tried to compete with the quicker, cheaper lunch places along Banff Avenue, but have since refocused on the early-dinner-through-late-evening crowd. It's a concept that seems a better fit.

As regards the food, it's a nice menu: a trio of scallop, tuna, and salmon tartars; Thai-style risotto with shellfish and green curry; seared salmon; beef tenderloin with foie gras and braised oxtail. It's an East-meets-West theme designed by Chef Gary Dayanandan. Even his New York steak entree is done with Indian spices and curried squash. He also does a four-course table d'hôte for $60 and a separate vegetarian menu of nine dishes, four of which are vegan. His roasted-tomato soup stands out as one of the best soups I've ever had, anywhere, any time.

A couple of things that have been consistent on my visits are the service and the wine. Banff can be a little spotty on service, but the staff here are exceptional. And so is the wine list. Both are the product of General Manager Anthony Chalmers, who used to be in charge of the Banffshire Club at the Banff Springs. Chalmers' wine knowledge is superb, and his service attitude is exceptional.

So Fuze is fine. Very fine. Maybe even finer.

www.fuzedining.com

Globefish

Japanese (Sushi & Izakaya)

326–14 Street NW
Phone: 521•0222
Monday–Saturday 11:30 am–3 pm, 5 pm–10 pm
Reservations recommended — Fully licensed — Corkage $15 — Patio — Non-smoking
V, MC, AE — $$

THE only thing that surprises me with sushi bars these days is that anyone can find a spot for a new one. So I have to give credit to the three partners who opened Globefish. They took what used to be a Vietnamese restaurant and opened this izakaya-style place, serving an astounding range of sushi and sashimi combos plus a realm of other dishes such as udon noodles and chicken teriyaki.

Izakayas are sake bars where numerous small plates of food are served with sake or beer over the course of a meal. Popular with Japanese salarymen—and increasingly with independent Japanese women—izakayas are livelier and more contemporary than traditional sushi bars and restaurants. They're gaining popularity in North America too.

Two of the partners in Globefish moved a few years ago from Japan to Vancouver where they worked for a big sushi company. After a while, they wanted to go out on their own so they relocated to Calgary, thinking the Vancouver market was pretty much saturated. They opened Chopsticks, a small room on Memorial Drive with thirty-odd seats but a challenging address. After a year or so, they sold Chopsticks, moved to a higher traffic location, and started Globefish.

These guys learned their trade well in Vancouver. They make a variety of the large sushi rolls that are popular on the coast, from the Rapture Roll and the mango roll to the Crazy Buster and the Moon Fantasy. This is one of the hot trends in sushi—big rolls. They're priced about $8 to $10 each. You get about eight slices out of a roll, and they're almost a meal in themselves. They come stacked or offset on long trays—the presentation is as exact as the cuts themselves.

I tried the large Crunch and Munch Roll of shrimp tempura wrapped with cucumber, avocado, rice, and nori and dressed with a wasabi cream. Good stuff. Then I had slices of Hawaiian snapper laid over what was left of my fish when the sushi chef was done with it. Creative, but um … perhaps a little scary looking. I followed that up with some beautiful red-tuna sashimi and more rolls filled with tasty, crunchy things. I do like my sushi.

It's hard to point to which of the local sushi bars is "the best," but I'll certainly give Globefish a nod for excellent sushi and creativity. And if you're a sake fan, this is definitely the place to go.

www.globefish.ca

Glory of India

Indian

515 – 4 Avenue SW
Phone: 263•8804
Monday–Friday 11:30 am–2 pm, Monday–Saturday 5 pm–10 pm
Reservations recommended — Fully licensed — Corkage $13.95 — Patio — Non-smoking
V, MC, AE, Debit — $$

'M often asked to recommend a good Indian restaurant. And for a very short question, I tend to give a very long answer. You see, India is a big country with a lot of food variation from end to end. There's the Punjabi style in the northwest with its great tandoori dishes and the Kashmiri style in the northeast with its fruits and creamy sauces. Gujarat in the west is known for its vegetarian dishes, and the southern states have their dossas. And that's just a start.

So, the first place I mention is my choice for best all round Delhi-style Indian food: Glory of India. (Delhi being the capital, the food there tends to be pan-Indian.) Glory does a better job of putting all the cultures together than any other place in town, and it consistently wows me with its flavours and quality.

And I'm not alone. Just try getting near Glory at lunchtime when the buffet is rolled out. You have to book well ahead for that. In the evening when you order off the menu, it can still be quite full even though they recently expanded the dining room.

Glory of India has the usual favourites: butter chicken, tandoori prawns, rogan josh, and so on. And they are good. But this is the spot to step out a bit and try some dishes you won't find in many other places. The chicken Chatinard is a fine example with its roasted spices and tamarind paste. It's not hot in a spicy sense, but it is spice intense. Then there's the navratan korma, a mix of vegetables in a creamy cashew sauce. Decadent. Even the Pindi chole—a chickpea dish—is heightened by the addition of mango powder. This is excellent food.

I'll even eat dessert here, something I rarely do at Indian restaurants—I often find them tooth-achingly sweet. But Glory serves what they call gulab jamun fudge, sliced gulab jamun with ice cream and mango coulis. Still pretty sweet, but darned good.

The fudge is not the only East-meets-West oddity on the menu. For something completely different, try the prawn cocktail served with an Indian-spiced cocktail sauce. This will have you rethinking every shrimp cocktail you've ever tried.

I like Glory of India a lot, enough that I named it Best New Restaurant of 2002 on my CBC Radio spot. And it hasn't disappointed me in the years since then.

www.gloryofindia.com

Golden Inn

Chinese (Cantonese & some Peking)

107A – 2 Avenue SE
Phone: 269 • 2211
Monday – Thursday 4 pm – 3 am, Friday & Saturday 4 pm – 4 am, Sunday 4 pm – 2 am
Reservations accepted — Fully licensed — Corkage $5 — Non-smoking
V, MC, AE, Debit — $ – $$

THE Golden Inn scared the bejeebers out of their late-night regulars for a while there. These hungry insomniacs couldn't get their fixes of 2 a.m. salt-and-pepper seafood. And the 3 a.m. moo goo gai pan was gone. The restaurant had forsaken their roots by moving closing time up to 1 a.m. Not that 1 a.m. isn't late enough for most folks, but the Golden Inn had always stayed open until 3 a.m., sometimes even 4 a.m. And even if I hadn't seen that part of the clock for a few years, it had always been reassuring to know that, in the early hours, a steaming platter of sweet-and-sour pork was just a call away. Fortunately, management saw the light (or perhaps, in this case, the dark) and quickly reverted back to the later-night status.

And just to clarify, the Golden Inn has never compensated by opening any earlier in the day. They've always eschewed the lunch crowd, choosing to open at 4 p.m.

Regardless of the hours, the Golden Inn is a Chinatown classic. It's been there for decades and has always had a traditional Cantonese menu that's different from everyone else's. There's a lot of seafood, including live lobsters and crabs in the tank by the front door. And they've always had cool-sounding dishes like Braised Eight Joe Duck and Singing Chicken Hot Pot.

And this is one of those places that has the mysterious—at least to my Western taste buds—Chinese menu. It's always helpful to go with someone who can read and order off of it. Now in truth, there are a lot of chicken feet and spleen dishes on it, but there are some other things that are friendlier to my palate too. Like a simple dish of garlic pea shoots, so fresh and lively and light. The garlic is well cooked, yet crispy and fresh.

That's the key to the Golden Inn's food and the food of Canton. It's all about the fresh, natural flavours. This style of Chinese food is less seasoned than most other styles, so the ingredients have to be particularly good. And I've always been happy with the Golden Inn's version. They are not hidebound either—the Golden Inn does a pretty decent version of ginger beef, that great Calgary-Chinese invention.

So even if my late-night dining excursions are but a bleary memory, the Golden Inn still stands the test in broad daylight.

Il Sogno

Inspired Italian

24–4 Street NE
Phone: 232•8901
Tuesday–Friday 11:30 am–2 pm, Tuesday–Sunday 5 pm–close
Reservations recommended — Fully licensed — Non-smoking
V, MC, AE — $$$

'LL bet I have received more comments about Il Sogno than any other restaurant. Some people love it, declaring it to be the best restaurant they've eaten in, anywhere, anytime. Others are less impressed.

I understand where both sides are coming from. Il Sogno is definitely not your checkered-tablecloth Italian restaurant. They've always tried to be unique, and those aspirations tend to polemicize people.

First, Il Sogno looks different. It's in the old brick De Waal Block on a southbound street that parallels Edmonton Trail. Inside, there are two high-ceilinged rooms with sleek, minimalist decor. It could be any kind of contemporary restaurant.

The owner labels the cuisine Inspired Italian, but I would narrow it down to predominantly contemporary Tuscan. I see grilled venison strip loin with Parma prosciutto, meatballs made from ground rabbit, and pasta with wild-boar bacon, sage, and pecorino—all of which fall broadly under the Tuscan sun. But spanning a range of Italian provinces, the menu does include sautéed baby squid, caramelized duck with chestnut gnocchi, and veal tenderloin with polenta.

This is one hard-working menu. Each plate is constructed unto itself, with its own side dishes. And I see a few items carried over from the lunch to the dinner menu, but mostly you'll find different choices on each.

I tried the Parma prosciutto with cheeses, oranges, and pea shoots in an orange-infused olive oil. Lovely, delicate flavours, a beautifully conceived and constructed dish. Then came the francobolli—a kind of small tortellini—stuffed with pumpkin and pancetta and topped with a cream sauce and parmesan. Again, delicate is the word I would choose to describe the flavours.

It's not big food at Il Sogno. And at $14 and $17 for the two lunch dishes I had, I wouldn't use the word delicate to describe the price. If you go in the evening, expect appetizers in the mid-teens and mains cruising up to $40.

I appreciate the amount of effort that goes into the food at Il Sogno. It's subtle and intricate and tantalizing to the palate. But it's not the kind of food that knocks you off your chair with robust jolts of flavour. This is satisfying and beautiful food, but it's also food you think about more than savour.

So, that may be why I hear so much about Il Sogno. Your pleasure here will depend on the kind of diner you are. Do you dine with your brain or your stomach?

www.ilsogno.org

Isabella's by Infuse

Alberta Market Cuisine

707–13 Avenue SW
Phone: 410•9288
Tuesday–Sunday 11 am–4 pm
Reservations recommended — Fully licensed — Non-smoking
V, MC, AE — $$

I F there's one place in this book that reminds me of my grandfather's farm, it has to be Isabella's by Infuse. Isabella's is in the historic Lougheed House, a beautifully restored mansion built in 1892 for Senator James and Mrs. Isabella Lougheed. A visit to the house is a great way to see how the upper class lived in Calgary at the turn of the twentieth century.

But that's not why the place reminds me of my grandfather's big old farmhouse, though both structures date from the same era. It's mostly the menu, put together by Wade Sirois and Jaclyn Labchuk of Infuse Catering, that takes me back a few decades. (Infuse took over the contract for Isabella's in the summer of 2006. Great Events Catering had it for the first year the Lougheed House was open, but released it in 2006 to concentrate on their other activities.)

The lunch menu—and they only do lunch—is short and rich. If you want to taste ingredients fresh from the garden, Isabella's is the spot. Infuse has a strong commitment to local producers, so you'll see loads of them named on the menu: Sylvan Star, Highwood Crossing, Gull Valley Greenhouse, Hoven Farms, and more.

The salad of Gull Valley tomatoes with Sylvan Star gouda ($7) reminds me of tomatoes from my grandfather's garden, still warm from the sun. And a pot pie of carrots, new potatoes, and beans in dill cream with a buttermilk biscuit ($14) is just the kind of dish my grandfather would tuck into for dinner. The natural flavours of vegetables and the simple dressing of dill cream are what really take me back. It's good, plain, simple cooking with flavours unsullied by excess. (We're talking farm "dinner" here. Most city folk would know it as "lunch." The later meal on the farm is "supper," and "lunch" is something you have mid-afternoon in the field.)

Isabella's menu will change seasonally (the summer 2006 menu was the first one Infuse put together at Isabella's), but here are the kinds of dishes you'll find: chicken-liver mousse with saskatoon mustard, cornichons, pickled cherries, and toasted baguette ($14); slow-roasted elk with caramelized peppers, gouda, cider-rye bread, and raspberry slaw ($16); and Bernard Callebaut bittersweet chocolate pot au crème ($7).

This is not cheap food, but then good ingredients never are. Even my grandfather would agree.

www.lougheedhouse.com

JoJo Bistro

French Bistro

#101, 2215–33 Avenue SW
Phone: 246•0082
Monday–Friday 11 am–2 pm, Monday–Saturday 5 pm–10 pm
Reservations recommended — Fully licensed — Corkage $20 — Non-smoking
V, MC, AE, Debit — $$–$$$

As the area around Marda Loop has developed, we've seen the arrival of some good places to eat. There's San Remo, the Belmont Diner, Karma Arts House, Kaffa Coffee, and the always outstanding Red Tree caterers. But one place that's been up and down is the corner that, over the years, has been called Trocadero, Pastis, and a few other things. For most of the time, it has been run by Mohammed Guelli, but for a while, he passed it over to someone else. It became spotty, and when I ate there in the summer of 2003, I did not have a good meal.

But Guelli has since taken the space back and moved his 17th Avenue bistro called JoJo into it. So today, JoJo resides in Marda Loop and looks pretty much as it did when the spot was called Trocadero. There are thirty-odd seats packed cosily into a warm, bright space. I mean "cosily" as in tight by North American standards, roomy by French bistro standards. And I mean "bright" as in daylight hours. In the evening, it is so dim that I need to read the menu using the outside street light.

What I like about the menu is that it is a true French bistro one—there is the expected bouillabaisse, some cassoulet, steak frites, and rabbit in mustard sauce. Prices for entrees are in the mid-$20s, with appetizers $6 to $12. Chef/Owner Guelli is capable of preparing all these dishes quite expertly.

I had cassoulet, a southwestern French baked-bean dish with sausage, lamb chops, and duck confit. Very good. And the Marseille-style mussel soup with a touch of cream was just fine. Lacking a certain depth, but still fine. The highlight of my meal was dessert, a tarte Tatin served sizzling hot from the oven, the caramel bubbling on the plate. This is actually a simple dessert often done badly. It's nice to see it in its pure simplicity.

Service is good in an understated bistro way. Don't go expecting extravagant Continental service and food styling. The food is nicely presented—no artifice here. And for those who find that restaurant meals sometimes come out too cold for their liking, this is the kind of place where plates arrive from the oven to the table in mere seconds—they're often smoking hot.

So, after all the changes in this spot, I hope JoJo is here to stay for a while.

Jonas' Restaurant

Hungarian

937–6 Avenue SW
Phone: 262•3302
Tuesday–Friday 11:30 am–2 pm, 5 pm–9 pm, Saturday 5 pm–10 pm
Reservations recommended — Fully licensed — Corkage $10–$15 — Non-smoking
V, MC, AE, Debit — $–$$

AFTER a friend heartily recommended a new restaurant, Catherine and I buzzed out to this unnamed (by me, anyway) place and had, well, part of a meal. The food was so unutterably bad, we couldn't eat much. Poorly seasoned, cheap ingredients, some items masquerading as others.

We made a hasty exit, but were left with significant appetites. Not to mention that Catherine was now a bit cranky. So we headed to a place that would cheer her up and remove both the figurative and the literal bad tastes from our mouths. We went to Jonas' Restaurant.

Jonas' is Calgary's only full-tilt Hungarian restaurant. It's hidden from the street in a long, narrow space. Even when it's open, it looks closed. But the owners are there almost every day, and they are a big part of the appeal.

Janos and Rosza Jonas owned restaurants in Budapest, but they immigrated to Canada in the late 1990s. Janos is the chef—a good, professional Hungarian chef—and Rosza runs the front end in a style that is part Hungarian mama and part stand-up comic. She will make you feel guilty if you don't clean your plate, but she will entertain you at the same time.

And cleaning your plate can be a challenge here. The food is big, from the chicken paprikash with homemade dumplings and the Wiener schnitzel with potatoes to the bowls of Hungarian bean goulash and the Wednesday special of roast duck with red cabbage. The food is substantial enough that two sizes of most things are offered, and if you're a first-timer, I suggest you start with the smaller portions. This is good Hungarian cooking. It's hearty enough for an afternoon of plowing the fields but elegant enough to elicit a fine Hungarian rhapsody.

Some sort of Hungarian music is always playing, whether it's classical, folk, or a polka. And the room is designed with a distinctly Eastern European feel to it; it's bright and floral, but discreetly private at the same time.

On the downside, prices have gone up lately. A small liver-dumpling soup has skyrocketed from $2.45 to $3.50. A small paprikash is up a couple of bucks to $9.50. And they have finally broken the $10 mark with a number of the regular-sized entrees such as the Thursday special of lentils and sausage, now priced at $11.50. This is still outstanding value for the quality and quantity of food.

I heartily recommend Jonas' Restaurant and guarantee you won't leave cranky or hungry.

www.jonasrestaurant.homestead.com

Juan's

Mexican

Downstairs, 232 Stephen Avenue Walk SW
Phone: 266•0051
Monday–Friday 11 am–10 pm, Saturday noon–10 pm, Sunday 4 pm– 9 pm
Reservations recommended, especially for lunch — Fully licensed — Patio
Non-smoking
V, MC, AE, Debit — $$

JUAN has gone underground.

He hasn't disappeared altogether, but he has become distinctly difficult to find. For years he had a high-traffic spot on 1st Street, but when the lease prices went up, Juan decided to go down—down to a basement spot beside Scotia Centre that is, with an entrance on Stephen Avenue.

When Juan's Stephen Avenue patio is open, the restaurant is easy to find, but in winter months, the entrance is a little too discreet. There's a thing that happens at Juan's every lunch hour about 12:10 p.m. Cellphones ring and you'll overhear one-sided conversations that go something like this: "Yes. I'm at Juan's. Yes, on Stephen Avenue. Yes, you're right outside. Just look for the door with the staircase leading down. See it?" A minute later, someone arrives. Of course all the regular clientele that Juan built over almost twenty years have long since figured it out. They wouldn't let their favourite Mexican restaurant disappear without a fight.

In a town with few good Mexican restaurants, Juan's continues to satisfy. A huge part of that is Juan himself, a seasoned service-industry professional. He's a perpetually upbeat guy, and he has the ability to pass that tone on to his customers.

The new place has allowed Juan to expand his menu—it has a real kitchen as opposed to the tiny space where he used to work. So you can find pechuga de pollo Oaxaquena (chicken in a spicy Oaxaca-style sauce) or carne asada a la Tampiquena (filet mignon with a chicken enchilada and mole sauce). Plus some chile rellenos and a range of seafood, salads, and enchiladas.

I always enjoy Juan's soups, one of the key indicators of a good Mexican restaurant. On warmer days, the chicken soup with tortilla strips, avocado, and cheese is light and refreshing. On colder days, the creamed frijoles (bean) soup is thick and hearty and warming. Or, you can throw caution to the wind and have the soup of the day.

Whichever you choose, Juan will tease you with tequila and tempt you with desserts. He serves the classic deep-fried ice cream, a fine crepas con cajeta (crepes with caramel spread), and the rich, dense chocolate mousse or the chocolate cake (remember, chocolate came from Mexico). No matter how you approach Juan's, you're not likely to leave hungry.

Just make sure you find it in the first place. Look down, look way down, and think about Mexico.

www.juansmexican.com

Kashmir

Indian (Mughlai)

507 – 17 Avenue SW
Phone: 244•2294
Tuesday–Saturday 5:30 pm–10 pm, Sunday 5:30 pm–9 pm
Reservations recommended — Fully licensed — Non-smoking
V, MC, AE, Debit — $$

SOME Indian restaurants are known for the abundance of their buffets. Others are known for their speed and value, and still others, for their rustic charm and intense spicing. At the Kashmir, it's mostly about the elegance of the food and the uniqueness of the flavours.

The Kashmir is one of the few Mughlai restaurants in the city. Its menu has similarities to many of our Northern Indian restaurants, but the use of nuts, fruit, and dairy is much higher here. Cream is used to balance the heat, crafting lovely flavours. The Kashmiri prawns come in a mild cream sauce with grated apple, and the paneer pasanda is layered with mashed potatoes, nuts, raisins, and another cream sauce.

Those ingredients, however, do not infiltrate all the dishes. A non-creamy Madras lamb curry is rated "hot," and the vindaloo chicken is "very hot." And they mean it. These dishes have plenty of zip.

The meat and seafood entrees at the Kashmir are as deep and rich and sultry as at any Indian restaurant in the city. The Kashmir offers almost forty of them, including a tasty list of prawns. But they also have sixteen vegetarian entrees, ranging from a thickly sauced jalfrazie of bell peppers, onions, tomatoes, cauliflower, carrots, peas, and spices to a dal makhani of kidney beans and black lentils with cream and butter. Plus there's a lengthy selection of breads, including the fruit- and nut-stuffed Kashmiri nan, the lamb-stuffed keema, and the buttered paratha. Excellent variety and all done with skill.

Beware the size of the dishes at the Kashmir. They look small, but they eat big. They can also add up quickly. The vegetarian plates are around $10, the meats are about $13, and the prawn dishes are all $15. Not exorbitant for the quality, however.

The space and the service match the tone of the food. The Kashmir is actually two rooms, prettily decorated, with windows facing 17th Avenue. It is discreetly Indian in decor with staff who quietly go about their business. They are not stoic; they simply provide a calm, helpful atmosphere for dining.

The Kashmir also has a short but well-selected and reasonably priced wine list. Markups are astoundingly low, with few bottles over $30. And the selections match the food nicely.

When you feel like elegant Indian fare, this is the place to go.

www.thekashmir.ca

Kinjo

Japanese (Sushi & Izakaya)

7101 Macleod Trail S
Phone: 255•8998
Daily 11:30 am–10 pm
Reservations recommended — Fully licensed — Corkage $12 — Patio — Non-smoking
V, MC, AE, Debit — $ – $$

THERE are many sushi bars around town. In almost every one, there is a quiet itamae, studiously toiling away at his craft. He concentrates on the seafood, the rice, and the assorted accoutrements and doesn't typically talk a lot. But there is one notable exception. His name is Peter Kinjo. He's worked in many places, but in 2005, he converted what had been a Tim Hortons into an izakaya-style sushi bar called, appropriately, Kinjo.

This place is very much about Kinjo himself. He's an entertainer, greeting people at the door with a loud welcome, bringing extra plates of sushi to folks just to try, and offering Japanese sweets on the way out. In between, he's an irrepressible force, singing karaoke, dancing, swinging his huge knives around. He's one of the few restaurateurs who can tell me I have sexy legs and get away with it.

So, if you're looking for a quiet Japanese food experience with water gently dripping and discreet, kimono-clad waitresses, I have other recommendations. Kinjo would not be one of them.

Kinjo offers the lively Japanese izakaya-style of food and drink that is so popular right now in Japan. You order drinks—sake or beer or whatever—and then a number of small plates of food to share and snack on. Some of those may be sushi, others may be teriyaki beef or tempura shrimp or fried gyoza dumplings. Kinjo has the whole range, with a big sushi boat bar, some teppan grills, and tempura fryers sizzling away.

The boat bar consumes most of the room, with stools along one side and a few booths along the other. Inside the big oval created by the boat bar, chefs prepare the food. So when you order tempura, it will come from the fryer to your table in seconds. It will be very hot.

And remember, this used to be a Tim's. It still has the vestiges of the past: indestructible tile floors, linear, industrial construction, and parking access through the Wendy's lot. It's not pretty, but it is one of the few independent restaurants on a stretch of Macleod that features way too much fast food. The funny thing is that Kinjo can be quicker than any of the chains if you grab a stool at the bar and start your sushi consumption immediately.

Then there's Kinjo himself. I keep expecting his batteries to wear down, but they never do. Did I tell you he's irrepressible?

Koi

Asian Fusion & Vegetarian

1011–1 Street SW
Phone: 206•1564
Monday 8:30 am–5 pm, Tuesday & Wednesday 8:30 am–10 pm
Thursday & Friday 8:30 am–close, Saturday 5 pm–close
Reservations accepted — Fully licensed — Non-smoking
V, MC, Debit — $

ABOUT the closest thing you'll find to koi on the menu at Koi is smoked salmon. And perhaps that's appropriate. Koi are the pet fish kept in ponds by many people. They are a descendant of wild carp and are thought to be gentle and rather bright for fish. So they are not typically found on menus.

Koi is a good name for this eclectic café with its gentle, holistic overtones and its menu that ranges from vegan to full-tilt carnivore. It is a crossover between healthy/organic and indulgent/mainstream. If you're vegan or vegetarian, you will find some good choices at Koi. For breakfast, there's homemade maple-almond granola with fruit and optional yogurt ($6.50). Or a bagel with organic apple butter ($4). In the evening, there's an organic soba noodle salad with vegetables ($7) or coconut curry bowls ($10). But there are also scallops served with ginger bok choy ($10) and Spolumbo-sausage-fried rice ($10).

I tried a good lunchtime panini special of chicken-apple sausage served with greens and a smear of house relish. Koi gets their bread from Daniel's Baguette, a good wholesale baker. The desserts come from Urban Baker, another reliable place. But the soups are made in-house, and in spite of my lackluster feelings toward broccoli, the broccoli-cheddar soup was good. So, for a $10 lunch near downtown, Koi was pretty decent.

What impressed me most, though, was the general tone and style of Koi. The look is edgy, with chocolate brown walls and an unusual, white, circular matrix thing that crawls up the walls. You just have to go see it. And then there's the seating. It ranges from tree stumps to stylishly uncomfortable chairs to a heavily foam-padded bench. The foam must be that memory stuff, because when you stand up, you leave a big butt-print behind (so to speak). Fun for the whole family.

And the soundtrack is the kind of music only found in edgy vegan cafés and high-end hair salons. So eclectic that you're bound to love some of it and hate some of it and ask yourself who the performer is and why the heck are they playing those songs one after the other.

And the staff. A friendly pierced and tattooed bunch they are. No holier-than-thou stuff here, just good service with a smile—a pierced lip smile, to be sure—but a genuine smile nonetheless.

I like Koi. It's simple, unpretentious, and fun. Just don't leave a big old butt print behind.

www.cafekoi.com

La Brezza

Italian

990–1 Avenue NE
Phone: 262•6230
Monday–Friday 11:30 am–2:30 pm, 5 pm–11 pm, Saturday & Sunday 5 pm–midnight
Reservations recommended — Fully licensed — Corkage $10 — Non-smoking
V, MC, AE, Debit — $–$$

WHEN the General Hospital came down in 1998, it looked like it might be curtains for some of the neighbouring restaurants too. Having your lunch trade disappear overnight can be a bit sobering. But I have to give credit to the folks along 1st Avenue NE for sticking out the eight long years it took to plan and build the Bridges project.

Today, folks like Marco Abdi look like geniuses. La Brezza's owner knew that if he stayed true to his principles of customer-first hospitality, good food, and controlled costs, he could weather the lean years. Now Abdi's La Brezza is as busy as it's ever been, with a whole new crop of upwardly mobile Calgarians replacing the medical professionals of the 1990s.

It seems as if La Brezza's prices have been locked in the 1990s too. While other places are cruising past the $40 entree mark, La Brezza has a rack of lamb for $25. And the most expensive pasta is $14. That's for the fettuccine mare monti with shrimp, smoked salmon, peppers, and mushrooms in a creamy tomato sauce. Then there's a nine-ounce New York steak in a mushroom sauce for $20, tiger prawns for $19, and veal piccata for $15.

And this isn't some discount diner. La Brezza offers both quality and volume for those bargain prices. Reviewing for this book, I had a huge lunch of tortellini Romanov with loads of pancetta and creamy tomato sauce finished with vodka. Tasty, filling, and $17 for that and a big bowl of bruschetta and endless focaccia.

La Brezza isn't some sleazy dive either. It's a little odd to be sure. It's a converted house, after all. But the forty-five-seat room has a comfortable level of style, the tables are topped with linens, the staff are all professional and friendly, and there's Abdi himself—always smiling, always the charming host, quick with the sambuca and espresso.

On my visit for this book, I tasked the kitchen severely. I arrived for lunch the day after Italy's late-night triumph over Germany in the World Cup soccer semi-final. I figured if they could do a good job in the afterglow of that event, they could do a good job anytime. And although the kitchen staff looked a little low on sleep, their execution was flawless.

So things are looking good for La Brezza these days. It passed twenty years in June of 2006, a major accomplishment in anybody's book.

www.labrezza.ca

La Chaumière

French Market Cuisine

139 – 17 Avenue SW
Phone: 228•5690
Monday–Friday noon–2:30 pm, Monday–Saturday 6 pm–midnight
Reservations recommended — Fully licensed — Patio — Non-smoking
V, MC, AE — $$–$$$

IT's difficult to string the words "grand" and "old" and "venerable" together in a sentence without sounding stodgy. But when I think about La Chaumière, those are the kind of words that come to mind. Not in a negative way though. La Chaumière has been around since 1978—old in restaurant terms. With its open vestibule (how many restaurants even have a vestibule these days?), spacious seating, and big, comfy chairs (how many places can boast those attributes either?), it's grand. And with the quality of its food and service day in and day out, it is, well, venerable.

All of the above can be credited to La Chaumière's founders Joe Mathes and Joseph D'Angelus, a couple of industry professionals who never waver in their sense of quality. And I have to also give credit to Bob Matthews, a talented local boy who has worked his way up from vegetable peeler to executive chef and partner. This is a dynamic team that, together, keeps La Chaumière among the elite of Calgary restaurants.

Since 1978, we've seen many high-end restaurants come and go. But La Chaumière came and stayed. Because they have never been content to stand still. The mille feuille of prawns and truffled celeriac purée wasn't on the menu in 1978. Nor was the sautéed sablefish with mushroom cannelloni. These are contemporary dishes developed from a classical background and are challenging enough to keep customers interested. Back in 1978, there was likely a rack of lamb and a beef tenderloin on the menu. And there still is. La Chaumière has never forsaken its traditions, but continues to update with, for example, a porcini pain doré for the tenderloin.

La Chaumière's prices consistently beat most of the market. While many newcomers are breaking $40 for their rack of lamb, La Chaumière has kept theirs at a reasonable $31.50. That makes it almost the most expensive item on the menu. (The big ticket is elk tenderloin at $32.50.)

La Chaumière also has one of the finest and deepest wine lists in the city, with over eight hundred labels and a private dining option in the cellar itself. And they have an outstanding dessert list. The Grand Marnier soufflé is one of the best desserts in the city. And I've never found the service here to be anything less than impeccable.

Perhaps I should add another word to the above list of "grand," "old," and "venerable." It would be "smart."

www.lachaumiere.ca

Las Palmeras

Mexican

3630–50 Avenue, Red Deer
Phone: 346•8877
Monday–Thursday 11:30 am–10 pm, Friday & Saturday 11:30 am–11 pm
Sunday noon–9 pm
Reservations recommended — Fully licensed — Non-smoking
V, MC, AE, Debit — $–$$

H ERE'S a question that I get more than I should: Just where the heck can you get good Mexican food in this province? There are some fine places in both Edmonton and Calgary, but my favourite remains Las Palmeras in Red Deer. They have been there since 1992 and in their "new" location for ten years. They've lasted that long for a simple reason: They do it right.

The biggest shortcoming in most Mexican restaurants in these parts is that they hold back on the spices and preparation; they don't cook the food in an authentic style because they're afraid customers won't like it. Which is totally wrong-headed. The worst thing any restaurant can do is fake a cuisine by reducing its natural flavours and spices. In reality, people who don't like Mexican food aren't going to like it no matter what. And people who do like Mexican food aren't going to like a diminished version of it. Consider how many Albertans spend time in Mexico and the American Southwest and love the food.

So, when you order the camarones escorpionados con salsa de chile rojo (that's prawns in one serious red-chili sauce) at Las Palmeras, you'd better be prepared for intensity. And when you bite into a taco de carnitas, you can expect a serious hit of spice. That's the way this food should work.

I'm happy to report that the carnitas, which is a spiced and roasted pork loin sliced into corn tortillas, is as good as ever. One of the tortillas was too thick last time, but I'm just happy to see that someone is actually making real corn tortillas. They just have to remember to press them thinner.

Las Palmeras looks and feels much like the Mexican places I've visited in the American Southwest. There are two large rooms with tables covered in plasticized tablecloths and paper-napkin dispensers. There are a few booths, some plastic palm trees, and lots of windows. On the one hand, it is fairly plain looking, and on the other, it has a certain charm that complements the food. And I've always found service here to be friendly and efficient.

Las Palmeras makes a pretty decent pit stop if you're passing through Red Deer. And it's a nice diversion from the many chain restaurants in the Central Alberta city. So Las Palmeras is still my favourite Mexican restaurant in the province.

Laurier Lounge

Fondue & Tapas

917–17 Avenue SW
Phone: 228•3771
Daily 3 pm – midnight
Reservations recommended on weekends — Fully licensed — Corkage $15
Smoking room downstairs
V, MC, AE, Debit — $–$$$

SEVENTEENTH Avenue is changing. And there's more to the change than just the party tone of the Red Mile phenomenon. The area has become a destination for those looking for interesting food, a lively time, and perhaps a drink or two. So on the one hand, 17th Avenue has serious dining establishments such as Brava Bistro and The Living Room, and on the other, it has casual bar-style places such as Melrose.

In between, capturing the essence of both sides, is Laurier Lounge. It's where JoJo Bistro resided for years before decamping to the quieter confines of Marda Loop. The space is long and narrow, perfect for the compression of a bistro, and it's equally appropriate for the energetic spirit of a lounge that is about food and fun.

Laurier Lounge—named after Sir Wilfrid himself—offers an eclectic list of tapas from $5 to $35. Now that's a serious range. What kind of tapas do you get for $35? A three-course fondue, starting with cheese, working over to beef stock, and finishing with chocolate. It's good fondue, though it seems more like dinner than tapas to me. At the $25 level, you can get a beef tenderloin with grilled asparagus and blue-cheese sauce or a seafood couscous. At $15, there's lobster ravioli or coquilles St. Jacques; at $10, there's prawn pizza, chicken-coconut curry, or baked brie; and at $5, there's corn and crab chowder or garlic escargot. There are other options at most of the price levels too. Suffice it to say, some tapas are bigger in size and concept than others.

Chef/Owner Martin Maheux draws from his French-Canadian heritage and international culinary experience to create this interesting mix of foods. His fare is richly flavoured and satisfying, and his clientele seem to enjoy the odd eclecticism. In the early evening, he draws from the more mature Mount Royal crowd, and as the evening progresses, his customers get younger. Many come for dinner at 11 p.m., having discovered Laurier Lounge as one of the better late-evening dining options around and as a good place for a creative cocktail.

So Laurier Lounge fills three local needs: First, it provides late-night dining with quality and style; second, there are interesting drinks; and third, there's fondue. I'm especially happy about that third one. I get lots of requests for fondue eateries, and it's great to finally have a place to send folks.

Le Beaujolais

French

Upstairs, Corner of Banff Avenue & Buffalo Street, Banff
Phone: 762•8374
Daily 6 pm–close
Reservations recommended — Fully licensed — Non-smoking
V, MC, AE, Debit — $$$

OUTSIDE, the intersection of Banff Avenue and Buffalo Street hums with foot and car traffic. Stately Mount Rundle looms in the background, framing the Bow River as it pushes toward Bow Falls. It's a fascinating view, especially from the comfortable confines of Le Beaujolais, located one floor above it all.

Le Beaujolais, an elegant oasis of fresh flowers, outstanding wines, great food, and fine service, has been parked above the corner of Banff and Buffalo since 1980. I've enjoyed serious corporate dinners here, brought in a few New Year's with friends, and indulged in leisurely dinners with Catherine. I've never been disappointed. Le Beaujolais is a classic.

We used to think of Le Beaujolais as expensive. And it is. But that was before the arrival of even pricier places just a few kilometres away and before the introduction of the $40-plus entree in Calgary. Nowadays, Le Beaujolais actually seems reasonably priced.

The most expensive dish on the menu is a $34 triple-tenderloin array featuring medallions of beef, veal, and pork, each with their own sauces, and loads of vegetables. Lobster meat even tops the veal medallion. This is a gorgeous plate of food. And $34? Excellent value. But there's more. The braised elk paupiettes with wild-boar bacon are $30, the roast lamb sirloin is $29, and the lobster vichyssoise is $10 (a huge, velvety bowlful too). And that's just the à la carte menu.

You can try the three-course prix fixe menu for $68 and have ahi tuna niçoise salad, then halibut cheeks and braised oxtail with fiddleheads, followed by a combo entree of duck breast and leg confit. Or start with a triple-tasting of salmon, move to the wild-boar civet with prosciutto, and then on to the rack of lamb, also all for $68. There isn't a thing on this menu I don't want to eat.

Not enough? How about the six-course dinner for $95, expertly paired with wines for $150? (Le Beaujolais has a stellar wine list.) And I haven't even mentioned the dessert list yet, which includes Grand Marnier soufflé, crepes Suzette, chocolate mousse, and crème brûlée. Classics, all.

I don't mean to portray Le Beaujolais as a bargain joint. That, it certainly is not. But I just can't believe how reasonable the prices are for the quality, the service, the room, the food, and the location. After twenty-six years, Owners Albert and Esther Moser have their business down to an art form.

www.lebeaujolaisbanff.com

Leo Fu's

Chinese (Szechuan & Mandarin)

511–70 Avenue SW
Phone: 255•2528
Monday–Friday 11:30 am–2 pm, Sunday–Thursday 4:30 pm–10 pm
Friday & Saturday 4:30 pm–11:30 pm
Reservations accepted — Fully licensed — Non-smoking
V, MC, AE — $$

O NE of the common themes you'll find in this book is that most of the restaurants are owner operated. You have to be at a place to make it work. And many of the best are family-run operations—operations where a tight group of folks work long and dedicated hours. One of the best examples is Leo Fu's. Run by the Koo family since the 1980s, it has been our favourite Chinese restaurant for almost two decades. And a good part of that is simply because the Koos are fine people doing a fine job.

That fine job revolves around top-notch Szechuan and Mandarin cuisine: General Tso's chicken, orange beef, salt-and-pepper seafood, Szechuan eggplant, and on and on. Sure, you'll find a version of ginger beef (a good one at that), but you'll see a number of dishes that you almost never see elsewhere.

That includes one of my favourite indulgences—Szechuan chicken wings. Fried to crispiness and soaked in chili-laced oil, these are positively addictive. But as the saying goes, too much of a good thing can hurt you. Oh, well. Perhaps it's better to stick to dishes with some redeeming value, like the beef and vegetables in black-bean sauce or the sautéed shrimp and vegetables with cashew nuts. All quality ingredients and well prepared.

Leo Fu's also qualifies as having one of the most obscure restaurant locations in the city. It's just off Macleod Trail, but far enough off to be almost invisible. Look for the Kinjo sushi bar on Macleod and you'll find Leo Fu's just a few doors west. You'll be surprised at just how many people are there ahead of you. This is a busy place.

Not long ago they gave the restaurant a makeover, installing hardwood floors and repainting with cheerful colours. They also tore down a wall sectioning off a private room in the back and inserted a folding door instead so that the room can be closed off as needed. And it's needed often. Leo Fu's is a popular place for family and group dinners, a place to get lots of excellent food in a casual atmosphere.

And aside from the Koo family and other good staff, Leo Fu's has one of my favourite servers. The diminutive Hua Lok is as pleasant and professional as they come. Her voice alone can cheer up my day, and I always feel especially well taken care of when she's on the job.

LeVilla

Chophouse, Seafood, Pasta

#404, 1851 Sirocco Drive SW (West Market Square)
Phone: 217•9699
Monday–Friday 11:30 am–2 pm, Friday & Saturday 5 pm–10 pm, Sunday 5 pm–9 pm
Reservations recommended — Fully licensed — Corkage $20 — Patio — Non-smoking
V, MC, AE, Debit — $$

'M always getting complaints that there aren't enough good, non-chain restaurants in the suburbs. And it's true. But occasionally, a place like LeVilla pops up.

LeVilla is the kind of solid neighbourhood place where you can get a nicely grilled piece of salmon, a plate of seared scallops, and some panko-crusted pork chops. Where the prices are a little less than downtown, the parking is plentiful and free, and the service is friendly. Where the whole atmosphere is casual, comfortable, and clean, and where you feel like you want to go back for more.

LeVilla is also very much about beef: steaks, prime rib, even steak salad. Chef/Owner Rick Chuk cooked at Buchanan's for seventeen years, so he knows a thing or two about beef. There are three sizes each of tenderloin and of strip loin and a couple of rib-eyes, all of which range from $28 to $34. Your choice from three sauces—Marsala-mushroom, brandy-peppercorn, or Béarnaise—is served on the side, so you can have as much or as little as you want.

We tried a slab of prime rib and a piece of tenderloin and they fulfilled our carnivorous desires. Nice beef, perfectly cooked to order, fine sauces. They both came with a selection of simply grilled vegetables and some mashed potatoes, providing a pleasant backdrop to the beef. We also shared a decent Caesar salad, but it's one of those that comes with the full pieces of romaine. So beware if you don't like that.

LeVilla has a food-friendly wine list with some big, beefy wines. A Spanish Tempranillo offered by the glass was perfect. And they have an elaborate water list of about a dozen choices, not counting Bow River. They've got Norwegian Voss and Italian Aqua Panna, and a limited edition Evian that goes for $16 a litre (ummm … it's in a very pretty bottle).

And what's a good neighbourhood restaurant without some heavy-duty desserts. LeVilla doesn't disappoint with their big, warm, gooey chocolate-rum cake and thick slabs of cheesecake. Great for weighing down all that beef.

Another thing I like about LeVilla is the setting itself. The dining room is pleasant enough, but a few years ago, previous operators glassed-in the patio, creating a bright and lodgy dining area with an indoor-outdoor feel. It's where everyone wants to sit in the winter and it's lovely.

So LeVilla is a great neighbourhood joint. And not just for the folks west of Sarcee. This one is worth the drive.

www.levilla.ca

Little Chef

Upscale Family Dining

555 Strathcona Boulevard SW (Strathcona Square Shopping Centre)
Phone: 242•7219
Monday–Friday 11 am–8 pm, Saturday & Sunday 9 am–8 pm
Reservations recommended — Fully licensed — Patio — Non-smoking
V, MC, Debit — $–$$

SOMETIMES we just want a nice, simple meal—nothing elaborate, but not fast food either. We might not feel like cooking at home, but we still feel like home cooking without a lot of glitz or high prices. And when that mood strikes, one of the top places on our list is the Little Chef.

It has been around for over ten years now, but I'm always surprised at how many people have never heard of it. I think it gets forgotten in the much maligned category of "family restaurants." Many of this style are last resorts offering lacklustre service, frozen, pre-packaged food with no character, and industrial furnishings that are indestructible for even the most active toddler.

But the Little Chef epitomizes what a true family restaurant should be: Pleasant staff serve up tasty, freshly prepared food at reasonable prices, all in an atmosphere that is comfortable for everyone from the local soccer team to a couple of seniors out for a nice dinner.

Now certainly, the Little Chef is no fashion plate with its mid-eighties pastel look. It's an angular room with a big overhead chalkboard announcing the specials and a large pop cooler humming away behind the counter. But it's pristine and always active with staff trundling out plates covered with clubhouse sandwiches, bison stew, beef dips, and meat pies.

Those pies—steak and kidney, steak and mushroom, and chicken—are among the best we've had. That should be no surprise considering the chef and owner is Arthur Raynor, an expatriate Brit and former president of the Canadian Federation of Chefs & Cooks. His pastry is superb.

But more than that, the side dishes that come with the pies, such as a spinach or Caesar salad, receive excellent attention. The spinach salad is loaded with hard-boiled egg, real bacon bits, mushrooms, and a pile of excellent spinach, all bathed in a delightful vinaigrette. The Caesar salad has real croutons and parmesan in a rich, creamy dressing. No bottles and packages here. The chefs actually prepare the food. And when a kitchen knows how to do things like that, the costs are reduced and the consumer benefits in value and quality. A meat pie with one of the salads or fries or mashed potatoes comes in at under $10.

There are way too few family places like the Little Chef. That's a pity.

The Living Room

Contemporary Interactive Cuisine

514–17 Avenue SW
Phone: 228•9830
Tuesday–Friday 11:30 am–3 pm, Daily 5 pm–midnight
Reservations recommended — Fully licensed — Patio — Non-smoking
V, MC, AE, Debit — $$–$$$

THE Living Room is in a renovated bungalow that went through a number of names and styles when it first became a restaurant. Since 1999, it has been comfortably The Living Room, one of Calgary's most innovative restaurants.

It has a great tone. The former living room, dining room, and a bedroom have been recreated as dining space. Banquettes wrap around one area, a long bar outlines one wall, and an elevated group table for a dozen takes the focus in the centre. There's a fireplace with curled couch seating and windows that look out onto a big patio. It's a pleasant patio, shielded just enough from 17th Avenue to allow for privacy.

The Living Room calls their food Contemporary Interactive, and it certainly is that with a number of entrees and appetizers for two or more. On the non-interactive side, the summer 2006 menu also included pistachio-crusted salmon with spinach tagliatelle tossed in a cranberry-mustard beurre blanc ($19). And a trio comprised of a maple-sugared duck breast, a confit-stuffed potato, and some caraway-braised duck drumettes ($28). It's creative stuff.

And certainly the dishes we had were pleasing. Catherine liked her pork loin with cassoulet, house-made sausage, and red-onion marmalade. And my braised short ribs with gnocchi in a Provençal sauce were quite nice, as was our shared appetizer of ancho-crusted soft-shell crab and the desserts of house-made ice cream.

The Living Room's menu shows some of the true creativity and quality available in the market right now. Good ingredients, well prepared. But do we really need all of them? They work in the skilled hands of Chef Kevin Hill at The Living Room, but a menu like this walks a tightrope. It relies on the quality being there day in and day out and on kitchen execution that is exact all the time. How else do you justify $15 for an appetizer of tiger-prawn and mascarpone ravioli in lemon and roasted garlic beurre blanc with black-truffle oil? Or $36 for a rack of lamb that's crusted in arugula and pine nuts and served with a wild-mushroom and ricotta lasagna? Mess up one ingredient or miss one step in the prep and you're working without a net.

Fortunately, The Living Room has the skill to pull it off. And the determination to make it happen every day, which maintains their status as one of the most creative restaurants in Calgary.

www.thelivingroomrestaurant.com

Marathon

Ethiopian

130–10 Street NW
Phone: 283•6796
Tuesday–Thursday & Sunday 5:30 pm–10 pm, Friday 5:30 pm–11 pm
Saturday noon–11 pm
Reservations recommended — Fully licensed — Non-smoking
V, MC, AE, Debit — $$

L OOKING for a different dining experience? Someplace where you can eat dishes you can't pronounce? Where you can eat with your hands? Where even the background music leaves you wondering what instruments are being played? Unless you come from the Horn of Africa or have eaten a lot of injera, ful, and yebeg alicha fitfit, you might consider Ethiopian cuisine. And a little place on 10th Street NW called Marathon.

The food here is a fascinating blend of vegetarian dishes, meat stews, and a sour, crepey bread called injera. It is typically served on a large tray under a conical-shaped, woven lid called a *messob*. The tray is draped with the spongy injera (made from the tiny grain known as teff), and the other dishes are then ladled over top. The idea is that you use the injera to scoop up your meal, much like eating Indian food with nan bread.

Since Ethiopian culture prescribes over two hundred vegetarian days a year, you'll find some great non-meat items on Marathon's menu. The yater kik alicha of split peas in curry is outstanding, and the yatkilt alicha of carrots and cabbage in ginger is very tasty. Many people like the ful—a dish of kidney beans with hot peppers and a butter called niter kibbeh; it's good, though not a personal favourite. The meat dishes are equally fascinating, from the yebeg wat of lamb braised in a hot Ethiopian berbere pepper sauce and the kitfo of lean ground beef served like steak tartare to the doro wat of chopped chicken marinated in lemon juice and cooked with ginger and berbere sauce. For the beginner, it's interesting to try one of Marathon's specials, combinations of these and other dishes.

What you don't find in Ethiopian food is much of a multi-course approach like you do in European and North American cuisines. Typically all the food is served at once. Only a couple of sambusas (savoury pastries similar to samosas) and a salad are listed as appetizers. And Ethiopian cuisine is not big on desserts. Also, the main starch is the injera bread, so if you don't happen to like its sourness, you might have to starch up on beans.

Still, the flavours are compelling, and the folks who run Marathon are charming. Enjoy the flavours, eat with your hands, and taste an Ethiopian beer. Or that great beverage of Ethiopian origin—coffee.

Mekong

Vietnamese

2885–17 Avenue SE
Phone: 248•1488
Monday–Saturday 10 am–9 pm
Reservations accepted — Fully licensed — Corkage $10
Separately ventilated smoking room
V, MC, Debit — $–$$

I F you rate your Vietnamese noodle shops by the volume of slurping going on around you, Mekong is one fine place. It's a noodle-slurper's paradise. Enter at any given lunch hour, and you'll be greeted by Mekong's owner, who will guide you to your seat, an overhead television, and a cacophony of noodles meeting their demise.

Don't expect anything demure about Mekong. It's not uncommon for customers to order their lunch while on the way to their table. "I'll have the number forty-seven today," one might say before being seated. "And what the heck, I'll have a number two too." Why waste time? A good Vietnamese noodle shop is partly about fresh, lively food. But almost as important, it's about efficiency, about getting you in and out in twenty minutes if you want. Mekong strives for both quality and expediency.

So don't expect any frills. One napkin. Plastic chopsticks. Basic decor and seats. No tablecloths. You'll get a pot of tea delivered to your table in seconds, and your order will arrive shortly. Then it's time to get to work.

Mekong's salad rolls, the number two on the menu, are among the best in the city. Crunchy shrimp are tightly rolled into rice paper with bean sprouts and noodles and served with a bowl of hoisin, chili sauce, and peanuts. Good eating. And I'll bet before you gnaw your way through a couple of them, your number forty-seven will have arrived.

So, assume the position. Pour the bowl of fish sauce, or nuoc mam, over the cha gio rolls, grilled shrimp, charbroiled pork, vegetables, and noodles, and you're off. Head bowed, mouth ready to accept the noodles, slurp diligently and scoop away. It's a big bowl of food—especially for $9—and it doesn't disappoint. The shrimp and pork have distinct grilled flavours, the vegetables are fresh, and the noodles aren't overcooked. It's amazing the range of flavour that can exist in a single $9 bowl of noodles.

Mekong does other big dishes too. There are fried noodles with various meats, steamed rice with various meats, and beef soups with various noodles. There are some Mekong special dishes that are more expensive, such as the goat hot pot, a sweet-and-sour fish hot pot, and some grill-it-yourself meats, but almost everything else is under $10.

Don't expect pretty at Mekong. Do expect good food, fast. And plug your ears if the slurping gets too loud.

www.mekongcalgary.ca

Mercato

Contemporary Italian

2224–4 Street SW
Phone: 263•5535
Daily 11 am–2:30 pm, 5 pm–close
Reservations recommended — Beer & wine only — Patio — Non-smoking
V, MC, AE, Debit — $$–$$$

I N 2005, Mercato opened as an upscale Italian deli with a little café attached. It was a big move for the Caracciolo family. They had run an Italian market in Bridgeland since 1974, but closed it when they moved to 4th Street. The new place immediately worked out well, and in no time, the café was swamped.

There are a couple of reasons for that. First, there's not much Italian in the Mission neighbourhood. Second, the food is market-fresh and contemporary. And third, you can sit at the counter and watch all the preparation in the open kitchen.

Anyway, not long after opening, Mercato expanded the café by adding a larger counter and more tables. The market side became a little smaller and the café got bigger, turning into more of a restaurant.

Mercato offers a dinner menu that is brief, and daily specials are added as their market brings in fresh ingredients. Their tomato bruschetta is as good as any I've had in Italy. They also use cannellini beans to top the grilled bread (bruschetta is not just tomatoes). A big appetizer for $9 and lots to take home.

If there is a knock against Mercato, it's that it is pricey. Dinner appetizers run $8 to $11 (or more for specials), pastas range from $14 for tomato, basil, and parmesan on tagliatelle to $26 for risotto with seared scallops and truffle oil. Main plates are up to $28 for braised pork shoulder with veal, pancetta, and grana padano. Then there are side dishes such as braised fennel, as well as wines and desserts. You're not getting out of there under $100 for dinner for two.

But the ingredients are top-notch, the preparation is skilled, and the service is excellent. I think what bothers some is that they are dining in a casual market atmosphere either elbow to elbow at the bar or on paper placemats at tables— it can be difficult to reconcile the atmosphere with the quality of the food.

Which, by the way, is good. Catherine told me with every bite how rich and tasty her braised rabbit in wild-mushroom ragout was. And I enjoyed the tiger prawns and pancetta in a lemon butter over pasta. I think the dessert menu is short and predictable, but otherwise, the food is exemplary.

One other thing about Mercato: It's loud. With all those people dining that close together and all those hard surfaces, it really reminds me of Italy.

www.mercatogourmet.com

Mimo

Portuguese

#203, 4909–17 Avenue SE (Little Saigon Centre)
Phone: 235•3377
Monday–Thursday 11 am–2 pm, 5 pm–10 pm, Friday & Saturday 11 am–11 pm
Reservations recommended — Fully licensed — Non-smoking
V, MC, AE, Debit — $$

MOST people can't find Mimo. Even with a map, it's not easy. It's removed from 17th Avenue, tucked in the back row of a double strip mall called Little Saigon Centre. The mall used to be called Portugal Plaza when they opened there in the 1980s, but things have changed and most of their neighbours are now Vietnamese.

Mimo did some serious renovations a few years ago, enlarging the bar and moving it into the back. The dining room is now out front where there are windows—not that there's much of a view. But it's a lovely room with tables nicely topped in crisp white and green linens and one wall covered with a big grape-picking mural. Unlike many restaurant murals, this one is actually quite nice.

The menu covers the Portuguese basics of pork and clams, paella, barbecued chicken, and bacalhau (salt cod) done various ways. It's a seafood-focused menu, and they carry it out well. The seafood appetizers range from $9 to $11, and the main courses pretty much top out at $16. That's excellent value, especially considering the quantity and quality.

The garlic shrimp are crusted in spices and grilled. The mussels Portuguese-style are rich and robust in a piri-piri sauce. The grilled squid is likewise plump and flavoured with hot spices. The folks who own Mimo are from Portugal's Azores Islands, and they love the piri-piri chili sauce, mopping it on almost everything. (If you'd rather have the more muted form of mainland Portuguese cuisine, just let them know.)

The food is also redolent of azeite, the rich, spicy Portuguese olive oil. In Portugal, they wait until the olives are almost bursting with flavour before picking them, and then they hot-press them, adding a depth of spiciness to the oil. But beyond the odd salad and fried potatoes—which are really good—there are not many vegetables in this cuisine.

Mimo is uncompromisingly Portuguese, to the point where they have a great Portuguese wine list and none from elsewhere. And that's fine by me. A good vinho verde goes great with the seafood, and the reds have gotten pretty good lately too. And for dessert, they make one of the deepest, darkest, best crème caramels possible.

Service at Mimo is always pleasant and professional. It can take awhile to prepare this food, but the staff are always eager to please. Mimo is very much worth the navigational effort it takes to find.

www.members.shaw.ca/mimorest

Moroccan Castle

Moroccan

217–19 Street NW
Phone: 283•5452
Tuesday–Sunday 5:30 pm–11 pm
Reservations recommended, especially on weekends
Fully licensed — Corkage $15 — Non-smoking
V, MC — $$

'M often asked where to go for something different, something that will break people out of their culinary ruts. One of the first places that pops to mind is the Moroccan Castle.

Why, you ask?

Cloth drapes from the ceiling to create a desert-tent tone. More draping separates dining areas that can seat up to six or eight people. Large brass tabletops are surrounded by cushioned benches. There's no Western table-and-chair seating here, and there's a suspicious lack of cutlery on the table. Because the style is Moroccan, and if you want, you can lounge back on the cushions and eat with your hands. Well, more accurately, with your right hand. And even then, with just the thumb and first two fingers of the right hand. (The left is used for, shall we say, other purposes.) Or you can just ask for cutlery. But where's the fun in that? As they say, "When in Rabat …"

The staff start your evening of Moroccan delights by bringing round a large silver basin, a pitcher filled with rose-scented water, and a towel. They then pour water over your hands in a cleansing gesture, a tradition inherited hundreds of years ago from Middle Eastern traders.

Moroccan cuisine is one of the more unique in our market, a descendant of the camel trains and the native Berber tribes of the desert. Much of it is made with dried fruits, nuts, and couscous, which were all relatively light for the trek across the sand, and it is flavoured with spices from across North Africa. And always there is sugar, answering the sweet-tooth desires of the area.

The harira soup features lentils in a broth enriched by harissa sauce, a condiment made from the hot chilies and spices of neighbouring Senegal. The lamb tajines are rich stews with prunes and almonds or olives and preserved lemons, and the couscous Fassi features chicken or lamb with raisins and chickpeas. These can all be scooped up with some Moroccan bread or with couscous pressed into an absorbent ball. (I never said this was easy. I also never said it wasn't messy.)

For the full effect, try the bestilla pie. This is a mixture of chicken, eggs, onions, cinnamon, ginger, and crushed almonds all wrapped in phyllo pastry and baked. (Sounds good, doesn't it?) Then icing sugar and cinnamon are dusted on top to add a sweetness to the pie. It's a gorgeous dish.

Now, how's that for something different?

www.moroccancastle.com

Mt. Everest's Kitchen

Nepalese

1448A–17 Avenue SW
Phone: 806•2337
Tuesday–Saturday 11:30 am–2 pm, Sunday & Holidays noon–2 pm
Tuesday–Thursday & Sunday 5:30 pm–9:30 pm, Friday & Saturday 5:30 pm–10 pm
Reservations recommended — Fully licensed — Corkage $15 — Non-smoking
V, MC, AE, Debit — $$

HAD a good plate of momos lately? How about an appetizer of choyla? Or some sekuwa, mala, or tarkari? If you're up on your Nepalese cuisine or are a regular at Mt. Everest's Kitchen, you may have had all of the above. But if you've never been to Nepal or to Calgary's only Nepalese restaurant, the words are probably unfamiliar.

Nepalese cuisine is an interesting hybrid of northern Indian and western Chinese cuisines with a lot of dal bhat (lentils and rice) added in. Momos are dumplings that look like they rolled in on a dim-sum cart, while tarkaris are the Nepalese version of curries. Choylas are grilled meat cubes served with green salad, and malas and sekuwas are meat and vegetables or just meat—both are cooked in a clay oven and served on sizzling hot plates. All these dishes show the influence of Nepal's large neighbours—India and China.

But where Nepalese cuisine really comes into its own is in the flavours. The food is full of spices that have no good English translation and is redolent of ginger, garlic, and mustard oil. Nothing else tastes like Nepalese cuisine. It's at once savoury and rich, with the mustard oil adding a bite and curry powders adding complexity. Using chicken, lamb, and shrimp, the dishes here jump in the mouth and satisfy the palate. Some dishes carry spicy heat, but most are just flavourful.

And fun. The Chicken Fruity is Nepal's answer to butter chicken. Chunks of chicken are served in a butter, cream, and cashew-powder sauce with slices of mango. Lovely dish. And the sweet bread (actually a bread, not to be confused with the meat of the same name) is filled with coconut and dried fruits. Tasty. You can also order chow chows of noodles stir-fried with various toppings.

The richness of colour carries over from the food into the look. The walls are a mango orange or, more accurately, an HB pencil orange—the same colour as the school pencils of my youth. On the walls are Gurkha regimental insignias, photos of Nepalese mountains, and notes from the many Calgarians who have visited Nepal. Tables are well spaced, and south-facing windows spill light onto the lunch buffet.

In the evening, ordering is off the menu, with most dishes ranging from $15 to $18. Good prices and no mountain treks required for these momos and tarkaris.

www.everestkitchen.ca

Muk-a-Muk

Rocky Mountain Cuisine

#1 Juniper Way (Base of Mt. Norquay Road in The Juniper), Banff
Phone: 763•6205
Daily 7 am–10 pm
Reservations recommended — Fully licensed — Corkage $18 — Deck
Non-smoking bistro & lounge, smoking on patio
V, MC, AE, Debit — $$–$$$

THE Timberline Inn hovered above the Trans-Canada Highway at the Norquay exit by Banff for about fifty years. But the building has recently been "boutiqued" by Decore Hotels and is now called The Juniper. By boutiqued I mean that they've re-done it in the current earthy tones, they've bought a bunch of duvets, and they've raised the prices. It's actually quite nicely renovated. They've maintained the kitschy 1950s tone, while at the same time, upgraded the old motel significantly.

For years, the Timberline had the best deck in the Banff area—the view across Vermilion Lakes out to Mount Rundle was, and is, spectacular. But the attached dining room seemed a bit shaky, at least in my memory. The Decore group has rejigged the restaurant, opened up the space, and created Muk-a-Muk Bistro & Lounge, named after a First Nation word for feasting or sharing.

Muk-a-Muk takes advantage of its location with a full bank of south-facing windows looking out over the deck. The floors have been uncovered to reveal polished concrete, an original stone fireplace separates the dining room from the lounge, and the tables have been well spaced to create a casual atmosphere.

The staff wear black, the current modern-bistro look, and are the typical Banff service crowd of snowboarding Aussies and Brits. Nice folks, doing a pretty decent job, with absolutely no guarantee they'll be there the next time you drop in. Their earnestness makes up for their occasional lack of expertise.

Muk-a-Muk's menus arrive on large sheets of heavy paper. That's a kind of modern-bistro approach too, as is the content itself: hot-smoked salmon with potato-crab gnocchi, for example, or sweet potato crab cakes with smoked tomatoes, or albacore tuna carpaccio. It's West Coast-ish and contemporary, with interesting choices. Top dinner dishes are $28 for braised bison short ribs and $32 for a ten-ounce rib-eye with sweet potato fries. Not bad prices.

We were there for lunch so we started with soup—the daily special of carrot-ginger and the menu's chicken-corn chowder. Both were surprisingly good. The chowder had crunch and flavour and richness, and it wasn't over thickened. The carrot-ginger escaped the blandness that sometimes creeps into carrot-based soups. The fish and chips weren't bad; the house-made tartar sauce was excellent, as was the gussied up ketchup. Pretty good stuff.

And that view—it's worth the price in itself. But the food at Muk-a-Muk is good enough to almost distract from it.

www.decorhotels.com/juniper

Murrieta's

Pacific Northwest Cuisine

808–1 Street SW	*737 Main Street, Canmore*
Phone: 269•7707	*Phone: 609•9500*
Monday & Tuesday 11 am–11 pm	*Monday–Thursday 11 am–11 pm*
Wednesday 11 am–midnight, Thursday 11 am–1 am	*Friday & Saturday 11 am–1 am*
Friday & Saturday 11 am–2 am, Sunday 4 pm–10 pm	*Sunday 11 am–10 pm*
Corkage $25 — Balcony	*Corkage $20*
Non-smoking dining room, smoking in lounge	*Non-smoking*

Reservations recommended — Fully licensed
V, MC, AE, Debit — $$–$$$

B ACK in 2001, the Alberta Hotel building in downtown Calgary was revitalized with the opening of Murrieta's. It's a great old sandstone structure on the corner of Stephen Avenue and 1st Street SW. They capped the courtyard with a huge skylight, creating a beautiful second-floor dining room. Second-floor restaurants typically fare poorly, and Murrieta's entrance was placed on 1st Street rather than on the busier Stephen Avenue. Regardless, Murrieta's became one of the most popular places in downtown Calgary and has been packing folks in ever since.

That's partly because it's such a lovely place. But it's also because the food has been pretty good and fairly priced, with most entrees under $25. They call the cuisine Pacific Northwest, indicating a lot of seafood mixed in with pastas, flatbreads, and steaks.

In 2003, a second Murrieta's opened in Canmore, this time in a brand new building in the heart of downtown. It's also on the second floor, but with a high-ceilinged, mountain-lodge look and a wraparound view of the Rockies. The menu echoes the Calgary one, but being in the mountains, they have added a few more gamey dishes such as wapiti rib-eye and buffalo penne. And again, they've been packing them in since day one.

Following the success in Calgary and Canmore, Murrieta's looked for the right spot to open in Edmonton, and they found it at *10612–82 Avenue* (*780•438•4100*), right next to the Varscona Hotel. Following a big renovation on what used to be a Sorrentino's, it's now another good-looking dining room, this time on the main floor though.

Each location includes 20 to 30 percent of their own dishes, which means you won't get cookie-cutter menus in all three Murrieta's. You'll find crab cakes and lamb meatballs in all, but they might be done in different sauces and with different plate presentations. Prices also vary slightly from place to place, but almost nothing breaks the $30 mark except the rack of lamb and the beef and bison tenderloins. (The least expensive spot is Edmonton's!) And I've always found service to be pleasant and professional no matter which location I'm at.

www.murrietas.ca

Muse

Contemporary International

107−10A Street NW
Phone: 670•6873
Daily 5 pm−close
Reservations recommended — Fully licensed — Small deck — Non-smoking
V, MC, AE, Debit — $$$

MUSE is a record-breaker. It's been in its Kensington location for over three years, which must be the longest a restaurant has resided on this site. Constructed in the early 1980s as Café Calabash, this building has seen far more eateries than it should have in its quarter-century.

But when Muse arrived in 2003, it came with an attitude of survival and a perspective that indicated they would be around for a while. With their Mardi-Gras-meets-*commedia-dell'-arte* look spread over numerous levels, Muse has an intriguing decor. And largely, their food lives up to it.

The problem with this space now and forever is the layout of those levels. They look great, but are all on the small side, creating awkward rooms for staff and customers alike. We have often ended up on the top floor, which isn't bad, but it has smallish tables and low lounge seats. Comfortable dining, it is not.

Which is not to say that Muse isn't a pleasant place. Quite the opposite. The staff are always accommodating, smiling, and knowledgeable. They do their darndest to make customers feel at home. It's just hard to eat if you're at one of these low seats and your chin is hovering a couple of inches above table height.

I like the food. It's contemporary and creative, full of rich flavours and interesting ideas. A summer salad of watermelon, cherry tomatoes, black sesame seeds, and watercress is refreshing in the mouth. A seafood chowder is as rich and creamy as I could ask. And a lobster risotto is packed with rich shellfish flavour. There's green-tea-marinated duck breast with sautéed cantaloupe, truffled tenderloin tartare, and spinach-stuffed poussin with fava bean risotto. Nice stuff.

What disappointed me on a recent visit was the size of the servings. The watermelon salad should have been bigger to justify its $9 price tag. And a piece of sablefish with bacon vinaigrette, mashed potatoes, oven-dried tomatoes, and broccolini was small compared to its $28 ticket. The food was good—very good, in fact—but there needed to be more of it.

For breads, Muse relies on the nearby **Charlie's Bakery**, which has the same ownership as the restaurant. Charlie's provides baking to about a dozen local restaurants and runs a retail operation at *1245 Kensington Road NW (670•0850)*. So they bake fresh croissants, breads, brownies, tarts, pies, and pain au chocolat for the public too.

www.muserestaurant.ca

Mysore Palace

Indian (Karnatakan)

4655–54 Avenue NE
Phone: 205•3672
Monday–Friday 11 am–3 pm, 5 pm–9 pm
Saturday & Sunday 11 am–10 pm

731–6 Avenue SW
Phone: 265•5800
Monday–Saturday 11 am–2:30 pm,
5 pm–9 pm

Reservations accepted — Fully licensed — Non-smoking
V, MC, AE, Debit — $–$$

HERE'S a question: Where in downtown Calgary can you find a huge carved wooden elephant? Try Mysore Palace, a Karnatakan restaurant. Never tried Karnatakan cuisine? It's Southern Indian, it's intensely spiced, and it features a lot of vegetarian dishes.

There are actually two Mysore Palaces, the other being up in the Castleridge-Westwinds area. They are named after an ornate royal palace that is now a major national monument in the city of Mysore in the Indian state of Karnataka. Calgary's downtown location has the elephant, but the northeast Mysore has an impressive carved wooden replica of the palace.

In the northeast location, the menu follows mostly the vegetarian side of Karnatakan cuisine. You'll find lentil-flour dossas (grilled crepes), lentil-batter vadas (doughnut-shaped savoury pastries), and rice utthappam (pancakes). The flours are ground in-house, so the dossas and vadas and such have a fresh, rich flavour. This Mysore Palace features some meatier dishes too, but the approach is strongly vegetarian.

The look and tone of the downtown Mysore Palace is quite different. They took over the former Mr. Munchie's and kept the diner look, which includes a lunch counter with twirly vinyl stools. There's something I like about the contradiction of a diner lunch counter juxtaposed with an Indian buffet and a carved elephant.

On the food side, the downtown Mysore offers a lunch buffet that covers a broad range of Karnatakan vegetarian dishes. It also includes a number of meat selections and other Indian dishes and costs a reasonable $14. In the evening, they do the same, mostly vegetarian menu as the northeast location.

One thing similar at both Mysore Palaces is the intensity of the spicing. Be prepared for some serious bite here. Spicing in the south of India can be quite strong and sometimes less complex than their northern neighbours. That doesn't mean it's less interesting on the palate though. And both locations make a good mango lassi.

Another difference between Karnatakan and Northern Indian cuisines is that the common bread in the southern state is chapati instead of nan. Chapatis are flatter than the fluffy nan and are made with whole wheat instead of white flour, but they are just as tasty.

So if you're looking for an alternative to all the Northern and Central Indian fare around town, Mysore Palace knows what they're doing. And there's an elephant and a castle!

www.mysorepalace.ca

New Berliner

German

#19, 2219 – 35 Avenue NE
Phone: 219•0961
Monday–Friday 11 am–2 pm, Wednesday–Saturday 5 pm–10 pm
Reservations recommended, especially on weekends — Fully licensed — Non-smoking
V, MC, Debit — $$

SCHNITZEL and rouladen fans were distraught when the Kensington Berliner closed in 2001. There's a general scarcity of German restaurants here because the food is perceived to be heavy and in opposition to leaner food trends. So for fans of the restaurant, there were no replacements.

The Kensington Berliner didn't close from lack of business. They needed a larger location, which they eventually found in a northeast industrial development. The New Berliner has great access off Deerfoot Trail and 32nd Avenue and also has loads of parking, especially in the evening when the body shops and printing houses around it shut down. The room itself looks nothing like the neighbourhood. It's done in soft gold and black, with about forty-five seats nicely spaced in what is still mostly a strip-mall bay.

Food-wise the New Berliner is as good as ever. One of their schnitzels is always a good choice for dinner. The Old World-New World Schnitzel is a pork cutlet lightly breaded, fried, and topped with white asparagus, shrimp, and hollandaise. The Tiroler Chicken Schnitzel is similarly prepared but with a sauce of double-smoked bacon, tomatoes, mushrooms, and paprika. Rich, intense sauces. Lovely. Both dishes come with braised red cabbage and a choice of either garlic spaetzle, potato dumplings, or fried potatoes. Not light food, but I have never found the Berliner's fare to be overly heavy. The contrast of the crispness of the schnitzels with the richness of the sauces is always a high point. Also good is their apple strudel, made in-house and topped with real whipped cream or ice cream.

It's good value too. The most expensive dish at lunch is $14. That pork schnitzel is $19, and there are lots of shrimp and white asparagus involved. The chicken schnitzel is a bargain at $16—we've had enough left over for lunch the next day. Nothing on the dinner menu costs over $23. And for that, you can order eisbein, the marinated pork hock dish that John F. Kennedy ate before declaring, "Ich bin ein Berliner."

Service is also sharp and professional and bilingual with both English and German. It's nice to see a restaurant that is successfully bucking current food trends with a strong adherence to a traditional style. The New Berliner may not be everyone's stein of beer, but when I get the urge for sauerbraten, it's where I go.

www.berliner.ca

Opus on 8th

Contemporary Market Cuisine

628–8 Avenue SW
Phone: 464•6787
Monday & Tuesday 11:30 am–midnight, Wednesday 11:30 am–1 am
Thursday–Saturday 11:30 am–2 am
Reservations accepted — Fully licensed — Corkage $15 — Non-smoking until 5 pm
V, MC, AE — $$–$$$

I have to admit that my first impulse when entering Opus on 8th was to give it a miss. It looks like a lounge, it sounds like a lounge, and it feels like a lounge. Nothing wrong with that, but it sets me up to think that the most creative dish will be a steak sandwich with, say, garlic butter.

But then I look at the menu and see melon gazpacho, house-made udon noodles, and a blue-crab, shrimp, and house-smoked bacon roll. Huh? I look closer and see Hotchkiss organic greens, ahi tuna tartare, and Diamond Willow organic beef tenderloin. I look around again. It still looks like a lounge. What's going on here?

Opus is what the owners call a Lounge Evolution. I suppose that means it has all the trappings of an older-style lounge enhanced by a thoughtful, contemporary menu. A long bar travels along one side of the room while booths line the other side. In the middle, there are tables of varying heights. Over the bar hangs a big plasma television. In the background throbs a killer sound system, laden with creative multi-generational and multi-genre choices.

And then there's the staff. Political correctness and my wife Catherine prohibit me from fully describing their charms. Just let it be said that the "little black dress" is in full force here. Delightful young ladies they are, calling you by your first name, smiling, and doing a good job. (Not surprisingly, the demographic is mostly male.)

The food doesn't have to be anywhere near as good as it is, although if Opus wants to build a solid lunch trade, it's not a bad idea to serve decent fare. The Shanghai street dumplings ($9) are better than most in Chinatown. They have distinct flavours of ginger, garlic, and five-spice powder and are served with a thickened soy sauce. Great dumplings.

I had to try the burger. Not only does it sound good ("homemade Galloway free-range cheeseburger with Asian root chips and firecracker salad"), it costs $21. How does a burger cost $21? It's good, layered with that house-smoked bacon and Sylvan Star gouda and piled into a Manuel Latruwe bun. The chips and salad are great too. But $21? That's steep.

Opus is not shy about charging. Actually, they're not shy about most things. They've got an energetic and lively attitude, which is appealing. Let's see how it works.

www.opuson8th.com

Orchid Room

Vietnamese-Thai-French Fusion

#244, 315 Stephen Avenue Walk SW (+15 Level, Bankers Hall)
Phone: 263•4457
October–March: Monday–Wednesday 10 am–7 pm
Thursday & Friday 10 am–10 pm, Saturday 11 am–10 pm
April–September: Call for reduced hours
Reservations recommended for lunch — Fully licensed — Non-smoking
V, MC, AE, Debit — $$

FIRST, a little history.
   Almost ten years ago, a great Vietnamese-French fusion restaurant called Indochine opened on the second floor of Bankers Hall. It took Vietnamese cuisine beyond the noodle shop by including more obvious French influences: The food was lighter, and it was artfully prepared and displayed; you could also get steak frites and crème brûlée. And the setting was more Paris bistro than Saigon café.

After a while, the chef went off to Penny Lane to open a restaurant called Sino, which served food similar to that of Indochine. But he kept a partnership in Indochine and eventually took over that space—he consolidated the two businesses into one, and the Bankers Hall spot is now called the Orchid Room.

And the Orchid Room is one fine restaurant. The owner and chef—a fellow named Ken Nguyen—spruced up the place, refreshing the green, brown, and white tones. He added red Chinese lanterns for colour and texture and renamed it to follow an orchid theme. The one-hundred-seat restaurant has fresh flowers on each table, on the walls, and on most of the dishes. (Nguyen also owns several flower shops and likes to spread the flowers around.)

Fans of Vietnamese cuisine will find a number of familiar dishes here. The Orchid Room does salad rolls, grilled la lot beef, lemon-grass chicken, and big bowls of soup. But you'll notice that the prices are higher than at your favourite noodle shop. Entrees range from $13 to $21. This is good food made from high-quality ingredients. It's well worth it—just don't expect any bargains.

At one dinner, we had caramelized salmon and tamarind prawns. These dishes are served as individual meals with rice and vegetables, but you can always share if you want. The salmon and prawns were perfectly cooked—the salmon in a lightly sweet caramelization, the prawns in a tangy tamarind glaze. Crunchy vegetables, nicely spiced, were piled on the plates, and the rice was wrapped in banana leaves. With a couple of purple orchids on the plates, this was gorgeous food that tasted marvellous.

The French influence on dessert is obvious, from one of the best crème brûlées anywhere to a stellar poached pear. Since we were already stuffed, though, we decided this time to go for a plate of freshly cut mango and pineapple instead.

So, the Orchid Room is a natural progression from both Indochine and Sino. This is beautiful food, skilfully prepared and well served.

Ouzo

Greek

2005–4 Street SW
Phone: 229•1400
Sunday–Thursday 11 am–10 pm, Friday & Saturday 11 am–11 pm
Reservations recommended — Fully licensed — Corkage $15 — Patio — Non-smoking
V, MC, AE, Debit — $$

Let's see: white plaster walls, Mediterranean-blue trim, wafts of garlic and grilled lamb. I wonder what kind of restaurant Ouzo is. Did the name give it away?

There's nothing subtle about Greek food, so why should there be anything subtle about the tone of Greek restaurants? It's comforting to think that most Greek places are white and blue and have that same smell. And Ouzo fills the Greek gap on 4th Street created when Paros was knocked down a few years ago. It also seems to have stopped the revolving door on a restaurant location that has seen everything from Dutch to Mexican to Turkish in all too brief a period.

So Ouzo seems to work. That's partly because people like Greek food—if it's done well. And they do a good job at Ouzo. They have one of the largest Greek menus in the city. It rolls from the mezethes (appetizers) of hummus, saganaki, mussels, and so on, up to the big plates of roast lamb and charbroiled veal chops, with loads of combo platters in between.

I tried one of those combo dishes, an appetizer one that included spanakopita, calamari, keftethes (meatballs), feta, olives, pita, and more. A nice variety and skilfully done. The calamari was excellent, lightly crusted and fried, and the keftethes were lean and well rolled. Even the dolmades—my least-preferred Greek dish—weren't bad. There's something about the slippery texture of vine leaves combined with a lightly seasoned mix of rice and ground meat that leaves me cold. But that's personal, and Ouzo's dolmades were okay. And I liked the horiatiki. This is a simple salad that just needs good ingredients, and Ouzo's was well balanced, not too oily, not too many peppers.

I'm not a big fan of Greek desserts—too sweet for me. (I know, I know—I sound like a curmudgeon.) Ouzo's rice pudding with a splash of Grand Marnier, however, was quite pleasant. It would have been better warm than cold from the fridge, but a good pud nonetheless.

True to its name, Ouzo does have its share of ouzo, plus a list of good Greek wines. I like the casual, friendly service at Ouzo—nice staff and the owners are always present, always willing to please. The biggest oddity here is that the owners themselves are not Greek. But the chef is, and that helps make Ouzo one of the better Greek restaurants in Calgary.

www.ouzo.ca

Palace of Eats

Montreal Smoked Meat

1411–11 Street SW
Phone: 244•6602
Daily 11 am–4 pm
Reservations not accepted — No alcoholic beverages — Non-smoking
V, MC, Debit — $

Is there a single more divisive food product in the Canadian market than the smoked meat sandwich? Is there a solitary food item that can cause more rifts between friends and family than a smoked meat sanger? How can a piece of cured and smoked brisket generate so much debate? Why can't we all just get along?

Similar but dissimilar to pastrami and corned beef, Montreal smoked meat is the legacy of Eastern European Jewish immigrants to Quebec. Sliced and layered onto rye bread with a slather of mustard and a side of dill pickle, it makes a good sandwich. On that, we can all agree. Everything after that is open for debate and discussion and filibuster. Just ask any Montrealer what their favourite smoked meat deli is (maybe Schwartz's or Ben's?) and then go for a coffee. Do some shopping. Have a nap. Don't worry—when you get back, they'll still be going on about the slicing (thin or thick, hand or machine), the fat (lean, fatty, extra-lean, extra-fatty), the bread, the mustard, the pickle (don't get me started), and on it goes.

In Calgary, one of the best places for good smoked meat is the Palace of Eats. The Palace of Eats uses Mello meat from Montreal, available here hand or machine cut, layered into Winnipeg rye bread with house-blended mustard and a side of dill pickle from—gasp!—Wisconsin. Fans of Mrs. White or Strub's may choose to disagree, but I say this before all humankind: It's a good pickle! And it's a good sandwich. I've always been a bit of a purist myself (I count myself among the Schwartz's faithful) and have always preferred the craftsmanship of a good hand-cut brisket. But I have to say, the Palace's new smoked meat slicer does a fine job. Try it!

The Palace doesn't have seating. You lean on one of the counters or take your sandwiches to go. But it is affiliated with the always-popular **Galaxie Diner** next door (*1413 – 11 Street SW, 228•0001*) and the **Belmont Diner** in Marda Loop (*#1, 2008–33 Avenue SW, 242•6782*). Both are small, classic diners that have great handmade foods, big breakfasts, and funky, fun decors. You may have to wait for a table at one of these places, but if a sit-down diner is what you want, these are good stops. If, however, you want the smoked meat, you'll have to go to the Palace. Or to Montreal.

www.palaceofeats.ca

Palomino

Southern Barbecue

109–7 Avenue SW
Phone: 532 • 1911
Monday–Friday 11 am–late, Saturday 10 am–late
Reservations accepted for groups over 7 — Fully licensed — Corkage $15 — Patio
Totally smoking restaurant, non-smoking patio
V, MC, AE — $$

IT's perplexed me for years why we don't have many southern barbecue joints around Calgary. Every Labour Day weekend, the BBQ on the Bow festival draws loads of barbecue fans and dozens of competitors, we have uncountable connections to the American south where real barbecue is popular, and we like the various meat-based food cultures.

Fortunately, in the summer of 2005, the Palomino Smokehouse & Social Club opened in the former Stirling Furniture building. It's the perfect setting for a smokehouse. They did minimal work on the building itself—just stripped it back to its essentials, leaving creaky floors and big holes in the ceiling and brick walls. It has a look that says it's been there forever, even if it is brand new. But it's very funky and appropriate for the genre. A big bar consumes the centre of the room, and televisions hang from the ceiling. Along one side is a honking-big smoker where all the meats are slow-cooked amid Okanagan apple and cherrywood smoke.

Palomino is as much a bar and roadhouse as it is a barbecue joint. As such, it sports numerous neon beer signs, it doesn't usually take reservations, there's often live and lively music, and it is one of the few new places to open recently that allows smoking. (So be forewarned: Until Calgary's smoking bylaw kicks in, you won't be able to take the kids.)

Southern barbecue is not subtle food. It's about flavour, lots of fall-off-the-bone meats, rich sauces, and sides like grits or Jack Daniel's sautéed apples. It's not delicate stuff, and you have to do it right or it's dry and dull.

I have had some good pulled pork and beef ribs at Palomino. I have also had some dry pulled pork and ribs that were hard to rip any meat from. I've had great coleslaw, but I've had refrigerator-soggy corn succotash. I've had a terrific slab of bread pudding, and I've had a bread pudding you could bounce off the wall.

The main chef at Palomino is excellent, and she has some good assistants. I know the initial food quality is fine, but what happens after the A-team leaves for the day is another thing. If Palomino can sort out some of their continuity problems, they could become a really fine barbecue joint.

Let's hope they can pull it off. We need a good barbecue spot downtown.

Panorama

Regional Canadian

101–9 Avenue SW (Calgary Tower)
Phone: 508•5822
Mid-September–mid-May: Monday–Saturday 11 am–1:30 pm, Sunday 9:30 am–1:30 pm
Monday–Thursday 5:30 pm–9 pm, Friday–Sunday 5 pm–9 pm
Mid-May–mid-September: Call for additional hours
Reservations highly recommended — Fully licensed — Corkage $25
Elevation charge (half price with reservation) — Non-smoking
V, MC, AE, Discover, Debit — $$–$$$

I like a room with a view. Like the one at the Panorama Dining Room. Hovering 525 feet above 9th Avenue and Centre Street and rotating a full 360 degrees every hour, the Panorama provides a great view of the Rockies, Stampede Park, downtown Calgary, and everything in between.

But the Panorama is about more than just the view. It's about some pretty good food, a kind of contemporary Western and Rocky Mountain cuisine that is partly innovative and partly comfortable. Admittedly that's a bit all over the map, but I don't think there's a restaurant in town with a bigger, broader, more difficult mandate.

The Panorama is a special-occasion restaurant for Calgarians, the place we go for a big birthday or anniversary. But it's also a major tourist attraction where thousands of international visitors have breakfast or dinner or just a glass of Canadian wine. So it must satisfy all palates, from the most conservative to the most adventurous. Not an easy task.

Chef Philip Gomes has a good handle on the market and has created a menu that includes a simple prairie-mushroom and wild-rice chowder, a platter of cured seafood and Valbella meats, a pork tenderloin with a sour-cherry and port reduction, and of course, several Alberta beef dishes. It's well-executed and well-served fare that covers a lot of bases.

Now it's not cheap. Dinner appetizers run $8 to $14. There are a couple of non-meat entrees for around $17, but the other entrees range from $28 to $38. So what do you get for $38? A bison rib-eye with a rose-hip and red-wine reduction, mashed potatoes, and fresh vegetables. The bison is very good, especially if you can focus on it instead of the view.

I particularly like the appetizers. The tiger-prawn martini is tasty with the chef's mango salsa. And the lightly grilled Caesar salad with prosciutto chips and asiago shards is delightful. I'd be tempted to order a couple of appetizers here instead of a full meal if I wasn't ravenous. The appetizers are creative, substantial, and cheaper. And they leave room for some pretty good desserts too.

One last hint: If you can book one of the outward facing booths, do so. It's the best way to view the view, and it's the most private dining experience the Panorama offers.

www.calgarytower.com

Parthenon

Greek

8304 Fairmount Drive SE
Phone: 255•6444
Monday–Friday 11 am–10 pm
Saturday & Sunday 4 pm–10 pm
Reservations recommended — Fully licensed — Non-smoking
V, MC, AE, Debit — $$

I'VE been going to the Parthenon for decades. The thing is, it's only been the Parthenon since 2003. Back in the 1980s, I gassed up there when it was an Esso station. Then in the 1990s, I bought doughnuts there when it was a Country Style outlet. And most recently, I've enjoyed it there as the Parthenon, one of the few restaurants I can actually walk to.

The Parthenon is a great example of how buildings can be recycled. It's just too good a location to pass up. Plunked on the corner of Fairmount and Heritage Drives, it draws traffic from all directions. And with the opening of Deerfoot Meadows (Meadows? Perhaps Deerfoot Asphalt would be a more appropriate moniker), this is one busy intersection.

The Parthenon is also a great example of a lively, tasty, neighbourhood restaurant. On any given evening—or any lunch hour, for that matter—the Parthenon is filled with Acadians and Fairmountese. And if you're outside the walking zone, there's a pretty good selection of free parking just outside the front door.

Inside, the former gas station/doughnut shop is now a pleasant sixty-seat, bi-level room decked out in the usual Hellenic trappings. There's the obligatory blue-and-white tablecloth and plaster-column theme, plus seaside wall murals and Greek busts. It's kitschy, but it works. The Parthenon is charming.

Not the least of that charm is the warm welcome offered by the owners and their staff. Chris and Dina Vlahos run the place with the skill of the seasoned restaurant veterans they are. The kitchen is a finely tuned operation, but the Parthenon somehow retains the casual tone of a Greek family restaurant.

They have a solid Greek menu of moussaka, souvlaki, calamari, spanakopita, garlicky dips, and lots of lamb—charbroiled chops, roast shoulder, tenderloin souvlaki. There are combination platters of appetizers, seafood, and other Greek dishes, and the pita bread is thick and warm, great for smearing with hummus and tzatziki. It's tempting to overdo it with the appetizers, so remember to leave room for that roast lamb.

Also remember to bring an appetite. Or some friends. The food is big at the Parthenon, so it's perfect for sharing. And for consuming with Greek wine. There are more and more good wines coming out of Greece these days, and it's always appropriate to match a food culture with its wine culture. So, indulge. And then walk home.

www.parthenonrestaurant.ca

The Pavilion

Chinese (Cantonese & Peking)

246 Hawkstone Drive NW
Phone: 208·3063
Monday–Friday 4 pm–midnight, Saturday & Sunday 11 am–11:30 pm
Reservations accepted — Fully licensed — Non-smoking
V, MC, Debit — $–$$

I wonder if the folks who run The Pavilion think Catherine and I have no friends or family. When we show up at the Hawkwood restaurant and want a table for two, it's a challenge for them. Table for eight? Sure, that can be arranged. Table for twelve? That'll just be a few minutes. Table for two? That can be a problem.

Not that they aren't accommodating. The staff are extremely helpful. It's just that most people seem to come to The Pavilion in large groups. So the room—which is fairly small to begin with—is set with big round tables. There's one table for two in a corner and another tucked under the service bar, but the pair of us may just as easily be seated at a table intended for eight.

The Pavilion is a blur of activity, of steaming platters of lobster in black-bean sauce and of bowls of fish, pepper, and vinegar soup being delivered to tables. The staff buzz about, taking orders, clearing tables, packaging takeout, and explaining daily specials. How they stay so pleasant is beyond me.

The Pavilion has a "regular" menu and a "Chinese" one. The regular version is a collection of 138 dishes that span a big chunk of China. They loosely call this style Original Peking, and it includes palace-style chicken, Peking duck, Szechuan-style shrimp, and pineapple sweet-and-sour pork. It's good stuff, but we look at the Chinese menu for Cantonese dishes we can't find at a lot of other places.

Dishes such as Chinese broccoli stir-fried with garlic; pea pods and prawns with candied walnuts; creamy tofu cakes with prawns and ginger-soy sauce. Bright flavours, crunchy vegetables, just delightful dishes. Wafts of grilled garlic rise off the broccoli. Slippery with just the right amount of sesame oil, the big plate of broccoli disappears instantly. Catherine steals most of the walnuts from the next dish, declaring them better (and cheaper) than those found in contemporary restaurants. I'm happy with the leftover celery, pea pods, and prawns. We both demolish the prawn-tofu cakes. Don't scoff—I'm not a tofu fan, but this dish is primo.

All around us, groups chow down on their meals. The Pavilion is loud, and the look is bland. Where there are no grey walls, there are windows looking out at the Husky gas station that The Pavilion sits beside. It's a classic location, perfect for some of the best Chinese food in Calgary. Especially if you have friends.

Pfanntastic Pannenkoek Haus

Dutch Pancakes

2439–54 Avenue SW
Phone: 243•7757
Tuesday–Friday 11 am–8 pm, Saturday & Sunday 8 am–8 pm
Reservations recommended Tuesday – Saturday, not accepted Sunday
Fully licensed — Non-smoking
V, MC, AE, Debit — $–$$

FROM a food perspective, Calgary is first and foremost associated with good old Alberta beef. Perhaps the second food association is the pancake. Long affiliated with the Stampede and the abundance of pancake breakfasts held during that July event, the flapjack can easily call Calgary home.

Which may explain why Calgarians have embraced the Dutch pannenkoek. Sure, it's not the thick, fluffy pancake we grew up on in these parts, but there is a familial resemblance. The Dutch pannenkoek fits somewhere between a crepe and a flapjack in thickness. It's usually about twelve inches in diameter, and toppings are typically cooked into the batter.

And while the flapjack is traditionally considered to be a breakfast food, Dutch pannenkoeks span the day, slipping easily into lunch and dinner and sweetening up for dessert. Pfanntastic offers over seventy versions to please almost any palate.

For those looking for a meal, savoury pannenkoeks, such as the ham and cheese or the shredded potato or the bacon, onion, and mushroom, are served at Pfanntastic. They are surprisingly filling. Then there are the sweet pannenkoeks for dessert—perhaps topped with warm blueberries or apple and cinnamon or maple syrup, all with powdered sugar and optional whipped cream.

For those who can't decide, there are combo pannenkoeks with both sweet and savory toppings—the bacon and raisins or the ham and pineapple and such. And for those who like their pannenkoeks just like back in Holland, a bottle of syrupy stroop sits on each table. Aficionados lace their savoury pannenkoeks liberally with this sweet stuff.

Pfanntastic also offers some open-face sandwiches, salads, and soups to round out the meals or to satisfy those who just don't want a pannenkoek. Although why that would be is beyond me—the pannenkoeks are such a delight. Only a few of them break the $10 mark. So for price, variety, and quality, they are a popular family dining choice.

Pfanntastic is an accommodating place too. Owner Denice Greenwald bends over backwards to make her customers happy, and she has staff that keep up their end too. Tables are pushed together for larger groups, the coffee is non-stop, and there is a comfortable, energetic atmosphere. The room is simply decorated with a light Dutch tone, and their shift to a non-smoking atmosphere a few years ago made the room fresher.

It may not be a Stampede breakfast, but the pannenkoeks at Pfanntastic taste mighty fine.

Piq Niq

French-Bistro Inspired

811–1 Street SW
Phone: 263•1650
Monday–Friday 11 am–2 pm, Tuesday–Saturday 5 pm–close
Reservations recommended — Fully licensed
Corkage $15, Free corkage Tuesday & Wednesday evenings — Non-smoking
V, MC, AE, Debit — $$–$$$

THERE has been a huge increase in downtown restaurants over the past few years, but there aren't many places that can say they've been doing the job for over a decade. Piq Niq, the tiny bistro in the Grain Exchange building, is one of the few.

Piq Niq seats about thirty-six at small, tightly spaced, paper-topped tables. I don't find the layout intrusive though. There's something about packing people that close together that creates a level of privacy. A bar consumes one-third of the room, and true to French bistro form, the bathrooms are downstairs (and are shared by Beat Niq, the jazz club directly beneath Piq Niq). In 2004, Piq Niq renovated, installing cork floors, long mirrors, some drapery and paneling, and an overall tan look. The only thing they kept was a great chandelier procured from the Westin when Piq Niq first opened.

Piq Niq also tastes like a French bistro. They say the menu is French-bistro *inspired*, which allows them to go beyond the confines of a strict French definition of bistro to include bruschetta, linguine, and ravioli. But there's enough onion soup, duck confit, and steak frites to satisfy any bistro purist.

This is good food, constructed skilfully from high-quality ingredients. A bruschetta appetizer of roasted tomatoes with truffled fireweed honey was sublime. Sparkling acidity balanced the sweetness of the honey and the depth of the tomatoes themselves. And I was impressed with the cassoulet, an excellent version with two full duck legs and a lamb merguez sausage in a steaming bowl of beans and vegetables. The duck had been perfectly salted, cured, and roasted, and the beans were likewise perfectly baked.

Chef Chris Spronk uses the weighty fats of French bistro cooking to build a base of flavour and then highlights it with points of acidity. This is not an easy thing to do. Most chefs are just happy with the richness of the pure French style, but Spronk's approach elevates and lightens the food at the same time.

Prices aren't bad considering Piq Niq is a downtown place. Dinner mains are in the mid-$20s, with appetizers from $8 up. The bruschetta at $9 is great for two. On Tuesday evenings, they do a three-course, prix fixe menu that is usually in the $30 to $40 range. And there's a smart list of wines by the glass too.

This is good bistro fare in a setting that makes it taste even better.

www.beatniq.com

Post Hotel

Continental

200 Pipestone Road, Lake Louise
Phone: 522•3989 or 1•800•661•1586
Daily 7 am–9:30 pm — Closed mid-October to mid-November
Reservations recommended for dinner — Fully licensed — Non-smoking
V, MC, AE — $$–$$$

WHERE to start? With the stunning view? Or the crisp service? Or the rustically suave dining room? With the string of accolades from influential magazines such as *Gourmet, Wine Spectator,* and *Travel & Leisure?*

Maybe I should just say that the Post Hotel is superb in all aspects of the hospitality business from check-in to check-out. And that they do it so effortlessly, I marvel that others cannot pull it off.

On the outside, the Post has the appearance of a rustic mountain hotel where one could lounge by a fire or in a hot tub. And in truth, you can, now that they have installed a sparkling new spa. The dining room follows the same tone as the outside. It's a low-ceilinged log room that curls around the kitchen—it's quaint and cute and mountainy. It could easily pump out mediocre food and still be fairly successful.

But it doesn't. The Post Hotel provides one of the most uncompromisingly superb dining experiences in the Bow Valley. The food is outstanding, the wine list is unparalleled, and the attitude is service first and forever.

Brothers George and Andre Schwarz have built the Post into an international destination since purchasing it from original owner Sir Norman Watson in 1978. In 2002, they were honoured by *Wine Spectator's* Grand Award, given only to those places with the very best wine lists. In receiving the award, the Post became the fourth Canadian establishment to achieve such a high level. That's what a carefully selected list of 1,500 wines and 28,500 bottles will do for you.

The food side of the Post matches perfectly. Open from morning to evening for the assembled guests and any other visitors who happen by, the 120-seat room keeps the kitchen busy. Oven-warm bread appears, hearty mountain breakfasts roll out, handcrafted soups elicit "oohs" and "aahs," and a fabulous burger and french fry lunch brings smiles of culinary joy to diners' faces. It's not precious in approach. It's just really, really good.

For the fully indulgent Post experience, a six-course tasting menu at dinner is hard to beat. There might be salmon tartar with saffron coulis and caviar; rabbit loin wrapped in sage and Parma ham; seafood in a roasted red-pepper coulis; filet mignon with oyster mushrooms; assorted cheeses; and a mascarpone cheesecake with Grand Marnier sauce. At $90, it won't be cheap, but it will be surprisingly good value. And there will be no problem matching any of your food with wine.

Now, where to stop?

www.posthotel.com

Prairie Ink

Café & Bakery

120 Stephen Avenue Walk SW (McNally Robinson Booksellers)
Phone: 538•1798
Monday–Thursday 9 am–9 pm, Friday & Saturday 9 am–10 pm, Sunday 11 am–6 pm
Reservations accepted for groups over 5 — Beer & wine only — Rooftop deck — Non-smoking
V, MC, AE, Debit — $

IT used to be a given that when you went to a bookstore, you did not eat food or sip on coffee. Then Chapters and Indigo changed all that with their cafés and Starbucks outlets. Food service became a big part of the bookstore experience.

So when McNally Robinson Booksellers opened their spiffy store on Stephen Avenue, it was no surprise to see a café component to it. But they've taken the food concept up a notch.

The café is called Prairie Ink, an appropriate name to come from a Western-based company. Situated on the second level of the store with a great south-facing view of the street, it seats about eighty on hardwood floors and in bamboo-backed chairs. It's casual and bright and covers a lot of territory—it's open during store hours, which means it's available for breakfast, lunch, brunch, afternoon tea, happy hour juices, and dinner. They offer a range of vegetarian dishes, and there's a bakery on-site. They even serve beer and wine, and there is live music on Friday and Saturday nights.

The menu itself is appropriate to the surroundings. It's a collection of contemporary salads, hot and cold sandwiches, pastas, pizzas, and a limited all-day breakfast. Plus a bunch of house-made desserts and a list of coffees and freshly squeezed juices.

I always enjoy their signature salad of pears and blue cheese for $8. Loads of toasted almonds and blue cheese are piled on a heap of greens with a mouth-puckering raspberry vinaigrette. And the sandwiches are substantial. At $7, they're a pretty good downtown deal, with lots of good ingredients.

Prairie Ink is big on desserts—slabs of chocolate cake or cheesecakes or coconut cake—that sort of thing. I often see waiters from other downtown restaurants whiling away their breaks over a cup of Prairie Ink's shade-grown organic coffee and a huge dessert.

I'm happy to eat here any time. The food is robust and thoughtful, meaty enough for the most avid carnivore and creative enough for those leaning to the soy side of the menu. And the setting is hard to beat. Especially on sunny days when you can get a seat on the quiet, second-floor deck. It's very nice.

Prairie Ink is a great option for downtown lunchers and weekend bookstore browsers. I'm glad to see it.

www.mcnallyrobinson.com

Priddis Greens

Casual Clubhouse & Continental

Priddis Greens Drive, Priddis
Phone: 931•3171
Golf season: Daily 7 am–10 pm
Off season: Friday 5 pm–10 pm, Saturday 11:30 am–10 pm, Sunday 10:30 am–2 pm
Reservations recommended — Fully licensed — Deck
Non-smoking restaurant, smoking on deck
V, MC, AE — $–$$$

MANY golf course restaurants make a good clubhouse sandwich, and a number of the private clubs have excellent cuisine. One of the few that has both great food and public access is Priddis Greens Golf and Country Club: Although you have to be a member to golf there, anyone can enjoy the food and the view.

And that view is worth the price of admission. The restaurant was smartly built to look over the course in a sweeping vista toward the Rockies. The high wraparound windows curve to the east too, adding a bucolic view of the Prairies. It's spectacular both in winter and in summer.

To answer the varying culinary desires of the members, Food and Beverage Manager Bernard Duvette, the ultimate host, and his excellent kitchen staff have created one of the most bizarrely diverse menus I've seen anywhere. It almost defies you to say there's nothing on it for you. There are burgers and salads and sandwiches, but there are also quesadillas, liver and onions, fish and chips, coconut prawns, venison tenderloin, lamb shanks, and lobster-stuffed mushrooms.

I've had outstanding duck confit at Priddis Greens, as good as any I've had this side of France. And I've had a near quintessential clubhouse here. They really understand the concept of this multi-layered sandwich. I've had superb soups, both hot and cold, and I've waded into buffet lines that forced me to take more food than I should. I've even had good sandwiches to-go when I've arrived late for a tee-off (as a guest—how rude) and had to eat lunch on the golf cart.

The culinary diversity carries over into desserts of pecan pie, a warm chocolate cake, crème brûlée, and sometimes a cold fruit soup. The dessert soup I've had was a chilled broth of fruits with strawberries and blueberries floating in it. Not for everyone, but definitely refreshing. For the traditionalist, the crème brûlée is an excellent, classic version.

Service at Priddis far exceeds the often-surly, frequently distant, and unconcerned style of service that plagues golf courses. (Why is the service at so many courses so bad? Is it because they have to deal with us golfers? Are we that difficult?)

The point is, whether you're looking for a quick post-golf feed or a tasty evening out, Priddis Greens comes through. A stunning view, great food, fine service, good prices. Does it get any better?

www.priddisgreens.com

Pulcinella

Neapolitan Pizza

1147 Kensington Crescent NW
Phone: 283•7793
Daily 11:30 am–late
Reservations not accepted — Fully licensed — Non-smoking
V, MC, AE, Debit — $–$$

FOR the first time in Calgary, we have a pizza parlour producing true Neapolitan pizzas. It's Pulcinella, in the location that once was the Stromboli Inn. Pulcinella is owned by Domenic Tudda, of the same family that opened Stromboli in the early 1970s. If you were ever there, you won't recognize it. Stromboli was totally gutted and rebuilt into a lively, loud, brightly white place with interesting lamps and backlit photos of Naples street scenes. The floor is of old wooden planks, there's an espresso bar at the front, and in the middle of the dining room is this honkin' huge pizza oven where the staff put the pies together.

Pulcinella follows the rules of the Verace Pizza Napoletana Association (VPN), the self-described arbiter of real pizza. Naples is considered to be the homeland of pizza, and the VPN has established numerous rules on what can and cannot be done to make an authentic Neapolitan pizza. The dough must be made from a certain blend of flour. It must be rested for at least three days before it is stretched—not tossed—into a pizza. The tomato sauce is made from crushed fresh or canned plum tomatoes from San Marzano and is not cooked until it goes on the pizza and into the oven. Most crucially, the construction of the wood-burning oven must include stones quarried from Mount Vesuvius. They do all this at Pulcinella.

The pizzas are all made individually as twelve-inch rounds. They're topped with prosciutto, mushrooms, salami, arugula, capers, anchovies, and such. All high quality. No pineapple here. The pizzas are cooked in about a minute at around 800° F and are served uncut. The crust is fantastically pillowy—neither thin nor thick, just great bread. The sauce is tasty and the toppings are near perfection. I love it.

But will everyone? I don't think so. This pizza is quite moist, not nearly as dry as some other Italian versions. The crust is very soft and is best eaten either with a knife and fork or by folding a piece and using your hands. It's also not pizza by the pound. But it is of such high quality, I think people will appreciate it even if they have other preferences.

Pulcinella also does calzone (the folded pizza), some interesting salads and antipasti, including some very fine calamari, and a great Nutella calzone dessert. Price-wise, almost everything is under $20.

I am ecstatic about Pulcinella. This is my kind of pizza.

www.pulcinella.ca

Puspa

Indian (Bengali)

1051–40 Avenue NW
Phone: 282•6444
Monday–Friday 11:30 am–2 pm, Saturday noon–2 pm
Monday–Saturday 5 pm–10 pm
Reservations recommended — Fully licensed — Corkage $10 — Non-smoking
V, MC, AE, Debit — $–$$

PUSPA is the kind of neighbourhood curry joint that I'd like to find in any area of the city. It's small, friendly, and well run; the food is good; and the prices are reasonable. It makes no pretense to grandeur, and over the past decade, it has built a loyal following for all of the above reasons.

Puspa is Calgary's only Bengali restaurant. As such, it features Northern Indian dishes such as chicken dhansak, aloo gobi, and rogan josh. You will also find the odd far-flung dish such as lamb Madras from South India. But in all these dishes you will find Bengali spicing and preparation, making them somewhat unique.

The Bengali approach is less complex than some other Indian food styles. But less complex does not mean less intense. Although the food stays in a reasonable heat range, the forcefulness of the spicing is front and centre on your palate. It may not include a great deal of subtlety, but it still offers a satisfying wallop to your taste buds.

The bhoona chicken, for example, is cooked in a thick sauce of tomato, pimento, onion, and spices. The chicken stays tender, and the sauce bounces flavour into your mouth. Likewise, the sag lamb is served in a rich, medium-spiced sauce, its spinach melding nicely with the meat.

Our favourites at Puspa remain the vegetarian dishes; for our palates, the spicing works best in dishes such as the mutter paneer and the tharka dal. The dense cheese and the peas of the mutter paneer blend especially well with the spices, making it a perfect dish to scoop up with piping hot nan.

Add an excellent chai masala and some rice pudding and we are happy Puspa diners. And with most dishes under $12, we're not badly off in the wallet either.

Puspa will never win any interior design awards, but its bright, sunny corner location offers a great view of Northmount Drive. It seats only a couple of dozen people, and most evenings it becomes busy with those dining-in plus a steady stream of others picking up takeout. At lunch it fills with more diners indulging in bargain plates of great food for cheap. Service is fast, friendly, and accommodating.

Puspa remains a neighbourhood classic with its unique food and obscure location. I wish there was something like it where we live.

www.members.shaw.ca/dattaj/puspa

Q

Haute Cuisine

100 La Caille Place SW (1 Avenue & 7 Street SW)
Phone: 262•5554
Monday–Friday 11:30 am–2 pm, Monday–Saturday 5:30 pm–10 pm
Sunday 5:30 pm–9 pm
Reservations recommended — Fully licensed — Non-smoking
V, MC, AE, Debit — $$–$$$

HAUTE cuisine. Is there a more unlikely term in the restaurant business these days? Do you see any other restaurant with that header in this book?

Restaurants serving haute cuisine have seen a serious downturn in business over the past decade or two. In fact, most of them are gone. The public wants good food, served pleasantly and well paced in comfortable surroundings, with a price tag that doesn't kill them. That's not what haute has meant.

So who would open an haute cuisine restaurant when the market seems to have headed in the opposite direction? Well, Michele Aurigemma, Gaston Langlois, Carmello Sangregorio, and Marcello Belvedere, that's who. One seriously talented chef—Aurigemma—and three seriously experienced service professionals, guys who really know what they are doing.

They know that their interpretation of haute cuisine has to be fresher than the stodgy, somnambulant, and slow haute cuisine of the past. The atmosphere has to be more casual. We're not talking sweatpants here, but neither are we talking required jacket and tie. They know that the customer has to be comfortable, that the food must be served at a pace the customer wants, and that the price should not be over the top. (Now Q is not cheap: Appetizers are in the mid-teens, and main courses are in the $30s. But you can pay that much in lesser places these days.)

They also know that the food has to be lighter, brighter, and more robust than its over-sauced predecessors. So how does poached lobster in a silky butternut-squash sauce sound? Or braised-lamb ravioli over a bed of lentils? Or sautéed strawberries with whipped cream? Big flavours, beautiful preparation. If that isn't haute enough, how about a wine list selected for its food friendliness with staff who know which wine goes best with what? And are willing to serve it all by the glass?

And while we're at it, how about a great view of the Bow River? Q consumes the upper level of what used to be La Caille. It has six rooms in all. The room with the nicest view is the public dining room. The rest—at least the part not taken over by the kitchen—is broken into rooms bookable for private functions.

Aurigemma and Sangregorio are also partners in **La Tavola**, a good Italian restaurant in Penny Lane Mall (*513 – 8 Avenue SW, 237•5787*). With Penny Lane slated for imminent demolition, La Tavola may well be in another location (hopefully) by the time you read this.

www.qhautecuisine.com

Quarry

Italian-French Bistro

718 Main Street, Canmore
Phone: 678•6088
Saturday & Sunday 9 am–2:30 pm, Call for weekday lunch hours, Daily 5 pm–close
Reservations recommended for dinner — Fully licensed
Corkage $15, Free corkage Thursday evenings — Patio — Non-smoking
V, MC, AE — $$–$$$

QUARRY is a great example of Canmore recycling—it used to be a gas station.

Although it's a bright room with high sloped ceilings, wood beams, and banquettes, Quarry owes its look not to a contemporary designer, but to Texaco. The kitchen is in the mechanic's bay, the scenic windows once displayed quarts of oil, and the patio fills the spot that housed the gas-pump pull in. It's the way Texaco stations were built in the fifties and sixties. It's now a stylish room and a great restaurant location right in the heart of downtown Canmore.

Quarry is popular with both locals and visitors for its contemporary cuisine, which is focused on local ingredients combined with French and Italian preparations. You'll find eggplant parmesan, olive-oil-poached halibut cheeks, a buffalo burger, and canola cake on the menu alongside linguine carbonara and a grilled Caesar salad. One thing that deserves note is Quarry's use of high-quality ingredients. It's good stuff. And it's consistently well prepared.

We tried a set menu of spinach salad, a choice from three entrees (fish and chips, a buffalo flank steak, or rigatoni all'Amatriciana), and a mixed berry shortcake, all for $30. The same items off the menu would have been about $35.

The spinach salad was very nice, a tart vinaigrette over spinach and brined onions with big chunks of stilton. The candied bacon was a nice touch, but I had trouble picking it up and I couldn't easily spear it with my fork. But tasty, regardless. My fish and chips were done with whitefish, an interesting spin. The delicate fish had been lightly dredged in flour and fried, very similar to campfire cooking, but it was then drizzled with a caper brown-butter. The pommes frites were excellent. Catherine's rigatoni was rich in smoky, stewed tomatoes, and the berry shortcake was made with a lovely biscuit and cream.

When I first visited Quarry, I felt that most of the elements of the food were excellent, but that sometimes those elements were better than the dish as a whole. I find the elements as strong as ever, if not stronger, and the food to be generally more unified in its approach. I would have liked more cohesion, though, in my spinach salad; I loved the ingredients more than the salad itself, if that makes sense.

But Quarry just fits and feels right. If there is a more "Canmore" restaurant in Canmore, I don't know where it is.

www.quarrybistro.com

Raw Bar

Pacific Rim Influenced

119–12 Avenue SW (Hotel Arts)
Phone: 266•4611
Daily 6:30 am–midnight
Reservations accepted — Fully licensed — Poolside patio — Non-smoking
V, MC, AE, Debit — $–$$$

IT's been a big project turning the former Holiday Inn on 12th Avenue into a boutique hotel called Hotel Arts. Aside from re-doing all the rooms, they wanted a restaurant that went beyond the hotel coffee-shop norm. So they created Raw Bar.

It's an odd name for sure. The food is not all raw, though it certainly is fresh. The chefs have designed a menu that focuses on seafood, Asian flavours, and creative presentation. Meat-eaters won't feel left out though. Lunch and dinner have a good showing of red meats and poultry, and there's an interesting breakfast menu too. The wine list suits the flavours well.

And flavourful it is. An appetizer of tuna tataki is lightly seared and served with marinated mushrooms and an Asian vinaigrette. Sushi fans will love this dish. It just jumps into your mouth and says, "Wake Up! It's time to eat." The salad of cooked tiger prawns with arugula, olives, dried tomatoes, and flaxseed croutons mixes textures and more zippy flavours. The Thai lobster bisque combines French technique with Thai tastes, and it works wonderfully. It is less creamy than French lobster bisque, but is just as rich and delicious. The chefs at Raw Bar bring out these toothsome qualities with bursts of acidity rather than loads of butter and cream. If you like lively food, Raw Bar has it. I love it— every mouthful makes me take notice. I sit there wondering how they got all that flavour on my plate.

What I'm not wild about is the room itself. It looks, feels, and sounds like a lounge. It's dark, with tiny overhead lights casting a blue palour over the guests and the food. And the chairs! They have four different styles, all of which are uncomfortable, none of which seem made for dining. Why? They're all lounge-style chairs. The best bet is to hope for a sunny day so you can sit by the pool. Now that's lovely, and the food perfectly matches a day at the pool.

Regardless, the food at Raw Bar is worth a little discomfort. Price-wise, it runs the gamut. Dinner appetizers and salads range from $7 to $17, and entrees sit reasonably in the mid- to high $20s. It is some of the most creative, flavourful, and elegantly presented fare in the city right now. Raw, cooked, fused, or infused, this food has style befitting Hotel Arts.

www.hotelarts.ca

Reader's Garden Café

Regional Garden Fare

311–25 Avenue SE
Phone: 245•3252
Monday–Friday 11 am–9 pm, Saturday & Sunday 10 am–9 pm
Reservations recommended — Fully licensed — Veranda — Non-smoking
V, MC, AE, Debit — $–$$

IT's not often we get to dine in a brand new, ninety-six-year-old house. Especially in a hidden park in the middle of Calgary. Reader's Garden Café in the Reader Rock Garden is such a place.

William Reader was Parks Superintendent for Calgary from 1913 to 1942. This house—well not exactly *this* house, but one that looked just like it—was built in 1912, and Reader moved into it in 1913. During the next thirty years, he planted and trialed over four thousand species of plants in the surrounding park, and he defined different areas with rocks that he and his friends collected. The house was disassembled in 1943, and over the next six decades, the 3.6 acre garden park fell into slow decline.

Fortunately, in 2004, funding became available to rebuild the park and house, and the Reader House opened in the spring of 2006. The results are stunning. The house has been updated to allow for a restaurant on the main floor, offices upstairs, and a classroom in the basement.

Witold Twardowski has the current restaurant contract and has opened a café in keeping with the tone of the park. It offers simple food, gussied up for goin' to town, farm food in its best outfit. It's nothing elaborate, but it's well conceived for the space and well executed by a professional team.

For lunch, you'll find an heirloom tomato salad with fresh basil and goat cheese pannacotta ($8) or an egg-salad sandwich with avocado on organic bread with soup ($8). At dinner, there's a baked salmon sandwich ($12), a roasted Cornish game hen with a mushroom and wild-rice pilaf ($22), and a beef strip loin with green beans and mashed potatoes ($25). And there's a nice list of desserts: cheesecake with orange-blossom syrup, chocolate-walnut cake with sour cherries, and lemon meringue tart.

The goat cheese pannacotta would be at home in any contemporary restaurant. It's light and fresh, yet punchy with flavour. And a beet and asparagus salad with candied pumpkin seeds is a wealth of subtle flavours and textures.

If the weather is nice, sit outside. Relax on the veranda and enjoy the view across the Stampede Grounds. Reader would have liked it. Except now a lot of his plants and trees have grown so much, you can barely see the city. Maybe that was his plan.

(Note: At press time, Twardowski was also in the process of resurrecting **Victoria's** at *306–17 Avenue SW, 245•5356*. Should be worth a look.)

Red Door Bistro

Country-French Inspired

607–11 Avenue SW
Phone: 233•2433
Monday–Friday 11:30 am–2:30 pm, Sunday–Thursday 5 pm–10 pm
Friday & Saturday 5 pm–11 pm
Reservations accepted — Fully licensed — Corkage $15 — Non-smoking
V, MC, AE — $$

ELECTRIC Avenue has been out of business for a while now, and the spaces that once housed Calgary's hot bars are slowly being converted to other things. One is now a day care, and another is Heavens Fitness centre. But there are a few holdouts. In the huge space that once was the King's Horse now sits the duo of Red Door Bistro and its affiliated (smoker friendly) bar, Amsterdam Rhino.

Like many recently opened places, Red Door calls itself a bistro. And it actually looks like a real French bistro. It's a large, airy, warehouse-type space with buckets of red paint splashed around. There are brick walls, heavy metal beams, wooden floors and booths, menus hand-drawn on mirrors, and small bistro tables. It looks the part.

Menu-wise, I had hopes that Red Door would adhere strongly to a bistro tone. When it opened, you could find boeuf bourguignon, duck confit in cassoulet, coquille St. Jacques, bouillabaisse, and a number of other bistro classics, including a serious oyster bar.

Maybe it's the Electric Avenue tone, but that initial bistro approach has been lightened. Most of the dishes are still there, but many have been renamed. The boeuf bourguignon is now braised brisket, the coquille is seared scallops, the duck confit is slow-roasted duck. Same dishes, but the bistro idea has become more of a theme than a commitment. They say the change is to help clarify to customers just what the dishes are. So be it.

I'm not saying that the food is bad now that the names are different. I've had good cassoulet and coquille here. And the house chicken soup has a fine roasted-pepper and tomato base. I even like their spin on the croque monsieur sandwich with ham and gruyère layered into a cinnamon-raisin brioche. But I've had some dull dishes here too, sometimes the same dishes I've had done well on other occasions.

I see Red Door as a party-bistro place, a decent French-inspired joint with good oysters and reasonably priced, mostly good food. And a primo cocktail list, perhaps the best in the city. They have a chef du bar who knows all the classic cocktails, from the sidecar and the Benedictine sour to the sazerac and the absinthe cocktail.

So if you're in that party-bistro mood, Red Door is okay. If you're looking for a true hard-core French bistro, maybe not so much. Still, I like the look, the service, the cocktails, and a lot of the food.

www.reddoorbistro.com

The Rimrock

Canadian

133–9 Avenue SW (The Fairmont Palliser)
Phone: 260•1219
Daily 6:30 am–2 pm, 5:30 pm–9 pm
Reservations recommended — Fully licensed — Corkage $25 — Non-smoking
V, MC, AE, Debit — $$–$$$

SINCE The Palliser Hotel (now The Fairmont Palliser) opened on June 1, 1914, uncountable kegs of beer, sides of beef, and bowls of clam chowder have been consumed in this space. Renovated and opened as The Rimrock Dining Room in 1962, the restaurant has a real sense of history that pervades every meal served here. It's a great room, adorned with Charlie Beil's huge Rimrock mural, sixty-eight hand-tooled leather columns, and a finely crafted fireplace. Right in front of that fireplace sits R.B. Bennett's favourite table. (Bennett was Prime Minister from 1930 to 1935.) When Bennett lived in the hotel for periods during the 1920s and 1930s, he would sit at that table and open his morning mail.

In spite of its history, The Rimrock has not let itself be stuck in the world of stodgy hotel dining. The Fairmont hotel group has corporately decided to honour the classic dining rooms in hotels such as the Fairmont Banff Springs and San Francisco's Fairmont as well as in Calgary's Palliser. Top-notch chefs have been given the mandate to use quality ingredients to create innovative cuisine with a regional spin.

So here you'll find a crab and coconut milk cappuccino, a local Hotchkiss tomato salad with buffalo mozzarella, and pan-seared Quebec foie gras. You'll also find great lamb and venison and beef prepared in interesting ways. You'll find prices that go along with the quality—$40 for the rack of lamb, $42 for the beef tenderloin—but there is sincere value. You'll find fine brunches and lunches and dinners of all sorts. And you'll find the trademark Palliser clam chowder, in all its creamy glory.

We sat at Bennett's table one evening just before Christmas when the hotel was decked out in seasonal finery. We enjoyed the warmth from the fire along with the professional service and fine food. The tables are well spaced—perfect for confidential deals. And the staff retain a discreet and pleasant demeanor.

Sitting by the fire and looking at the unique coat of arms hung over the carved mantel, you can hear the echoes of the Big Four planning the Stampede, the liquid toasts from the Prince of Wales (the one who would become Edward VIII), and the celebratory cheers of victory in the World Wars. This is Calgary's history at its best. And its tastiest.

The Palliser is also Calgary's best option for high tea. It's served in the Rimrock's sister lounge—**The Oak Room**—every Monday through Saturday from 1:30 p.m. to 4 p.m. ($25).

River Café

Seasonal Canadian

Prince's Island Park
Phone: 261•7670
Monday–Friday 11 am–11 pm, Saturday & Sunday 10 am–11 pm — Closed in January
Reservations recommended — Corkage $20, Free corkage Sundays — Patio — Non-smoking
V, MC, AE, Debit — $$$

WHEN the Smithsonian Institution showcased the best of Alberta cuisine at their Folklife Festival in the summer of 2006, the sole Calgary representative chosen was River Café. And in a normally friendly but competitive market, I heard a unanimous nod from local restaurateurs and chefs. "Oh yeah," they said. "River Café. Good choice." I agree.

Proprietor Sal Howell's unwavering dedication to local ingredients, seasonal products, small producers, and organic foods and wines has established River Café as a standard for Calgary—and Canadian—restaurants. Her monthly Canadian menus consistently bring interesting foods to the table, while at the same time, provide support to our agricultural industries.

Which is not to say that River Café's food belongs in a museum. It deserves to be touched, sniffed, gazed-upon, and above all, tasted. (And that's how the Smithsonian treated it at their interactive kitchen theatre.) A recent menu included morel and pea perogies with crème fraîche; elk carpaccio with blue cheese, apple, and hazelnut vinaigrette; wild-boar prosciutto with eggplant caviar; and maple-brined pork tenderloin with braised pork belly. Sound staid to you?

Alberta has always been known for great beef, corn, wheat, and such, but there is so much more to savour from our country's talented farmers and ranchers, as well as from our fishers, winemakers, and orchardists. Howell and Chef Scott Pohorelic search for the essence of Alberta and regional Canadian cuisine and capture it in River Café's kitchen.

You can't beat their location either. It's the only building on Prince's Island (not counting the new bandstand), and it looks the part of the sun-washed, lodgy, greenery-surrounded restaurant. The patio is outstanding, and the window-wrapped interior is lovely in any weather. The furniture leans to the rustic tree-branch and hewn-slab style, but it's not trite. The style works for the stone and wood building and for the park setting.

River Café is a short walk from downtown, accessed from the south by either of two bridges or by a walk from a parking lot across Memorial Drive. The footpaths are paved and cleared frequently when it's snowing, but because there is no vehicle access to the island, a walk of some kind is in order. Plan ahead if arriving in inclement weather.

A walk is also the best way to prepare for a meal at River Café. A lungful of fresh air, a good look at the Bow River, and a stroll through the greenery—or the snow—helps set the table for a true Canadian meal.

www.river-cafe.com

Rose Garden

Thai

Upstairs, 112 Stephen Avenue Walk SW
Phone: 264·1988
Monday–Friday 11 am–2:30 pm, Monday–Saturday 5 pm–10 pm
Sunday 5 pm–9 pm
Reservations recommended — Fully licensed — Patio — Non-smoking
V, MC, AE, Debit — $–$$

O N any given weekday, in the waning minutes before high noon, furtive-looking individuals lurk in front of a narrow door on Stephen Avenue. They glance about, checking for others of their ilk and then disappear quickly through the small doorway. They climb a steep stairway and arrive in a warm, darkened room.

Those meeting friends squeeze into the main dining area. Others, those without reservations, may find a high chair at the bar or, more likely, be turned away by the smiling hostess, directed to try again another day. Those in the know have called ahead, ascertaining correctly that a lunch table at Rose Garden can be hard to come by.

It wasn't always so. Rose Garden used to have a surface-level location about a block west of their current address, but they left there when the rent became excessive. There was a heady transition period when both locations were up and running, and both were quite full, though a table could usually be found. Eventually, when the lease on the original place ran out, Rose Garden downsized to the one new location.

Many Rose Garden frequenters consider the second-floor restaurant a hidden gem in the downtown core, one of the cheaper, faster, better places to have lunch on Stephen Avenue. But others think Rose Garden closed for good, without opening a new place. And, thanks to the fact that the new restaurant is smaller and more obscure than the original, Rose Garden has become the secret of those many. It doesn't hurt that businesses of questionable status used to reside here and that the room is long and dark. Dining at Rose Garden is akin to belonging to a secret club.

A club that has a long lineup at the lunch buffet, that is. That's the real reason everyone is here. Rose Garden's Thai buffet is quite good: It's fresh, nicely spiced, has a good deal of variety, and the price is right ($13). That doesn't mean you won't find the odd piece of calamari glued to its neighbour and that you'll get in line before the satay is gone. But I always feel I get my money's worth. (At dinner, Rose Garden offers an extensive Thai menu from which to choose, and prices top out at about $15.)

So, just watch for the furtive souls on Stephen Avenue. And for the Thai flag flying overhead. And, oh yeah, make a reservation, especially at lunch.

Rouge

Calgary Cuisine with a French Twist

1240–8 Avenue SE
Phone: 531•2767
Monday–Friday 11:30 am–2 pm, Monday–Saturday 5:30 pm–10 pm
Reservations recommended — Fully licensed — Patio — Non-smoking
V, MC, AE, Debit — $$$

WHERE to start with Rouge?

The location? The historic A.E. Cross home on the banks of the Bow with the huge caragana-enclosed yard is lovely. The patio is gorgeous on long summer nights, and the interior captures the Victorian tone of Calgary a century ago. Rouge is just a nice place to be.

The Chef? Paul Rogalski—also part-owner—is simply one of the most talented chefs in these parts. Ask serious chefs around town whose food they want to eat and the most common name to pop up is that of Paul Rogalski. He seizes flavours from food and holds them captive on the plate. His combinations— smoked trout with pickled fennel, frog-leg consommé with fiddleheads, chateaubriand with lemon-grass Béarnaise—are odd and astounding. His commitment to local products and the Slow Food movement are commendable, and his passion for quality is to be admired. His obsession with truffles leads truffle-heads into ecstasy, and his desire to bring the best of the best to his table can almost bring diners to tears.

And the service? Partner Olivier Reynaud brings Andorran elegance and a level of skill to the front end that is often lacking these days. I just relax at Rouge, knowing that everything will be taken care of, that everything will unfold as it should.

It all comes together at Rouge. In this book there are good, very good, and excellent restaurants. Rouge borders on superb.

It is not, however, for the neophyte diner. First, it is not cheap. Most dinner entrees are over $30, with a couple pushing into the mid-$40s. But I'd say this is one place where you do get what you pay for. Second, the food can be intimidating—did I mention the frog legs? We don't see a lot of pheasant breast served with pear-butter clafoutis or prawns laced with a Sylvan Star gouda cream accompanied by a squash-lentil compression. There's no doubt this is excellent food, but some people think it's just a little unusual.

So, Rouge is not as busy as some of its lesser counterparts. Partly that's because its location is a bit out of the way. And partly it's because the food is challenging. Great, but challenging.

That's fine. I'd rather not see Rouge compromise its standards. Someone has to be at the top of the heap. And in Calgary, that's Rouge.

www.rougecalgary.com

Route 40 Soup Company

Contemporary Alberta Cuisine

146 Main Street, Turner Valley
Phone: 933·7676
Monday–Wednesday 11 am–8 pm, Thursday–Saturday 11 am–9 pm
Reservations recommended on weekends & for groups over 6
Fully licensed — Corkage $9 — Patio
Non-smoking restaurant, non-smoking section on patio
V, MC, Debit — $$

ROUTE 40 Soup Company used to be in Black Diamond, but it moved into larger quarters in Turner Valley in 2005. Don't be fooled by the name though. They're not actually on Route 40, which is the main road through Kananaskis.

The new Route 40 is a forty-seat restaurant in a renovated building, nicely done with old furniture, vintage tablecloths, and no air conditioning. There's a large kitchen in the back for Chef Mark Klaudt to work in. And there's a killer seasonal dinner menu that includes dried blueberry- and brie-stuffed pork tenderloin and elk-blackcurrant meat loaf. There's a swack of salads, a pasta or two, and a selection of soups, among other choices.

We arrived for lunch just after the roasted-tomato soup ran out, but they still had lots of stinging nettle soup. Perhaps that's no surprise, but seriously, if you have a chance to try this, go for it. These were locally grown nettles, picked young and tender, before they get woody and start to sting. The soup tasted fresh and green and had a light citrus bite. Delightful. We also tried the butternut squash and peanut soup—could have been more peanutty for my taste, but otherwise, creamy smooth and excellent. A huge bowl is $7.50, but it's a meal. A half-bowl, which is still pretty big, is $5.75.

And they do sandwiches for those of us who feel there is no greater culinary accomplishment than a good sandwich. Chef Klaudt is one of those people who truly understands the sandwich and the sandwich lover. The Cajun-seared, twenty-eight-day aged, AAA Charolais beef tenderloin on baguette with roasted peppers, marinated tomatoes, and chipotle mayonnaise was an outstanding sandwich, the best in this book. Catherine had the red-wine and rosemary-baked lamb wrap with smoked cheese, arugula, black-currant ketchup, mint-infused olive oil, and caramelized red onion. It rendered her speechless for a good fifteen minutes (no easy feat, if I may say so). For $10 or $11, each with a side dish, these were extremely good value. The side salads of locally grown greens were great. So were the fries of Yukon Gold and blue potatoes—nicely seasoned, fried, and served with a couple of creamy dips. I was in heaven. I noticed some people coming in just to have a big plate of them.

I like Route 40 so much, I dubbed it Best New Restaurant of 2005.

www.route40.ca

Sage Bistro

Canadian Bistro

1720 Bow Valley Trail, Canmore
Phone: 678•4878
Mid-October–mid-May: Monday–Friday 5 pm–10 pm, Saturday & Sunday 9 am–10 pm
Mid-May–mid-October: Call for additional hours — Closed in November
Reservations recommended — Fully licensed — Corkage $20 — Deck — Non-smoking
V, MC, AE, Debit — $$

WHENEVER I find a good breakfast place, I wonder why more restaurateurs don't offer this meal. I receive so many requests for breakfast joints, and there are few good options. But Sage Bistro is one of them, on weekends anyway. There are only seven items on their breakfast menu, but they are well conceived and well executed.

They offer the standard bacon and egg dishes, but they use first-rate eggs, thick back bacon, maple sausages, and multi-grain bread. Their pancakes are whole wheat, the eggs Benedict come with a choice of smoked trout or back bacon, and the French toast is made from banana bread and served with vanilla yogurt and maple butter. Don't you just want to run out there right now?

The whole wheat pancakes ($9.50) are delightful. I know they sound healthy, but they're topped with warm blueberry coulis, maple butter, and house-made lemon curd. And they don't mess around—there are enough blueberries for every bite. I would have liked an egg, and I suppose I could have gotten one, but eggs aren't listed as a side dish.

But then, I could also have ordered the Three Sisters Breakfast of three eggs, three sausages, three pieces of back bacon, hash browns, pancakes, and toast, all for $12.95. Come to think of it, why didn't I? It would have been a better deal. Hmmm. I'm obviously not that bright early in the morning.

Sage Bistro has a lengthy tea list, and why not? Everyone else is doing coffee, so someone has to do it. They offer a nice selection for those who like the flavoured side of the drink. I'm hard-core and prefer black tea, and they only have two of those. Served in a plunge pot, it's great tea though.

And, of course, Sage does lunch and dinner, and all accounts—including my own—rate it highly. My in-laws, new Canmorites, tout dinner at Sage as memorable, and who am I to argue?

This is also a great place for train fans. Although the trees have grown up around its log-cabin structure, Sage is still only a few metres from the train tracks. Train buffs and kids rush to the windows every time one goes by, which is often; the rest of us dine without conversation for a few minutes, since it's hard to hear at train time.

Which is fine by me. I like to focus on my food, and it's worth focusing on at Sage.

www.sagebistro.ca

Sahara

Lebanese

739–2 Avenue SW
Phone: 262•7222
Monday–Friday 11:30 am–2 pm, Sunday–Tuesday 4:30 pm–9:30 pm
Wednesday–Friday 4:30 pm–10:30 pm, Saturday 4:30 pm–midnight
Reservations recommended — Fully licensed — Corkage $15
Smoking after 11 pm Saturdays only
V, MC, AE, Debit — $–$$

LEBANESE food has become popular for its broad appeal (it's great for carnivores and herbivores alike), its comparatively low cost, and the mostly casual atmosphere of its cafés. Sahara takes the concept up a few notches with linen tablecloths, belly dancing, and other live entertainment.

It's in the building that, for you old-timers, used to be Orestes. Sahara spills onto two levels, seating 165. The upper-level lounge has north-facing windows, while the lower-level dining room is larger and has some booths and room for the entertainment too. Tables are spaced with flexibility for both large groups and couples.

Sahara covers the usual range of Lebanese cuisine from shish taouk of chicken with garlic sauce and shawarma of grilled, shredded beef to tabbouleh, kibbeh, falafel, and baba ghannouj. There are also different items than we typically see on Lebanese menus around town—say, the beef tartar with cracked wheat, for example, or the grilled sea bass with taratour sauce. The difference at Sahara, though, is not so much in what is on the menu as in what is done with the dishes.

We started with some hummus and baba ghannouj, the familiar chickpea and eggplant purées. But from the first taste of hummus, we knew there was a difference. A big one. While most cafés use canned chickpeas in their hummus, Sahara starts with dried. The result is stunning, creating a texture and taste like I've never had before. The baba ghannouj, roasted eggplant mixed with tahini and lemon, was likewise superlative. I'm usually unimpressed with this dish. Now I see why people like it.

Our main dishes were equally impressive. The shish kafta of minced beef was seasoned with aromatic spices, laid over a rich tomato sauce, and served with vegetables and rice. All the elements jumped with flavour. Even the rice was excellent. The beef itself was lean and tasty, not greasy or dry at all. The fattoush filled our mouths with flavour, and even the pickled turnips they served with dinner were delightful.

Every element of the food was a step beyond what I expected. I even liked the phyllo-layered desserts, which I usually find way too sweet. The prices aren't bad either, with appetizers $7 to $10 and main courses mostly in the teens. Sahara also does a weekday lunch buffet, a fine way to sample the variety and quality of the food.

So this Sahara is no desert. Actually, it's a bit of an oasis.

www.saharacalgary.com

Saigon

Vietnamese

1221–12 Avenue SW
Phone: 228•4200
Monday–Saturday 11 am–10 pm
Reservations recommended — Fully licensed — Non-smoking
V, MC, AE, Debit — $–$$

I T seems like yesterday that Vietnamese cuisine was an unknown commodity in these parts. Back in the early 1980s, a few places opened and struggled for acceptance. But it wasn't long before Calgarians were drawn to the freshness, the bright flavours, and the economy of Vietnamese cuisine. By the late 1990s, Vietnamese noodle houses and sandwich shops were popping up all over town, and soon those bowls of noodles called bun became a weekly lunch staple for many.

Over the years, I've eaten in lots of those places and usually leave satisfied. But my favourite Vietnamese spot remains one that first appeared on the local scene in 1987—Saigon Restaurant. Catherine and I discovered Saigon the night before the first edition of this book went to print, and all we could do then was add an addendum to a page, pointing people to our find. Saigon has moved since those early days, but they are still going strong in their current location.

The Saigon's food is just a little lighter, a bit brighter, and more flavourful than most of the other places. The salad rolls are a symphony of flavours (did I really say that?) and crunchy textures. Their cha gio rolls are surprisingly light for something deep-fried. And the bun is always zippy—my favourites include the lemon-grass chicken and the barbecued pork versions. Catherine's is the satay sautéed shrimp topped with some sliced cha gio.

Saigon's menu includes a number of wrapping dishes such as the la lot beef. These are oblong beef meatballs wrapped in Hawaiian la lot leaves and grilled. They are brought to the table for you to then wrap in rice paper with greens and hoisin sauce. Delicious. Saigon is also one of the few places to offer the Genghis Khan grill, an open-flame grill that is placed on your table. You cook your own meats—presented raw—and wrap them with more greens and sauces, again in rice paper.

Saigon follows the tried-and-true Vietnamese style of quick service and reasonable prices. If you want, you can be in and out in twenty minutes. Now that's fast food done right.

If Saigon has a flaw it's that little has been done to the space since they replaced a moribund Italian joint years ago. A few renos would go a long way here. But maybe then Saigon would be harder to get into. Right now, the food exceeds the surroundings, and that's just fine by me.

Saint Germain

Bistro-Inspired Regional Cuisine

115 – 12 Avenue SW (Hotel Arts)
Phone: 290•1322
Monday–Friday 11:30 am–2 pm, Sunday–Thursday 5 pm–10 pm
Friday & Saturday 5 pm–11 pm
Reservations recommended — Fully licensed — Corkage $25 — Non-smoking
V, MC, AE — $$$

I N early 2006, Saint Germain opened in what used to be Mountain Jack's Café. It is attached to the new Hotel Arts, a former Holiday Inn that has been boutiqued into a stylish, upscale, independent hotel.

The restaurant is a beautiful makeover of the former plain café. The floors have been taken down to the concrete, and new walls, a granite bar, a wine storage area, leather banquettes, and huge white lampshades create a spacious sense of style. The operators have placed about seventy seats in the room without crowding tables. I really like this space—it's the next evolution of the post-millennium minimalist look that has been defining restaurants lately.

Saint Germain's food is largely bistro classic, adhering to its Parisian name. You'll find onion soup and moules frites, plus cassoulet and duck confit. And you'll see a number of dishes done with local, organic products: The grilled strip loin from Eckville's Hoven Farms is marinated in twenty-five-year-old balsamic vinegar, and Sunworks Farm's organic chicken is roasted in a simple bistro presentation. Then there's pear and mâche salad, roasted sablefish, and steak tartar. Classic French westernized with a regional spin.

The food I've had at Saint Germain goes well beyond good. Some has been very good and some has been superlative. Some has even bordered on definitive. A bowl of onion soup was the best I've ever had, and the cassoulet was one of the best. Chef Paul McGreevy, a local, SAIT-trained guy, has a real touch with the cuisine. Now it's not cheap. Appetizers run $8 to $16, and dinner entrees, $26 to $39.

But it's not just about the food. Service is far more mature than I would expect of a new restaurant. That's because two of the four partners involved—Jay Daniels and Ritchie Breen—are veterans of the restaurant scene and well know the service side of things. The third is Jesse Glasnovic, who also owns the Auburn Saloon and knows the lounge scene. (Chef McGreevy makes the fourth partner. It's a very good team.)

The star of the show, however, is the pastry chef, a young lady from Quebec City named Karine Moulin. Her breads, pastries, and desserts are outstanding. I predict that fights will break out over her cheese scones, and customers will be seen bowing down to Moulin, begging for more macaroons and migniardises.

I may well be one of them.

Sakana Grill

Japanese

116 – 2 Avenue SW (Harmonious Centre)
Phone: 290 • 1118
Sunday – Thursday 11 am – 11 pm, Friday & Saturday 11 am – midnight
Reservations recommended — Fully licensed — Corkage $10 — Non-smoking
V, MC, AE, Debit — $$

SOMETIMES it's easy to forget that there's more to Japanese food than just sushi. Every time I think the sushi craze is fading, I see another sushi bar opening. But one place that has always presented a balanced approach to Japanese cuisine is the Sakana Grill in Chinatown.

Part of their balanced approach is due to the sheer size of the place. The Sakana Grill is, I believe, the largest Japanese restaurant in Calgary, allowing it space for teppan grills, a sushi-boat bar, tatami rooms, and a variety of other booths and tables. Customers can dine discreetly in a booth or have a lively group party wrapped around one of the grills. Wherever you sit, however, the energetic tone of Sakana will likely invade your space.

The Sakana Grill had the first sushi-boat bar in town (nowadays there are many fleets plying the waters of Calgary), and it still serves a good round of sushi. For big sushi eaters, there's the $32 Love Boat dinner for two, which comes with soup, salad, ice cream, and a whole whack of sushi and sashimi.

But the parties happen around the teppan grills where the chefs wield their knives skilfully. They slice, they dice, they toss their knives in the air while the meats and vegetables and noodles sizzle away. Sauces are added with flare, and the food is scooped onto plates and served bracingly hot. Sure, it's just a fancified version of the mall-based Edos around town (or more accurately, the Edos are a simplified version of the teppan grills), but it's entertaining and pretty darned tasty.

For those wanting more cooked food, there is an evening list of tempura, noodles, and various dishes ranging from breaded chicken cutlets and salmon teriyaki to lobster and steak teriyaki. And at lunch there are lots of combo specials for $8 to $10 in addition to more noodles, gyoza dumplings, and other good things.

Service can bog down a little when lunch gets rolling. That's due to the instant crush of lunchers descending from nearby office towers and the strain it puts on the kitchen. Otherwise, though, service is efficient and pleasant, performed by traditionally clad staff.

The Sakana Grill also offers classes for those who want to make sushi at home or for those who just want a little more knowledge about the food they're eating. I guess the sushi craze still has some staying power.

Sandro

Italian

431–41 Avenue NE
Phone: 230•7754
Monday–Friday 11:30 am–2 pm, Monday–Saturday 5 pm–10 pm
Reservations recommended — Fully licensed — Non-smoking
V, MC, AE, Debit — $$

THIS book attempts to answer a question I'm frequently asked: "What's your favourite restaurant?" I usually respond with a jolly, "Why, I have a whole book of them." But when it comes right down to where Catherine and I most often spend our hard-earned dollars to be assured of a comfortable, reliable, reasonably priced meal, the field narrows quickly. And one of the few that rises to the top is Sandro.

Now don't go expecting a spacious room with soft Italian violin music and elegant staff. Don't go expecting elaborate plate presentation and exotic ingredients. Just go to Sandro if you want a good pizza, well-crafted pasta, a gulp of wine, and friendly staff. Go if you like character in a restaurant.

Because character is what Sandro has in abundance. It's a smallish, low-ceilinged, second-floor place overtop an automobile accessories shop. The tables and chairs are nothing special, and a framed replica of Mona Lisa and some plastic grapes are about the only decorations. But who cares? You want a real Italian, thin-crust pizza? Go to Sandro.

Sandro is a family-run operation where two brothers, Michael and Alfredo Rea, run the service side of the business, while their mother, Maria, presides over the kitchen. Maria makes her pizza dough three times a week, and insiders say it's always better on the second day.

She presses it out to a medium thinness. It's neither a cracker nor a super-thick crust. Then she coats it lightly with her tomato sauce, not too much, not too little. The sauce is there to provide a crucial adhesion between the toppings and the dough. And then there are the toppings themselves: fresh, high quality, applied in reasonable, well-balanced amounts. Maria spreads the cheese on lightly, creating a presence, but not an overwhelming one. It's there as an ingredient, not an oily blanket to inundate the flavours of everything else.

The most popular pizza here is the Sandro Special of capicollo, mushrooms, olives, green pepper, and prosciutto. But we always go for a simplified version of the Dom Special—a light coating of the house tomato sauce, a healthy sprinkling of mushrooms and crisp pancetta, and that modest amount of cheese.

You can also find a range of pastas and other Italian dishes at Sandro. And occasionally we try them and are happy. But it's the pizza that keeps us coming back. That and the character.

Santorini

Greek

1502 Centre Street N
Phone: 276•8363
Tuesday–Thursday 11 am–10:30 pm, Friday 11 am–11:30 pm
Saturday noon–11:30 pm, Sunday 4 pm–9:30 pm
Reservations recommended — Fully licensed — Patio — Non-smoking
V, MC, AE, Debit — $$

EVER since the success of *My Big Fat Greek Wedding*, there has been a resurgence in the popularity of Greek restaurants. The public returned to the fragrant foods of the Greek isles and the lively atmosphere that accompanies it. And no place does it better than Santorini Greek Taverna.

Santorini looks the part of the typical Greek restaurant with an exterior of white plaster and blue trim. Inside, there's a patina to the wood floors and more plaster walls. Plants have overgrown parts of the room, and a small fountain trickles in one corner. It looks like it's been there since the days of Odysseus. It's really only been there since the mid-eighties, but that practically rates it as an antiquity in Calgary restaurant terms.

Quality has never wavered over the years—the food is uniformly excellent. The arni kleftiko (roast lamb) is consistently tender and moist. It pulls apart in long, juicy strands. The calamari is among the most skilfully prepared we've had. They pay attention to it, cooking it twice in hot oil and changing the oil frequently to ensure clarity of taste. With a little tzatziki for dipping, it is a superior squid dish. The moussaka is a comparatively light dish of potatoes and ground meat. Some versions are heavy and oily; this one is not. Then there is the pastichio, a fairly uncommon dish on Greek menus in Calgary. Similar to moussaka, the potato is replaced with pasta, but it is still layered with béchamel—a sauce claimed by the Greeks as their own. It's a savoury blend of creamy flavours and textures.

The difficulty is in deciding what to order at Santorini. So the owners have created various combination plates too, ranging from a collection of cold appetizers ($12) through to seafood appetizers ($16) to a big dinner platter for two with six dishes ($45). But the best way to sample their food is with the mezethes special at $26 per person. It combines smaller portions of eight dishes, providing a broad array of tastes. It's a lot of good food—I speak from experience here.

Throughout a Santorini dinner, there will likely be fine Greek wine, some ouzo, and lots of music and dancing. Owners Andreas and Maria Nicolaides say that every day is a party at Santorini and that everyone is invited. It's no wonder they have survived the test of time.

Shan Tung

Chinese (Cantonese & Peking)

332–14 Street NW
Phone: 283•3388
Monday–Friday 11 am–2 pm, Sunday–Thursday 4:30 pm–10 pm
Friday & Saturday 4:30 pm–11 pm
Reservations highly recommended — Fully licensed — Corkage $4 — Non-smoking
V, MC, Debit — $$

THE Shan Tung has been around since the 1970s when it was on the corner of Crowchild and Kensington. After that intersection was enlarged, it moved to 14th Street and has been there ever since. But it changed hands in 2004 and is now owned by the folks who used to run the Grand Isle in Chinatown.

The Grand Isle was a popular place, partly because it had that neat flatiron space overlooking the Bow River and partly because it had good contemporary Hong Kong cuisine. Much of the food in Chinatown restaurants is a combination of century-old Cantonese cuisine, Chinese regional dishes, and Calgary's ginger beef. But contemporary Cantonese and contemporary Hong Kong cuisines are different than that. They are lighter on the oils and the deep-fried stuff. They are lighter on the salt too. And they include flavours from other Asian cultures. That's what a lot of the new Shan Tung is about, though they still have the ginger beef and the deep-fried wontons.

We tried the prawns in curry sauce for $13 and the crispy chicken with garlic in teriyaki sauce for $10. Both were excellent. Their Hong Kong curry is not as complex as an Indian one or as distinctive as some Thai curries. It still has flavour though—it just doesn't hit you on the palate with too much of a statement. It has a sweetness and creaminess in spite of the fact that there is no cream or coconut milk in it. And the crispy chicken is just that—a chopped half-chicken that is crispy on the outside, tender and juicy on the inside. Topped with crispy fried garlic and bathed in teriyaki sauce, it has a heap of flavour. And although there is salt from the teriyaki, it's not overwhelming. And there's no grease slick left on the plate.

We also had some pea shoots in garlic sauce. Crisp, lightly sautéed greens, beautifully prepared, again lightly but appropriately seasoned. A great dish. The Shan Tung does use some MSG, so if that's a concern, make sure to ask and they'll leave it out.

I like the look of the new Shan Tung too. The old version was quite dark, but the new owners have brightened it up with lots of light splashed on white walls. The lines are clean and simple and flexible. And I like the display cases that are filled with big shark fins. A bit scary but still nifty.

Shikiji

Japanese

1608 Centre Street N
Phone: 520•0093
Sunday–Thursday 11:30 am–9 pm
Friday & Saturday 11:30 am–10 pm
Reservations accepted — Fully licensed — Corkage $5 — Non-smoking
V, MC, AE, Debit — $–$$

SHIKIJI is a fine example of a Japanese noodle shop, albeit one with a strong side of sushi. Most of the menu is focused on the udon, the ramen, and the soba noodles of Japanese cuisine. Udon are wheat-flour noodles done here in two sizes (fat and skinny); ramen are egg noodles that have become quite popular in Japan in the last few decades; and soba are buckwheat-flour noodles that are common to the northern islands of Japan.

Shikiji, which means "the way of the four seasons," is a small, unassuming room that seats about forty around a central service area. The tabletops are loaded with the usual soy sauce as well as bottles of rice vinegar and chili oil and pots of dried garlic. Depending on which noodles you order, you'll receive more stuff—maybe a dish of sesame seeds or a wooden ladle or an assortment of additional bowls. In the latter case, you can eat directly out of a big noodle bowl or you can remove some of the noodles to a smaller bowl and add in the other ingredients that have been delivered to your table. It's complex, so go, order, ask questions, have fun. This is a style that gives the customer options.

I've tried both the thick udon and the ramen at Shikiji. You get a lot for the price tag. Noodle dishes range from about $7 to $11, and they are packed with stuff. The Nabeyaki udon had mushrooms, green onions, sea legs, and an egg all swimming in a broth with the noodles. And my bowl of ramen was filled with barbecued pork, nori, slivered vegetables, and more broth. Both dishes had a variety of textures and flavours, and the broths, expertly prepared on-site, were great.

One note about the food at Shikiji: Those stocks are highly salted, and they don't offer low-salt soy sauce, even with the sushi. But I admit that the saltiness is part of the food culture.

The sushi, by the way, is quite good. They offer a reasonable by-the-piece menu and a list of combos, including a nine-piece selection for about $9.

Service at Shikiji is pleasant. I think I confused them a bit by asking lots of questions about how to manage the food, but they were unfailingly helpful.

Just remember, you're dealing with long, slippery, wet noodles here, so expect a dry-cleaning bill to go along with your meal.

www.shikiji.ca

Silver Dragon

Chinese (Cantonese, Peking, Szechuan)

106 – 3 Avenue SE (Chinatown)
Phone: 264•5326
Monday – Thursday 10 am – midnight, Friday & Saturday 9:30 am – 2 am
Sunday & Holidays 9:30 am – 10:30 pm
Reservations recommended — Fully licensed — Corkage $7.50 — Non-smoking
V, MC, AE, Debit — $$

WE love the simple beauty of dim sum. Take a seat, grab a pair of chopsticks, and wait for the steaming carts to roll over to your table. There's the anticipation and surprise of a Christmas morning (ooh ... what's in the next package or steamer?) combined with the savoury satisfaction of small bites quickly consumed. And underlying it all is the suspense of strategically planning the meal. Will we get full before the shrimp dumplings arrive? Do we want another round of black-bean chicken? Why does that table over there seem to get better stuff than we do? And how many times have we seen the same cart full of duck feet and tripe roll by? Dim sum is fun, fast, tasty, and challenging.

And at the Silver Dragon, dim sum is a tradition that's been going on for forty years. Most restaurateurs consider themselves lucky if they're still in business after two years, so it's a marvel to see the Silver Dragon still going strong with the same overall food concept, the original owners, and some of the most loyal customers in the city.

I started visiting the Silver Dragon for dim sum in 1974. At the time, this Sunday morning treat was largely unknown to those outside Chinatown, and there were few non-Chinese faces in the crowd. But the food was good—steamed dumplings, rice pancakes, sticky rice—and the prices were low. The crowds grew and grew, and before long, the dim sum hours were extended until eventually dim sum became a daily event.

The Silver Dragon dedicates seven cooks just to the task of dim sum. (An additional ten cooks prepare the regular menu.) They slice, dice, roll, and steam dishes quickly, preparing Cantonese staples such as pork dumplings and shrimp balls. These dishes showcase the natural flavours of the ingredients and are fairly low on spices. But savvy to the trends of the market, the Silver Dragon also includes various Peking and Szechuan dishes on the dim sum carts. And, of course, a fine version of the classic Calgary-Chinese creation known as ginger beef. These dishes bring more spices and a broader range of flavours to the table, satisfying those who need their Peking fix.

That's how the Silver Dragon survives. They've held on strongly to their traditions while allowing for new ideas. They have grown with their market and continue to be a leader among Chinatown restaurants.

www.silverdragonrestaurants.com

113

Silver Inn

Chinese (Peking)

2702 Centre Street N
Phone: 276·6711
Tuesday–Friday 11 am–2 pm, Tuesday–Sunday 5 pm–10 pm
Reservations recommended on weekends — Fully licensed — Non-smoking
V, MC, AE, Debit — $$

N the fall of 1980, I got a call from CBC Radio saying that the *Calgary Eyeopener* was looking for a restaurant reviewer. I had been writing reviews for a local magazine and was asked if I would be interested in applying for the job. I was, so I prepared a sample review of one of my favourite places, the Silver Inn, a Peking-style restaurant that I'd been going to for about six years.

It's amazing that the Silver Inn is still around today, in the same location and owned by the original family. The Silver Inn has actually been around since 1975, when they opened in a down-at-the-heels location on 4th Street SW. They were one of the first places to serve Peking-style cuisine in a town that was more familiar with Cantonese food. Peking-style back then didn't have a lot of beef options, and the family decided they needed a good beef dish to appeal to the local crowd. So they pulled out a recipe that had been adapted over the years, tweaked it again, and started selling deep-fried shredded beef in chili sauce—now more commonly known as ginger beef. They've sold a lot of it since then and now offer ginger chicken and ginger squid too.

The Silver Inn moved into their "new" location in 1978, and they're still going strong. The room itself is nothing special. It was expanded sometime along the way so that there are now two distinct areas. It's simple and straightforward.

On a recent visit we thought we'd go beyond our usual litany of Peking-style food (chicken and cashews in yellow-bean sauce, grilled dumplings, and ginger beef). But the dumplings are so good (they are one of the few remaining places that actually make their own pork dumplings) that the two of us shared a half-dozen. We did have Szechuan eggplant instead of chicken and cashews. In a rich, hearty sauce, this was an excellent dish even for non-eggplant fans. Just to be wild and crazy, we had ginger chicken instead of ginger beef. And it was good. The Silver Inn uses a fairly sweet approach—many places go for a hotter one. The texture is great—crunchy outside, tender inside.

So the Silver Inn remains a classic. It still has the quality, the service, and the consistency, and after more than thirty years, it's a comfort that they are still around in these ever-changing restaurant times.

Simone's Bistro

Continental

636–10 Avenue SW
Phone: 263•6661
Monday–Friday 11 am–2 pm, Tuesday–Saturday 5 pm–close
Reservations recommended — Fully licensed — Corkage $30 — Non-smoking
V, MC, AE, Debit — $$–$$$

S IMONE'S Bistro is a little place on the south side of the railroad tracks that offers a good business or social lunch and a romantic, mature tone in the evening.

I want to define my use of the word "mature." I don't want it to be interpreted as stodgy or dull. Many customers complain that too many restaurants are noisy, overly active, and bent on moving diners in and out quickly. One of the things I like about Simone's is that it is a calm and relaxed place that seems more concerned about the comfort of guests than about pushing bodies around. That's what I mean by "mature."

Simone's is named after Nina Simone, the American blues-jazz-soul singer. The soothing tones of her voice are a perfect match for the space. And Simone's features live jazz on Friday evenings.

To accommodate the music and create a unified look, the owner of Simone's opened up the room and partly closed in the kitchen left over from the days of Il Girasole. The look is brown and beige, there are hardwood floors and elegant wall treatments, and comfy couches are parked in the middle of the room.

Simone's menu is good, better than my first glance at the list of salads, pastas, lunch sandwiches, and dinner entrees of beef tenderloin and rack of lamb led me to believe. Fairly standard fare, I thought. On closer inspection, though, I noticed a port-fig demi-glace served with pork tenderloin, a fruit salsa poured on grilled halibut, and a mango chutney used to balance a curried chicken breast. Much more interesting.

And I'm impressed with Simone's food. An appetizer of mussels in a mustard cream sauce was superb. Creamy, rich, great mussels. None of that sauce went back to the kitchen. A daily special of rotini with smoked salmon and capers in a light cream sauce showed a delicate and deft touch in the kitchen. I was even more impressed with dessert, one of the best sticky toffee puddings I've had.

Simone's biggest challenge is the location, a touch too far out of downtown for the lunch crowd and not quite far enough into the Beltline for the evening biz. But it has free parking out front (now that's a bonus), and it appears to be aimed at a dining savvy public that wants more maturity in a meal. So Simone's is finding its fans.

Sobaten

Japanese Noodle House

#105, 550–11 Avenue SW
Phone: 265•2664
Sunday–Thursday 11:30 am–10 pm, Friday & Saturday 11:30 am–11 pm
Reservations accepted — Beer & wine only — Non-smoking
V, MC, AE, Debit — $–$$

SOBATEN (which means "heavenly buckwheat noodles") occupies the corner of 5th Street and 11th Avenue SW, overlooking one of the busiest intersections in the city. But inside, it is a surprisingly serene Japanese noodle house.

It's a long, narrow space split into two rooms, and it seats about eighty. The look is minimalist contemporary with solid, straight-backed chairs, black-topped tables, big windows, and simple overhead lamps. The view of the busy streets and the glaring sun is dampened by large pull-down blinds.

At the north end of the room, in a glass booth, sits the noodle machine. Imported from Japan, it pumps out soba and udon noodles on a daily basis. The udon flour mix comes from Japan too, ensuring the most authentic texture for these wheat-flour noodles. The soba are a blend of North Dakota buckwheat flour and Alberta wheat flour. Both noodle styles are popular in Japan, served with various toppings and either hot in broth or cold with sauce on the side. Owner Yosh Shima can be found most days making these noodles, and he is very good at it. Few chefs in town even try to make their own.

Sobaten also does some donburis, rice dishes with toppings such as salmon or breaded pork. You will find a limited amount of tempura and yakitori here, and I have seen more sushi creep in over time. But the menu is mostly about noodles.

And that's what I go for. I tried a bowl of soba in a hot broth topped with broiled duck breast, grilled green onions, spinach, and watercress. The broth is marvellous—a rich, deep brown that is still clear, filled with soy and seafood flavours. It's the perfect backdrop for the al dente soba noodles. Soba are not soft like many wheat and rice noodles; they have a denseness to them. It's like the difference between fluffy white bread and dense multi-grain. The grilled greens add lightness and more flavour to the bowl. The udon are likewise tasty, perfect with tempura and vegetables.

This is lovely food with only two downsides. The main one is that it is salty. The other is that it can be messy as you flip the broth around while slurping up those noodles.

But for soup and noodle fans, Sobaten is a must-visit. And you can take your sushi and tempura friends too.

www.sobaten.com

Spolumbo's
Italian Deli & Sausage Makers

1308–9 Avenue SE
Phone: 264•6452
Monday–Saturday 8 am–5:30 pm
Reservations accepted for private room only — Wine & beer only — Non-smoking
V, MC, AE, Debit — $

IT used to work like this: People searching for a sausage place they'd heard about in Inglewood were told to head to the south end of the Zoo bridge on 12th Street SE, keep going south a block or two, and then look for a big brick building at the corner of 9th Avenue. Now it works like this: People searching for the Zoo are told to head for Spolumbo's and then go north across the bridge. Easy.

It's fascinating that a sausage factory cum café has become a culinary landmark for Calgary. The energy of the owners, combined with the intensity of the food, is a perfect fit with the personality of the city.

Spolumbo's is owned and operated by three large, retired Calgary Stampeders, brothers Tony and Tom Spoletini and teammate Mike Palumbo. (Get it? *Spol*-etini and Pal-*umbo?*) They have managed to parlay some family recipes for sausage and meatballs into a mini-empire of sausagedom. They started out in a small deli with a rudimentary sausage machine in the back and a single ordering station. When the lineups extended into the parking lot, they decided to build their own place a few blocks away. Not being into half measures, the boys built a hundred-seat café with a large federally inspected sausage plant attached. The lineups are still long, but they move pretty quickly (now there are two ordering stations).

Spolumbo's is crowded most days with avid Spolumbites, eyes glazed over, mouths caught in a rictus of tomatoey delight. It's not a pretty sight. They're diving into meat loaf sandwiches, big piles of cold cuts stacked into Italian rolls, and tomato-sauced sausages. And they are loving it.

They are not alone. In 2002, *Gourmet* magazine writers Jane and Michael Stern visited Calgary and found the sausages equal to those back home in their sausage-savvy neighbourhood. That's lofty praise from people who know their meats.

Spolumbo's twenty varieties of sausage can be found not only in their deli, but also in local grocery stores and at community events around the city. And one of their promotions takes them to Eskimo games at Edmonton's Commonwealth Stadium where they grill sausages on the sidelines for fans. Occasionally they make a foray into the end zone, unfamiliar territory for former linemen. Once there, they do a little dance, but so far have resisted the temptation to spike a sausage into the turf.

www.spolumbos.com

Sushi Club

Japanese Sushi Bar

1240 Kensington Road NW
Phone: 283•4100
Monday & Wednesday–Friday 11:30 am–2 pm, Monday–Thursday 5 pm–9:30 pm
Friday & Saturday 5 pm–10 pm, Sunday 5 pm–9 pm
Reservations recommended — Wine & beer only — Corkage $15 — Non-smoking
V, MC, AE, Debit — $$

WE have reached an interesting point in the development of sushi houses in Calgary. There has been such a sushi explosion over the past few years that some of the newer places are approaching things a bit differently. Towa Sushi is into big sushi, and Wa's does a lot of warm sushi filled with hot tempura and such. Meanwhile, Sushi Club has gone for more elaborate sushi. There are a few other dishes on the menu, but not many. The name pretty much says it: Sushi Club is all about sushi.

It is a fairly small space, the only sushi house in the Hillhurst-Sunnyside area, aside from the new Globefish on 14th Street. It's odd that this section of town is so bereft of sushi, so Sushi Club is a welcome presence.

It seats about thirty, at tables and at a sushi bar. The room is done in the current dark-mustard tones. It's simple, clean, and fresh.

As is the sushi. The owners are a pair of sushi chefs who worked at Sukiyaki House and Kyoto 17. Between them, they have about forty years of experience in the business and have trained many of the other sushi cutters around town. They know what they are doing.

Lunch features almost seventy different sushi pieces, from individual nigiri to giant rolls and cones. In addition, they offer a couple of combo plates that come with soup and salad. The combos are good, if somewhat limited in selection. You get the basic salmon and shrimp and tuna nigiri with a couple of slices of rolls.

That's what I had one lunchtime. To broaden the selection, though, I added a prawn tempura Dynamite Roll. Filled with crunchy prawns, it was a nice accompaniment. Especially since it was still a little warm from the cooking.

Sushi Club does more creative sushi in the evening. That's when they make mango rolls with cream cheese, shrimp tempura, avocado, and of course, mango. Or Alaskan Shake Rolls with broiled salmon, cucumber, daikon, smoked salmon, and mango. I've tried the crunchy calamari roll with tempura calamari, jalapeno, salsa, and sour cream. Nice ideas, all of them. Lovely crunch. Great flavours. Strong salt presence.

So if you want the really creative stuff and a slightly slower pace, check out Sushi Club in the evening. That's when the experience and the creativity of the sushi chefs really shine.

Teatro

Modern Italian

200 Stephen Avenue Walk SE
Phone: 290·1012
Monday–Thursday 11:30 am–11 pm, Friday 11:30 am–midnight
Saturday 5 pm–midnight, Sunday 5 pm–10 pm
Reservations recommended — Fully licensed — Corkage $20 — Patio — Non-smoking
V, MC, AE, Debit — $$$

A lot of new restaurants have opened over the past ten years, and a number of higher-end places have appeared in the downtown core. And although there's always an excitement about heading out to a hot, new place, I find it even more interesting to go back to restaurants that have been around awhile. Like Teatro, one of the first of the tony, contemporary spots downtown, now with more than a decade under its belt.

Teatro has been through it all: the buzz of opening, the crush of people trying to get a reservation in the first few months, the drop in business as the fickle first-time crowd moves on, chef and ownership changes, and times of stability.

That's where Teatro is at today—stability. It is now owned by a single person, Dario Berloni, and the kitchen has been under Chef Dominique Moussu, a skilled practitioner from Brittany, for several years. Teatro has always done a spin on Mediterranean cuisine, and they now call their food Modern Italian, featuring dishes like rack of lamb with zucchini cannelloni, rigatoni con pendollini with asiago and pecorino, and carpaccio with parmesan granita. And there's the one dish that has not left the menu since day one—the lobster and scallop lasagna.

I think there's a fair bit of French on this menu too, if only because the chef is from France. The foie gras ravioli with truffled celeriac purée and duck jus is a cross-cultural effort that is outstanding. And the roasted Quebec poussin— that's literally a spring chicken—is a French country-style dish served with a fricassee of fresh vegetables. The poussin is roasted in Teatro's sparkling new French rotisserie, part of their new kitchen installed in 2006.

Teatro is not cheap—it has always been one of the pricier places around town. The lobster and scallop lasagna is $32, the poussin, $34, and a beef tenderloin with foie gras ravioli, $46. (This is a good place to be taken as a guest.)

Teatro has also built one of the better wine lists in the city, with over six hundred labels and a couple of sommeliers to navigate you through it. The staff are among the best in the city—professional, pleasant without being cloying, good at making customers comfortable.

Overall, Teatro has matured nicely. It truly is one of Calgary's better restaurants. Pricey yes, but you get the full package of good food, wine, and service.

www.teatro-rest.com

Thai Boat

Thai

#108, 2323–32 Avenue NE
Phone: 291•9887
Monday–Friday 11 am–2 pm
Monday–Thursday & Sunday 5 pm–10 pm, Friday & Saturday 5 pm–11 pm
Reservations recommended — Fully licensed — Non-smoking
V, MC, Debit — $–$$

THAI Boat is part of a family of fine Thai restaurants that includes Thai Sa-on and Thai Nongkhai. But Thai Boat, located in a northeast strip mall, is quite different from the other two places in both food style and decor.

The location is unusual. It's in chain-restaurant country in a stretch that includes Joey Tomato's, Hooters, Cactus Club, and every burger joint imaginable. The subtle purple tones of Thai Boat appear refreshingly out of step with the area. Thai Boat's space—a former strip-mall bank—is done in a nautical theme with dock-like booths and a bar that's shaped like a boat. The room is also filled with herds of decorative elephants, including cute teacups with elephant handles. It's very attractive.

The food style focuses on the cuisine of Bangkok. On my first visit a few years ago, I had the best pad Thai noodles I'd ever had and a definitive yam nua beef salad with fresh mint and grapes. I also had a dish called Crying Tiger that brought tears to my eyes with its rich flavours of grilled beef, lemon grass, chilies, and roasted rice. Almost everything I've eaten at Thai Boat since has been outstanding. The flavours are intense and bright, and there is a strength and clarity to the food. They don't add MSG—they use palm sugar to amplify the taste instead. It adds a little sweetness, but it balances the flavours too.

I'm also impressed that the most expensive dinner item is only $14 and that's for a whole fish. The main dishes generally fall in the $10 to $13 range. They offer combination dinners at reasonable prices too if you prefer to let the experts choose.

At lunch, there is a longer list of noodle dishes topped with things like barbecued pork or green curried chicken for around $8. You can add side dishes of satay or spring rolls or some of that Crying Tiger for another $5 to $7 and make a rich, filling meal. At Wednesday lunch, they do a buffet that consistently packs the place. Book long ahead for that.

Service is pleasantly professional in the warm Thai style. The Boaters are a welcoming bunch, the perfect complement to a kitchen that pumps out tasty Thai food on a daily basis.

So it's great to find good Thai food in the northeast, especially in an area so overwhelmed by chains.

Thai Nongkhai

Thai

#10, 7400 Macleod Trail S
Phone: 705·3329
Monday–Friday 11 am–2 pm, Sunday–Thursday 5 pm–10 pm
Friday & Saturday 5 pm–11 pm
Reservations recommended — Fully licensed — Corkage $10 — Non-smoking
V, MC, AE, Debit — $$

THAI Nongkhai is a direct offshoot of Thai Sa-on and has an almost identical menu and approach to Thai cuisine. Not only does it have the same great food and service as Thai Sa-on, but it has a shorter, though no less tasty, wine list. And since Thai Nongkhai is run by members of the same family that operate Thai Sa-on, this all makes sense.

For me, though, Thai Nongkhai has a couple of advantages over Thai Sa-on. It has loads of free parking, and it's about five minutes from my house. What's a person to do? The newcomer, Thai Nongkhai, provides a great option for all southerners, not just for me. Until recently, there really wasn't a Thai restaurant south of the Beltline area, so we've had a fair drive to downtown or up north. But top-notch Thai at 74th Avenue and Macleod? Now, that's a bonus.

Thai Nongkhai is about a lot more than just convenience though. This is good food. The larb nua—that's a spicy beef dish with roasted rice and lemon grass in a lime dressing—is mouth-puckeringly good. The swimming rama with chicken or prawns, spinach, and peanuts is silky smooth—one of Catherine's favourites. And the panang kai of red-curry chicken in coconut milk and basil is creamy and rich. If you want it spicy hot, they have it spicy hot. If you want it mild, there are lots of those dishes too. The menu is long and the chefs are creative, so just tell them what you want.

They've also followed the model of Thai Sa-on in offering a surprisingly wide and affordable list of wines, high-acid whites such as Sauvignon Blanc, Gewürztraminer, Riesling, Viognier, and such. (They have good reds too, but if you're going big-chili, don't go big-tannin—stay with the whites.) The list is not as expansive as Thai Sa-on's, but it is good and so are the prices.

Thai Nongkhai—which by the way refers to the name of the Thai province from which the family comes—is an attractive, simple restaurant. It is in a strip mall, so the bay is rectangular and low-ceilinged. They've painted the room a soft yellow and have brought in comfortable Thai chairs. Service is handled by friendly and colourfully clad staff who know their food, so you'll be fed well here.

And then there's that free parking, day and night. You gotta like that.

Thai Pagoda

Thai

1306 Bow Valley Trail, Canmore
Phone: 609 • 8090
Monday – Friday 11:30 am – 1:30 pm, Monday – Saturday 5 pm – 9 pm
Reservations accepted for groups over 5
Wine & beer only — Corkage $6 — Non-smoking
V, MC — $ – $$

THAI seems like a natural cuisine for Canmore. I'll bet that on a per capita basis, there are more citizens from this mountain town who've been to Thailand than from any other place in Canada. It's a well-travelled bunch who live around here, and the bright, fresh flavours of Thai food fit perfectly with the mountain crowd (and with most other crowds too, for that matter).

Anyway, it's a little surprising that the first Thai restaurant in Canmore did not open until the summer of 2006. Thai Pagoda moved into what had been a Japanese restaurant, renovated a bit, and opened to full houses almost immediately.

There is no shortage of experience behind Thai Pagoda. Owners Peter and Khampiene Gran-Ruaz have decades of food-service background between them. Khampiene also runs Banff's only Thai restaurant—the tiny, tasty **Pad Thai** at *110 Banff Avenue (762 • 4911)*. Peter spends most of his time at the larger Thai Pagoda, supervising newly arrived staff from Thailand and running the service end of things.

The menus at the two restaurants are quite simple and similar, but Thai Pagoda's has a few more choices. They're both basically "best of" listings of Thai dishes, running from Thai salad rolls and tom yum soup to pad Thai noodles and a range of curries. But with chefs from different areas of Thailand at each restaurant, the food tastes slightly different from one place to the other.

Thai Pagoda's food is lively and spiced in a medium range. The pad Thai is a simple but spirited mix of noodles, bean sprouts, egg, and peanuts (with optional meats). It's not at all greasy or heavy. The panang curry with chicken is robust and creamy, a full-bodied curry that goes well with coconut rice. And the salad rolls are among the best I've had. The rolls themselves are simple and fresh, but the nam pla dipping sauce jumps with flavour. I could lunch on a few orders of these alone.

Thai Pagoda also has an unusual wine list. Although many wines are available in the typical twenty-six-ounce bottles, most are sold in smaller 375 or 200 millilitre sizes. This allows patrons who want just a single glass to choose what they want to drink without requiring the restaurant to keep a number of bottles open. A little like drinking on an airplane, but it works. And the small bottles are also a reminder that you don't have to fly all the way to Thailand for good Thai food.

Thai Place East & West

Thai

1947–18 Avenue NE
(Best Western Airport Inn)
Phone: 291•4148
Tuesday–Sunday 5 pm–10 pm

2359 Banff Trail NW
(Quality Inn University)
Phone: 338•4405
Daily 11 am–2 pm, 5 pm–10 pm

Reservations recommended — Fully licensed — Free corkage
Indoor patios by pools (West location also has rooftop patio) — Non-smoking
V, MC, AE, Debit — $$

'M a sucker for poolside dining. How many places in Calgary can you sit by the pool, listen to kids running around the deck, and dodge splashes when they jump in the water? All while dining on a good Thai meal?

Turns out there are actually two options: Thai Place East in the Best Western Airport Inn and the new Thai Place West in the Quality Inn in Motel Village. Both Thai Places are owned by the mother-daughter team of Juree and Chaja Trentham.

The east location appeared a few years ago, morphing out of the Best Western's breakfast room and also consuming tables around its enclosed pool. Then, following a renovation to the Quality Inn in 2006, a forty-seat restaurant was created for the west location. It's got a big kitchen, a sunny and nicely decorated room, and extra tables around the enclosed pool too.

And it has good food. The menu at Thai Place West is enormous. They serve lunch and dinner daily, and they do both Thai and Western cuisine. At dinner, there are seventy-eight Thai dishes and six pages of Western foods. That's a lot, but they have both Thai and Western chefs to prepare it all. Thai Place East has a similar, though slightly smaller menu and also includes some Western items. Personally, I'm more inclined to do the Thai food, including the $13 Thai lunch buffet, only available at the west location though.

Both Thai Places do a chicken-wing appetizer where the wings are stuffed with chopped chicken, onion, noodles, and herbs. These are huge things and served with a sharp peanut sauce and a sweet, clear sauce. Their panang curry prawn dish is loaded with green and red peppers and covered in a creamy panang curry sauce. Nice and fresh. And the som tum salad of green papaya and tomatoes in a chili-lime-peanut coating makes me sit up and take notice. If you like it hot, these places are for you.

Pricing is mid-range at both locations. Appetizers run $6 to $13, main courses, $12 to $15 for the Thai side. Thai Place West gets a bit higher for the Western part of the menu with items like a strip loin for $22 or a rack of lamb for $30. There's always the beef dip at both locations, though, for around $10.

But if you're looking for a little Thai poolside dining and can't afford the flight to Bangkok, the Thai Places can do the job.

Thai Sa-on

Thai

351–10 Avenue SW
Phone: 264•3526
Monday–Friday 11:30 am–2 pm, Monday–Thursday 5 pm–10 pm
Friday & Saturday 5 pm–11 pm
Reservations recommended — Fully licensed — Corkage $10 — Non-smoking
V, MC, AE — $$

TENTH Avenue across the tracks from downtown is not prime restaurant territory. It's largely populated with places that attract the after-work crowd for a drink or six. But in-between all the busy bars is one place that is very much about food—Thai Sa-on. It has been one of Calgary's best Thai restaurants since it opened over a decade ago.

Thai Sa-on has built a substantial following over the years. It's highly advisable to reserve well ahead to ensure a table. Although it's a large room, it's always full and almost impossible to just walk into most days.

So what makes Thai Sa-on so popular? Partly it's the gracious service that includes a willingness to meet customers' wants. Partly it's the calm Thai decor, the lovely green plates, and the filigreed tin rice pots. But mostly it's the food, a collection of "heating" and "cooling" dishes, all freshly prepared.

This fare is actually good for those who like Asian food but don't want the heat. Although Thai cuisine produces some of the hottest, most chili-filled dishes in the world, it is designed to balance those hot dishes with cool ones that are flavourful in different ways. The pad pug tua (stir-fried vegetables in a peanut sauce) is a fine example for the mild of palate. The goong narm mun hoi (shrimp with oyster sauce) is another richly flavoured dish without extreme heat.

For those into the heat, Thai Sa-on has curries in green, yellow, red, and masaman styles, and they can be inflamed to any degree. I don't suggest going to ridiculous lengths though; Thai cuisine has so many lovely flavours, you'd hate to lose them under excess chilies.

Thai Sa-on is constantly changing their menu, incorporating new dishes to keep the regulars intrigued. But they maintain a long list of favourites too. Over 140 dishes are offered to satisfy everyone.

They also have one of the best wine lists of any Asian restaurant in town. Actually, make that one of the best wine lists of any kind of restaurant in town. Although it can be a challenge to match Thai dishes with wines, Thai Sa-on has spent much time and effort building a list that works well. That's just another sign of a fine restaurant doing its best for its customers.

Sa-on means "to have a passion for something." In this case, the passion revolves around presenting the best Thai food and service possible.

www.thai-sa-on.com

Thomsons

Regional Canadian

700 Centre Street S (Hyatt Regency)
Phone: 537·4449
Daily 6:30 am–1:30 pm, 5 pm–9:30 pm
Reservations accepted — Fully licensed — Patio — Non-smoking
V, MC, AE, Discover, Debit — $$–$$$

MY golf buddies hassle me that my interest in the post-golf meal is greater than in the game itself. (If you saw my golf game, you'd understand why they say that.) And if truth be told, I am on a lifelong quest for my own personal holy grail, the ultimate clubhouse sandwich. I've had many and when I see one on a menu, I am sorely tempted to try it.

As I was at Thomsons. A hotel, like a golf course, should be able to do a decent clubhouse. A Hyatt should be able to do a great one. Perhaps the ultimate one. So I eschewed the lamb burger, the short-rib rigatoni, the seafood salad, and the balance of the lunch menu in deference to Thomsons' clubhouse. Except, that is, for the cauliflower bisque.

In addition to my quest for the perfect clubhouse, I am always intrigued by anything that makes cauliflower sound interesting. Not that cauliflower is horrible. It's just dull. So when I see a cauliflower bisque advertised with toasted pecans and sage foam, I have to try it. Just to see. And man, this one was good. As in, I'd order it again and recommend it to others.

It was a good preamble to my clubhouse, which was comprised of multi-grain bread layered with grilled organic chicken, crisp bacon, aged cheddar, and tomato. Two slices of bread, not three as most places do these days. A nice plate of food. A very good plate of food. Close to Hall of Fame level. Not quite, but close. The fault lay with the fries—they were dull. The organic greens would have been better for me, but a great clubhouse requires great fries.

Now to Thomsons itself. I've always loved this reworked sandstone room. And the fact that the Hyatt has kept and used the arched, brick delivery bays that were formerly part of the Thomson brothers' shop, built in 1893. More renovations in 2006 reduced some of the formality of the room while retaining its high-tone, Western look. Thomsons is a comfortable, friendly, all-purpose hotel dining room.

Note: Don't be confused by the address. Thomsons is inside the Hyatt, which faces Centre Street. But the restaurant itself faces Stephen Avenue Walk (8th Avenue), though its entrance is inside the hotel. If you want, you can enter the hotel on Stephen Avenue too rather than going all the way around to the Centre Street entrance.

www.thomsonsrestaurant.com

Tibet on 10th

Himalayan

#C2, 314–10 Street NW
Phone: 313•6561
Daily 11 am–2 pm, 5 pm–10 pm
Reservations recommended — Wine & beer only — Non-smoking
V, MC, AE, Debit — $

WITHOUT getting into politics, I will just say that Tibet is a small area that borders on Nepal and is currently controlled by China. The food has similarities to Indian, Chinese, and Nepalese fare, but since many Tibetans have lived for a time in India, the food tends to lean more in that direction.

It's impossible to have even a quick lunch at Tibet on 10th without getting a quick political primer on the situation. There's a shrine to the Dalai Lama in one corner, and there's information on the Free Tibet movement by the door. It's not heavy-handed in any way; it's just part of the Tibetan circumstances.

On the food side, you'll see momos and shogo khatsa, some of the basic dishes of Tibet. Momos are a kind of steamed or fried dumpling filled with such ingredients as beef or vegetables and cheese. You won't find seafood on this menu, but you will find vegetarian dishes such as the shogo khatsa. This is a dish of spicy, cubed potatoes. And when they say spicy, they mean it. This food bites back.

Much of Tibetan cuisine is aimed at keeping people warm. You'll sometimes see tea mixed with yak butter to help stave off the cold. They don't serve it that way at Tibet on 10th, but on request, they'll do it with cow butter. I did find some warming Then Thuk soup, though, which translates literally as pulled-noodle soup.

With the Indian influence, you'll also see butter chicken showing up on the lunch buffet—which, by the way, is a very decent $12. The butter chicken was the least interesting of the buffet dishes I tried; the sauce was lighter and thinner than Indian versions I've had. But the rest of the dishes were great. The momos were fresh and lively, a dish of mixed vegetables and chicken was nicely flavoured, a lentil soup was creamy and rich, and the rice was particularly tasty.

The lunch buffet, which is served daily, is a good way to try Tibetan cuisine. In the evening, you order off the menu, and the most expensive dish is $10.

I think Tibet on 10th could easily become a hot new place in Calgary. The flavours are really interesting. And I don't expect them to be in their tiny twenty-seat location for long. I think it will become too popular for the space and will need to move to a bigger location in the not-too-distant future.

www.tibetontenth.com

Ticino

Swiss-Italian

415 Banff Avenue (High Country Inn), Banff
Phone: 762•3848
Daily 5:30 pm–10 pm
Reservations recommended — Fully licensed — Corkage $10–$15 — Non-smoking
V, MC, AE — $$–$$$

Over the years, I've ranted about the inconsistencies of Banff restaurants, but lately we have seen some good places arrive and stay. And remain consistent, often because they are owner operated. In talking with Banff restaurateurs, I often hear a common goal expressed: They'll frequently tell me that they want to achieve the same level of consistency as Ticino, where owners Erwin Widmer and Markus Wespi do a quality job, day in and day out.

Using Ticino as a role model is admirable. The service here never disappoints. It is a rock of reliability; some of the staff have been with the place since well before Ticino relocated to the High Country Inn in 1995. The food and the ambience are also comfortably reliable, making Ticino a place we like to go.

Ticino is adorned in the trappings of the Swiss canton after which it is named. Lamps are shaded by stained glass motifs of the Swiss and Ticinese flags, cowbells and ski memorabilia dot the walls, and a large alphorn hangs over the room. An enclosed sun room faces the east, providing an outstanding view of the mountains. It's a little bit of Switzerland on Banff Avenue.

The menu follows the theme, with appetizers of air-dried beef and melted raclette and main courses of veal with wild mushrooms on pasta, pork tenderloin baked in a potato crust and plated on savoy cabbage, and venison with pear and caramelized chestnuts. And then, for those who like to play with their food, there are the fondues. You can choose from beef cooked in oil, beef and shrimp poached in broth, or bread dipped in cheese. These are excellent fondues, and Ticino is one of the few places in our area where they can be had. Overall, the menu is hearty, rich, indulgent fare made for satisfying the appetite after a long day of hiking or skiing.

Ticino is only open for dinner these days, serving breakfast and lunch only to large, pre-booked groups that are in Banff for hiking and skiing excursions. That's too bad. I loved Ticino's breakfast, a workout of cold meats, cheeses, fruits, muesli (of course), and buckets of coffee. Maybe I'll have to don my lederhosen and blend in with a group.

Regardless, dinner at Ticino is a mountainy, decadent delight. It's nice to relax there, sip some schnapps, and enjoy the pleasant service and food after a day in the Rockies.

www.ticinorestaurant.com

Towa Sushi

Japanese

2116–4 Street SW
Phone: 245•8585
Tuesday–Thursday 5 pm–10 pm, Friday & Saturday 5 pm–11 pm
Sunday 5 pm–9:30 pm
Reservations not accepted — Beer & wine only — Patio — Non-smoking
V, MC, AE, Debit — $–$$

How many sushi bars does 4th Street really need? Sushi Kawa and Hana Sushi do a good job along that restaurant strip, and for that matter, there are boatloads of other good sushi joints around Calgary too. To be impressive, a new place must provide something better or something that sets it apart from the crowd. Towa Sushi does just that.

It opened in 2003 in the north part of what used to be 4 St. Rose. Designed by Robert Sweep Interior Design in tones of saltwater and natural cherry, it's gorgeous inside. There are tables and a sushi bar and a counter that overlooks a patio. There are no boats or trains here, no cute delivery gimmicks, just good sushi.

And it is some of the best—and largest—sushi I've had. Towa doesn't do the small-sized sushi that has only a few bites to it. They make a larger style that was popular in Japan a hundred or more years ago and of which I've seen more in the States. Each piece of fish on the nigiri sushi is about four times the size we usually see. But it is not just big—it is fresh, well-cut, high-quality fish. And they do little things such as topping the nigiri with sprouts and sliced pickles, creating plates that are as lovely as the room itself. At $2 to $3 a piece, it also costs more, but it is still a bargain for what you get.

Towa uses a couple of automatic sushi rollers to make their rice balls. This allows them to use less water and create a slightly denser ball. These machines can work exceptionally well, but need to be tended carefully. When sushi chefs loose the hand touch of making rice balls, they must ensure that the machines are intricately adjusted. So far, so good at Towa.

The only thing I can fault Towa on is once there was some damp nori inside my tekka rolls which made them tough to bite through. This then made them fall apart. Other than that, I have had excellent sushi on a number of occasions. Especially a spicy tuna cone. And I have to commend them on having three kinds of soy sauce—regular, low salt, and sweet. More attention to detail.

Towa Sushi has changed some people's perceptions of what sushi can be. It's a little loud a times, but that's just folks enjoying their raw fish.

www.towasushi.com

Treo

Global Contemporary

1005 Cougar Creek Drive, Canmore
Phone: 678•8802
Tuesday–Sunday 4:30 pm–10 pm
Reservations recommended — Fully licensed — Corkage $15 — Patio — Non-smoking
V, MC, Debit — $$–$$$

MOST of Canmore's restaurants reside in fairly prominent locations along Main Street or Bow Valley Trail. As such, they are destinations for locals and tourists alike. But a few are hidden elsewhere around the mountain town and seem aimed more at residents than at visitors. Treo is one of these.

Treo is located in a mostly residential area of Canmore. It's not hard to get to, just a bit off the usual restaurant track. Opened in 2005, it has quickly gained a reputation for good food.

Treo breaks their menu loosely into five plate sizes and price categories. There are "small plates" at $7, $11, and $15, "large plates" at $20 to $28, and desserts at $7.50. The general idea is that you can order a meal any way you want—a variety of small plates perhaps, maybe a small and a large one or a large one and a dessert and so on. Or, you can order a number of plates to share à la many Asian cultures.

This free-form style of Western menu has never been my favourite—I'm not sure how certain things, like a bowl of soup or a duck taco or a beef tenderloin, are to be shared. I prefer more structure in the approach to my meal.

Having said that, though, I like the food at Treo. The Mexican Miner Soup of roasted peppers, tomatoes, avocado, sour cream, and tortilla chips is one of the best soups in this book. It's rich and smoky and salty, with the avocado and sour cream providing just the right counterbalance. A little cornbread would complete this dish and send me to soup heaven. The warm baguette was nice, but too wimpy for the forceful soup. (Note: I shared this soup with no one.)

The "crispy seared" chicken with cranberries, almonds, leek, and maple vinegar sauce was nice too, but though it was seared, it wasn't crispy. A skinless chicken breast is just not going to be crisp without the skin. Still, nicely prepared, especially if you like a sweeter, fruity style of sauce.

The almond-Grand Marnier cake with vanilla ice cream and candied orange zest was a dense piece of cake with a big wallop of ice cream. Also nice.

Treo has a sleek, contemporary, black and tan look, and there is a patio so that you can enjoy Canmore's sunny days away from the bustle of its busier streets.

The Tribune

Forgotten Fare

118 Stephen Avenue Walk SW
Phone: 269•3160
Monday–Thursday 11 am–11 pm, Friday 11 am–1 am, Saturday 4 pm–1 am
Reservations recommended — Fully licensed — Corkage $25 — Small patio
Non-smoking
V, MC, AE, Debit — $$–$$$

AMONG the hot new restaurants around Calgary, one of the hottest is The Tribune. It's in the 1892-built, sandstone Tribune Block. It is the fifth restaurant from the folks who own the three Murrieta's and the Siding Café, and it is their showcase.

They've done a great job on the rooms and have taken an unusual and brilliant approach: The basement is the dining room, and the main floor is the bar. This tends to equalize the crowd. If the bar were downstairs, I think it would be empty during the day. As it is, the bar is packed for lunch, and so is the dining room.

The Tribune has big tables, nice glassware and cutlery, leather chairs, a sumptuous look, and service to match. And it features the Continental style of the early twentieth century. Chef Andrew Keen calls the dishes Forgotten Food. It's classic cooking that is high on fat and salt and takes time to prepare.

They make a croque madame sandwich of brioche layered with rosemary ham and aged gruyère, topped with mornay sauce and a fried egg. They do a rabbit rillette of slow-cooked rabbit pounded and mixed with fat and served with baguette. Marvelous. A dish of braised lamb over a lentil ragout takes hours to cook, and a shellfish spaghetti is coated in a real tomato sauce. It's how I always want this dish to taste but rarely does.

I like the food at The Tribune a lot. It's got depth and richness, and for the quality, the prices aren't bad. The croque madame is about $15 with soup, salad, or frites. The braised lamb is about $23, and a lunch of the shellfish spaghetti, about $20. Big ticket dinners for two are a chateaubriand for $76 and pressed duck at $63.

So, criticisms. I don't care for pommes allumettes, the small, matchstick french fries. Too fiddly. And much as I like all the fat and salt, some may find it too heavy, antithetical to current culinary trends. But again, personal preference. That being said, The Tribune is one hot and happening place. I think it's one of the best to open in Calgary—ever.

For a more casual option to The Tribune, the **Siding Café** is just a block away at *100–7 Avenue SW (262•0282)*. It started life as a diner, but was converted to a comfort-food bistro when the bistro craze hit Calgary in 2006.

Trong-Khanh

Vietnamese

1115 Centre Street N
Phone: 230·2408
Sunday–Thursday 11 am–9 pm, Friday & Saturday 11 am–10 pm
Reservations recommended — Beer & wine only — Non-smoking
V, MC, AE, Debit — $

IT hasn't been that long since Vietnamese was a mystery cuisine in these parts. Only fifteen or twenty years ago, there were less than a handful of Vietnamese restaurants, and those few struggled for customers. One of the first was the Trong-Khanh.

I remember trudging up the concrete steps to the Trong-Khanh back in the late eighties; it was a homely room then, with worn carpets and glaring lights. But they stuck it out and helped popularize bowls of bun and salad rolls. And as a reward for their tenacity, they seem to have been packed solid for at least the last eight or so years.

The look has improved a lot since the early days. The walls are now soft pastels lit by sleek wall and ceiling lamps. The ceiling itself has been opened up to give more height, and it's painted deep blue. They've even fixed the washroom doors (part of the Trong-Khanh's early charm were washroom doors that tended to lock people in). They have, however, retained the pop cooler that dominates the tiny room with its size and its incessant hum.

The tables are all numbered, as are the dishes on the menu. That way regulars can reserve their favourite table (say, number eight) and order their favourite dishes (perhaps a number four and a number fifty-five) with greater ease. It's a user-friendly place. And it's fast. It's the kind of restaurant where you can easily be in and out for lunch in a half-hour. And you can feel good about it.

The food is always tasty. The salad rolls (number four) are a classic: The shrimp is tender and crunchy; the greens, fresh; and the noodles, lightly al dente. With a spiked brown-bean sauce, they are among the best in town.

The bowls of bun are likewise filled with freshly prepared ingredients and topped with richly grilled meats. The barbecued pork (number fifty-five) is a salty partner to the rice vermicelli, the greens, and the light nuoc mam sauce. Occasionally I've found the meats a touch oily here, but that is a minor complaint.

The prices continue to amaze me. Most dishes remain under $10, like the deep-fried quail with chopped egg on broken rice for all of $8.50. And that brisk service remains friendly.

The Trong-Khanh is nothing fancy, but it is fresh, hot, fast, and cheap. And you won't get locked in the washroom anymore.

Velvet at The Grand

Contemporary Canadian

608–1 Street SW (The Grand)
Phone: 244•8400
Monday 11 am–2 pm, Tuesday–Friday 11 am–5 pm, Tuesday–Saturday 5 pm–close
Reservations recommended — Fully licensed — Non-smoking
V, MC, AE, Debit — $$–$$$

THE Grand theatre beside the Lougheed Building was built in 1912 as a vaudeville house and saw acts ranging from Sarah Bernhardt to the Marx Brothers. Now The Grand has been redeveloped into a new home for Theatre Junction and Velvet. It's very Euro cool.

The theatre itself is a beautiful performing space with flexible seating for up to four hundred. The old entrance has been restored with what was remaining of the original Grand. The former lobby, plus some of the old seating area, has been turned into Velvet, and theatre doors split Velvet in two, with a lounge to the left and the restaurant to the right.

The restaurant seats about sixty-five at a long banquette and at tables. It's a black, mirrored space with an open kitchen and polished concrete floors. Overhead hang exposed light bulbs and a zigzag pattern of old planks that were once used as a catwalk in the theatre. There are also steel-mesh-enclosed fluorescents and a stairway to the second floor mezzanine where you'll find another unique aspect of The Grand: a large, unisex sink area outside of the bathrooms.

But back to Velvet. It's part of Canadian Rocky Mountain Resorts, the folks who own Divino, Cilantro, The Ranche, and a number of mountain properties. I would say the food at Velvet has a contemporary sensibility somewhere between Cilantro and Divino. You've got your seared tuna with arugula pesto, your duck confit salad, and your flatiron steak with brie-mashed potatoes. The menu accommodates the breadth of clientele that arrive for business lunches, pre-theatre meals, and post-theatre snacks.

The food I've had at Velvet has been good. The tamarind-glazed duck breast with a truffle risotto is perhaps the best non-confit duck I've had this side of the Atlantic. The portobello mushroom pâté is also a winner. And the caribou-elk burger, from Canadian Rocky Mountain's own game ranch, is really good. Nice attention to detail.

Velvet is not cheap. That duck is $31, the pâté, $10, and the burger, $16. But I guess you have to pay for such coolness.

Velvet is definitely worth a look. Not everyone will like it. It's extreme. But I think it's one of the best combinations of old and new I've seen. And then there's the theatre itself.

As mentioned above, Velvet is a sibling of **Cilantro**, a California-Southwestern restaurant at *338–17 Avenue SW (229•1177)*. I've reviewed it many times over the years, and I continue to enjoy its ambience and its food.

www.velvetgrand.com

Village Restaurant

Pakistani

#834, 5075 Falconridge Boulevard NE
Phone: 509•2559
Tuesday–Sunday 11 am–9:30 pm
Reservations accepted — No alcoholic beverages — Non-smoking
V, MC, Debit — $

I should explain how to find Village Restaurant because it can be tricky. It's just north of McKnight Boulevard, south of 50th Avenue NE, and between 47th and 52nd Streets NE. The area is comprised of a series of malls that intertwine with each other, and I find it quite confusing. But it's a fascinating part of the city to me, with the bulk of the businesses here featuring products from the Indian subcontinent.

Village Restaurant is Calgary's only sit-down Pakistani restaurant. Their mall bay is filled with decorative tin rice-cookers, brightly painted chairs, and overhead televisions that churn out Bollywood films non-stop. It's lively.

As is the food. I tried the shami kebab because it sounded so interesting. Ground beef and ground split peas are mixed together and formed into hamburger-like patties. The patties are cooked and served on a sizzling hot platter with vegetables and chutneys. They're good, but have an unusual texture—smooth, perhaps too smooth for those expecting a hamburger type of mouth feel. They won't be everyone's favourite.

The Lahori chargha is Pakistani-fried chicken. The Colonel has nothing to worry about, unless you like your fried chicken spicy and less battered, that is. Then he'd better watch out. There's also the murgh tikka masala, tandoori-baked boneless chicken marinated in yogurt and spices and served in a tangy sauce. This is a lovely dish—moist chicken with layers of rich spices. Beautiful.

And the cheeker chanay, a chickpea curry that I've come to think of as "cheeky chanay," is a dish that bites back. Blazing with heat, loaded with flavour, it's great.

Village specializes in goat, and they do it well. If you've been hankering for goat korma with ginger and garlic or goat palak with spinach or goat karahi in a spicy tomato sauce, Village is the place. (FYI, we raise a lot of good goats in Alberta.)

And they do kulfi-on-a-stick at Village. This is an ice cream made with pure cream and flavoured with pistachio, mango, almond, or vanilla. Again, it's not going to excite everyone, but I really enjoyed their vanilla version.

So Village is unique. It may take awhile to get your food (pretty much everything is made to order), but it benefits from that handcrafted quality. I like the flavours here a lot, and almost everything is under $10.

Village is worth the effort it takes to find. Go for the goat. Stay for the kulfi.

Vintage

Chophouse

322–11 Avenue SW
Phone: 262•7961
Monday–Wednesday 11:30 am–midnight, Thursday & Friday 11:30 am–2 am
Saturday 5 pm–2 am, Sunday 5 pm–midnight
Reservations recommended — Fully licensed
Non-smoking dining room, smoking in tavern
V, MC, AE, Debit — $$–$$$

WHEN Calgary's fresh-air bylaw finally kicks in, few places will benefit more from it than Vintage. (Note: If, by the time you read this, it *has* taken effect, replace "kicks" with "kicked," "will benefit" with "benefited," and skip the next paragraph.)

When Vintage opened in 2003, it was beautifully designed to have the elegant dining room sweep into a lively tavern. Problem was, they decided to allow smoking in the tavern. So unless you are seated well inside the dining room, a smoky hue will taint your meal. And if you are seated in the elevated area that adjoins the tavern—well, forget about having a smoke-free meal. The smoke from the tavern curls smartly into this area. Vintage is one of the few smoking holdouts in this book.

Enough ranting. Vintage also rates notice for being one of the few chophouses to open in recent memory. It has the rich wood and leather look of East Coast chophouses as well as servers attired in white jackets, crisp linens, and a great wine list. Plus lots and lots of meat. I counted fifteen beef dishes on the summer 2006 dinner menu. There's top-quality Alberta beef done in various cuts and sizes, from tenderloin tartare ($16) to a grilled sixteen-ounce, bone-in tenderloin ($60). (Bone-in tenderloin? Yeah, I thought that was odd too. Seems to be a bit of a fad these days.)

I always enjoy the Vintage Burger, an eight-ounce house-ground patty with wild-boar bacon, smoked gruyère, and chipotle aioli ($12). But I thought I should check out the prime rib lunch sandwich with spiced onion rings and red-wine demi-glace ($16). I could hear the primal murmur from within: Mmmm, good meat.

The onion rings aren't the kind you'd get at, say, a drive-through burger joint. These are the lightly frizzled, trendy variety. You can get fries on the side or a salad (who does that?), but the fries are of the frozen variety. Please! Peel some potatoes! The demi-glace is decent, but the focaccia mostly dissolves in it. Still, good meat.

Vintage has also opened **Redwater Rustic Grille** (*9223 Macleod Trail S.,* *253•4266*), a chain-in-the-making. Aimed at being a cut above the Earls of the world, Redwater is a nice room with a great concept. At press time, execution of the Southwestern-influenced menu still needed some tweaking, but it could become a fine suburban joint. And it's been non-smoking from the start.

www.vintagechophouse.com

Wa's

Japanese

1721 Centre Street N
Phone: 277•2077
Monday–Friday 11:30 am–2 pm, Saturday & Sunday noon–2 pm
Monday–Saturday 5 pm–10 pm, Sunday 5 pm–9 pm
Reservations recommended — Fully licensed — Non-smoking
V, MC, AE, Debit — $$

W A'S is one of the most simply named restaurants in town, suitable for its tiny space and discreet street presence. It seats only a couple of dozen at booths and along a short sushi bar.

I've never seen any advertising for Wa's. It's the kind of place that has become popular by word of mouth. And I can see why. They do a good job.

Although there are a number of sushi chefs, or itamaes, out there who have taken courses in Japan (it takes years of study to become a true itamae), there are some who have almost no training at all. Not long ago, I asked a fellow from an unnamed restaurant what kind of sushi training he had, and he told me that the boss had shown him what to do in a few hours. That lack of skill shows up in restaurants where the sushi falls apart, the cuts are ragged, the nori is tough, and the flavour and presentation are uneven or sloppy.

You are not going to see that at Wa's. This is elegant sushi. I ordered a series of rolls where the seafood was combined with other ingredients and rolled in sushi rice and nori. I was impressed with the quality of the rice, which was just right. It stuck together without being gluey and was lightly sweet, complementing the seafood. This is much more difficult to do than it sounds. The cuts were clean and sharp too, creating a balance in the rolls. Nothing was off-centre or sticking out unless it was supposed to.

The Dynamite Roll, for instance, had shrimp tails sticking out of it because that's the way it was intended to be. And the house special, a giant roll of tuna, salmon, pollock, shrimp, cucumber, avocado, and fish roe, was beautifully prepared and, in spite of its size and variety, held together through eating. The Flames Roll and the spicy tuna roll were just that—spicy. No holding back at all. But my favourite was that Dynamite Roll. They had used freshly cooked tempura shrimp, not cold, limp stuff. Steaming hot, crunchy tempura in a roll— it doesn't get much better.

Wa's also offers a short menu that includes various appetizers, tempuras, teriyaki chicken, and such, but it seems most go for the sushi. Wa's is skilled at putting out good stuff nicely and quickly. So sushi purists can delight in Wa's. Short, skilled, and to the point.

Wild Horse Bistro

Contemporary Alberta Cuisine

126 Centre Avenue, Black Diamond
Phone: 933•5800
October–April: Tuesday–Thursday 11 am–3:30 pm
Friday & Saturday 11 am–8:30 pm, Sunday 11 am–3 pm
May–September: Call for summer hours
Reservations recommended, especially on weekends — Fully licensed — Corkage $10
Small patio — Non-smoking restaurant, smoking on patio
V, MC, AE, Debit — $–$$

WHEN the Route 40 Soup Company first opened, they were located on Black Diamond's main drag. After they moved to Turner Valley, their space was quickly taken over by Amy and Jessie Smulders and renamed Wild Horse Bistro. With a similar philosophy to Route 40, these two sisters support local producers and work with seasonal products. So, you'll find organic bison, baking made from Highwood Crossing organic flour, and home-grown herbs.

But they don't limit themselves to local food stylings. Though it's a fairly short menu, it bounces around the globe. They have, for example, artichokes with spaghetti, couscous with veggies and feta, a smoked salmon bagel, tandoori-chicken pizza, and several Mexican dishes. Normally I worry about such eclecticism. But at Wild Horse, they pull it off because they keep the concept tight and the ingredients strong.

The couscous bowl is overloaded with goat feta, pine nuts, local vegetables, and an herb dressing. For $7, it's a huge lunch. You can make it even bigger for another $4 if you add some chicken or smoked salmon. They also do a good lemon chicken burger ($10) that's layered with olives, more feta, lemon zest, and spinach.

And they make a Tex-Mex burger ($10) that really could be called an Alta-Mex burger. It's loaded with salsa, peppers, guacamole, and slabs of cheddar. This is one really large and lean house-made beef burger that was too big for me to finish. That could have had something to do with the side of roasted vegetables and the accompanying herbed mayonnaise dip. Plus the bowl of clam chowder I started with. Regardless, I finally met a hamburger that got the better of me. And it was good.

So was the chowder, the daily soup special. They called it Manhattan-style, but although there are many variations on that theme, I thought this was more of a hearty vegetable soup with some clams in it. Still, a nice soup.

Most things at Wild Horse are made in-house and to order, so it may take awhile to get your meal. Don't be in too much of a hurry. It's a small restaurant and a kind of community visiting place where everyone seems to know everyone else. But it's not one of those spots where you feel like an outsider. Wild Horse has a warm, sociable tone that envelopes you even if you're not from Black Diamond.

Wildwood

Rocky Mountain Cuisine & Brew Pub

2417–4 Street SW
Phone: 228•0100
Daily 11:30 am–2 pm, Sunday–Thursday 5 pm–10 pm, Friday & Saturday 5 pm–11 pm
Reservations recommended — Fully licensed — Patio
Non-smoking restaurant, smoking in pub
V, MC AE, Debit — $$–$$$

WHEN the hankering for a piece of bison liver or a slice of wild-boar-bacon pizza hits, just where are you gonna go? And when you just have to have veal tenderloin topped with cambozola cheese and served with a fricassee of mushrooms, where do you head? And where can you find caribou scaloppine with a sour-cherry and ginger sauce?

Wildwood.

When the game craving hits and you don't have time to head for the hills yourself, Wildwood answers nature's call. This is a place for the serious carnivore, for those who like their game gamey and their prawns wrapped in double-smoked bacon. Wildwood is unrepentantly meaty, from a simple bison carpaccio to pan-seared elk medallions with an elderberry sauce.

But don't confuse Wildwood with those fusty, safari-themed restaurants of generations past. There's plenty of meat to be sure, but it's done in a tasty, contemporary way. And there are adequate greens and veggies on the menu to round out your meal. But don't take your vegan friends to Wildwood. That is not a good idea.

I'm particularly fond of Wildwood's lamb burger, a slippery concoction that includes melted cambozola cheese and a berry chutney. And the steaks here are always good. (Yes, there are some good old beef steaks in the mix.)

Wildwood also pours a line of house-brewed beers to go along with their food. They are clean, sharp, well-brewed beers that pass the time nicely, with or without food. For those who want to hide away, the Wildwood pub downstairs offers a den-like tone and a smaller food menu.

The main Wildwood dining room is a high-ceilinged, airy room with south-facing windows spilling light into the space. A large, open kitchen lines one wall, and a popular patio tracks the southern side of the room. A private dining area seats about twenty behind a room-dividing fireplace. Wildwood is a nice space, contemporary in its tone and lighter in look than a glance at its meaty menu might first indicate.

And it's a busy place. With such a key location on the 4th Street restaurant strip and its closeness to Stampede Park, it's a natural meeting place for local activities. And what better way to kick off a Flames game or a day at the Stampede than with a big hunk of meat in your stomach.

Wildwood's sister restaurant, **Bonterra** (*1016–8 Street SW, 262•8480*), is a reliable rustic-Italian joint with a great patio and a fine wine list.

Yuzuki

Japanese

510–9 Avenue SW
Phone: 261•7701
Monday–Friday 11:30 am–2 pm
Reservations recommended — Fully licensed — Corkage $12 — Non-smoking
V, MC, AE, Debit — $$

WHENEVER I'm asked where to find good sushi, I spiel off a whole group of places. And I always mention Yuzuki, a favourite of mine for over fifteen years. It's usually about then that the querulous looks start. "Yu-what?" they seem to say. "Yu-where?"

Yuzuki is almost invisible to all but the most discerning sushi-phile. With a dust-covered canopy protruding over the 9th Avenue sidewalk, it's missed by the thousands of cars that buzz by each day.

But just try to get a lunch seat without a reservation. (If you can find it, that is.) You might get lucky, but chances are, you'll be cooling your heels for a while. Because over the years, Sam and Cheryl Oshiro have built up a loyal clientele for their sushi and their cooked Japanese food. So on any given lunch hour, all eighty-odd seats are usually filled.

Many of the regulars angle for tables along the miniature train tracks that run from the sushi bar into the middle of the dining room. It's fun to have the sushi delivered by train. Others prefer the relative privacy of the tatami rooms that line one side of the room. And a select few get the handful of seats at the sushi bar itself, the perfect place to watch Sam's skills.

Don't expect a lot of other decor at Yuzuki, however. They've spruced it up in recent years, but the bathrooms still need work and the carpets have looked better. Regulars bypass the frills for the sushi though—the kind that makes you realize there is good sushi and not-so-good sushi. Yuzuki's is the good kind, from Sam's precision-cut rolls to his fresh, fresh nigiri.

It has to be fresh; it's only made to order. If you don't know what you want, order the assorted sushi. Then supplement it—if you have room—with a salmon-skin cone. It's the best of its kind in town. I think I've tried them all, and Yuzuki's cone has the best balance of fish, crispiness, and taste.

So if you can find Yuzuki, you'll be treated to quality sushi and Japanese food. It's been years since I ordered anything cooked here, but every time the servers carry a bowl of donburi or a sizzling teriyaki past me, I think that next time I *must* order that. Maybe some day I will.

Note: With redevelopment of this area looming, don't be surprised if Yuzuki moves to a different downtown location in the near future. Call ahead.

Little Eats

A & A

1401–20 Avenue NW, 289 • 1400

At any lunch hour, you'll likely find a long lineup flowing out the door of A & A Foods & Deli. A lineup at a convenience store? Why?

It's all about the fast Lebanese food of donairs, tabbouleh. and falafel. And the floor show provided by the staff. Jimmy Elrafih, the master of the one-liner, zings out jokes as quickly as he wraps pitas in tinfoil.

There are a couple of canopied tables outside, but most of A & A's food is for takeout. The chicken "roasted-with-love" shawarma laced with garlic sauce, tomatoes, pickles, and greens is the big seller. (Note: At press time, Elrafih was putting the finishing touches on **Mediterranea** at *1304–4 Street SW, phone number TBA*, featuring similar food but in a café setting.)

Barpa Bill's Souvlaki

223 Bear Street, Banff, 762 • 0377

Ah, the sweetly pungent aroma of garlic and roast lamb wafting on the fresh mountain air. Ambrosia to some, not so much to others. Barpa Bill's is uncompromisingly Greek, something of an Hellenic Pied Piper to me.

Bill's (and yes, there is a Bill) is a tiny space where the grill is bigger than the seating area: Sixteen stools are pushed up against a wraparound counter. Bill can almost reach out to the farthest corners of his shop without leaving his station.

Try his spanakopita (superb), his pita (outstanding), and his Caesar salad (garlicky), along with a souvlaki. And have a chat with Bill. He's an affable fellow and a great ambassador for all things Banff.

www.barpabills.com

Beamer's Coffee Bar

737–7 Avenue, Canmore, 609 • 0111
1702 Bow Valley Trail, Canmore, 678 • 3988

You have to love a community whose citizenry will sit outside at a coffee shop when it's below zero. Check out Beamer's next time you're in Canmore on a frosty day. If the sun is shining, there will be a gaggle of Cowichan-sweatered, Tibetan-toqued, Serengeti-sunglassed addicts sipping their caffeine on Beamer's downtown patio. Why? Because it's there, of course. And because they love their Beamer's coffee in any weather. With a blueberry bran muffin. And a bowl of ice water for the pooch.

Indoor or out, Beamer's does decent coffee and hearty baked goods to go with it. Yes, you can sit inside if you want. Wimp!

www.beamerscoffeebar.ca

The Better Butcher

385 Heritage Drive SE (Acadia Centre), 252•7171

SOMETIMES I just like to stand in front of the counter and look at all of The Better Butcher's chops and roasts and sausages. They don't have a huge meat cooler here, but it's always filled with excellent, and often organic, slabs of meat.

The beef, lamb, and pork are particularly well cut, and the cold cuts—especially the ones prepared in-house—are always of high calibre. The Better Butcher has also been my source for the holiday turkey for years. They know where to get their meat, how to age and trim it, and how to serve it with a smile. So what if they always have big knives in their hands?

The Bison General Store

211 Bear Street (The Bison Courtyard), Banff, 762•5550

THE ground-floor entrance to The Bison Mountain Bistro doubles as The Bison General Store, a terrific pit stop for all your cheese, pickle, jelly, and meaty mountain needs. The store makes great use of space that might otherwise have been filled with fake plants and perhaps a couch or two.

A couple of coolers wrap around the base of the stairwell that leads to the second-floor restaurant, and staff diligently toil at sandwich-making, cheese-slicing, and pickle-pickling. The products are local and/or Western Canadian, with as many organic foods as possible. How great to finally have a gourmet takeout shop to fill that gap in Banff.

www.thebison.ca

Boca Loca

1512–11 Street SW, 802•4600
777 Northmount Drive NW, 289•2202

FINDING just the right chili for that mole or some fresh cactus paddles can be difficult in Cowtown, so Renette Kurtz opened Boca Loca. Fans of Central and South American foods flock to her stores for tortillas, chipotles, and epazote. Each day she makes a couple of fresh salsas, such as the basic pico de gallo or her popular mango one. She also does enchilada sauces with tomatillos and roasted poblanos, and she makes tangy tamales. Her guacamole is outstanding, and her meals-to-go have saved many a Friday night for folks. Look for cooking classes, catering, and cookbooks too, all focused on the warmer side of the Americas.

www.bocalocacalgary.com

Boogie's Burgers

908 Edmonton Trail NE, 230•7070

Ah, the smell of the open grill, the lingering waft of the deep fryer. The heyday of the independent burger bar is past, but a few soldier on, defying the big chains with (gasp!) quality. One of the best is Boogie's, an Edmonton Trail institution for decades.

Boogie's has changed hands in recent years, but the style has remained the same. They now serve beer and wine with their food, but the grilled-to-order burgers, the handmade shakes, and the blazing-hot fries remain a treat. The mushroom burger is popular, but the chicken burger is right up there too.

Brûlée Patisserie

Downstairs, 722–11 Avenue SW, 261•3064

Started in 1997 as an offshoot of the then-hot but now-extinct Florentine restaurant, Brûlée Patisserie has seen many changes. One constant, however, has been the present owner, Jennifer Norfolk, who has been there baking cakes and squeezing frosting since day one. So the Diablo Torte and the walnut brownies and the lemon tarts are as good as ever.

Norfolk took over Brûlée in early 2006 and has broadened its retail hours to include Thursday, Friday, and Saturday. (It was just Saturday for a while.) You can now also place orders and pick them up through the week. And if you just stumble in off the street in need of a good cookie, she has those too.

Bumpy's Cafe

1040–8 Street SW, 265•0244

In my humble opinion, the current title for "Best Espresso in the City" goes to Bumpy's. They pump out rich cupfuls of Big Mountain coffee for the truly addicted. (Bumpy's used to be Big Mountain's retail shop before the mountain folk focused solely on roasting and wholesale.) But aside from espresso aficionados, there is a whole flock of Bumpites who come for the breakfast cereals, the fruit crumbles, the sandwiches, and the funky ambience. Not to mention the cleanliness. Bumpy's is right up there for "Cleanest Café in the City" too.

Note: To find Bumpy's, look down the alley between Bonterra and Brewster's on 8th Street SW and follow your nose.

www.bumpyscafe.com

Cadence Coffee

6407 Bowness Road NW, 247•9955

THIS Bowness hideout features some of the best espresso in the city (it's easily in the top five coffee shops). They do it with Oso Negro beans roasted in Nelson, BC. Many of the beans are organic and/or shade grown and/or fair traded and/or farmers' co-op grown. So when you go to Cadence, you can feel politically correct as well as caffeine-buzzed.

The baked goods here—brownies, rice krispies squares, and such—are made in-house and go well with the coffee. Cadence is one of the more spacious coffee shops in town, it's filled with what could charitably be called "vintage" furniture, and it maintains a well-worn funkiness that is as scruffy and comfortable as an old pair of runners.

Café Metro

7400 Macleod Trail S, 255•6537

THE debate rages on about who has the best Montreal smoked meat sandwich in town. While others wrangle with this, I choose to nosh on Metro's sanger and enjoy the oddly captivating Montreal street-scene ambience. They make the sandwiches—using Delstar meat—in regular and "big mouth" sizes, and they serve them with the requisite mustards, pickles, and slaws.

The Macleod Trail location is handy for those who live or work in the south. I don't think there's another smoked meat sandwich anywhere nearby. So when the smoked meat jones hits, there's always lots of free parking out front and some extra fatty brisket on the slicer.

Caffè Beano

1613–9 Street SW, 229•1232

BEANO is the favourite coffee spot for many Calgarians because they make a darned good espresso, some tasty molasses-soaked muffins, and a decent sandwich. For others, it's the tone of the place, the let's-hang-out, time-doesn't-matter feeling. And for others, it's because Owner Rhondda Siebens is so endearingly charming and enthusiastic.

Beano satisfies with all of the above, attracting a broad cross-section of Mount Royalites, youthful Beltliners, 17th Avenue strollers, and double-parkers looking for a quick cup of joe. It's a busy place, but the line moves pretty quickly and service is usually cheerful. Just a brief coffee at Beano will often buff up your entire day. In a good way.

Caffè Mauro

805A–1 Street SW, 262 •9216

A good sandwich is a joy to behold. And to consume, for that matter. Salvatore Malvaso, the former chef at Da Salvatore, is whipping up some tasty Italian ones in his Caffè Mauro downtown. He roasts peppers and eggplants and slides them into house-baked focaccia with capicollo and Calabrese salami. Or he'll build you one, perhaps using bread from the Rustic Sourdough Bakery and your choice from various cheeses, cold cuts, and other fillings. There are a few tables for dining in, but most people haul the sandwiches back to their offices.

Sal also makes the best traditional Italian espresso in the area. It must be consumed on-site to truly appreciate the crema.

Calgary Farmers' Market

4421 Quesnay Wood Drive SW, 244 •4548

I could write pages about my favourite market. The old military airplane hangar is the perfect location for over eighty producers, processors, and purveyors of fine food. There's Lund's organic carrots, Vital Green Farms' cream (at Sunworks), Hoven's beef, Grazin' Acres' eggs, Sunworks' chickens, Gull Valley's tomatoes, Jackson's house-roasted beef, Habina's cherries, Cherry Pit's pineapples, Labybug's Belgian pastries, Going Nuts' roasted almonds, Sylvan Star's gouda, Wee Bit O' Spice's waffles, Innisfail Growers' asparagus, Walker's peaches, Simple Simon's pies, Le Chien Chaud's hot dogs, and on and on. Great stuff, all.

And then there are Henry and Debbie Mandelbaum and all the staff at Tutti Frutti, whose smiling faces alone are enough to make us head out to the market on a frosty Saturday morning. (They make a good coffee and the best gelato in the city.)

www.calgaryfarmersmarket.ca

Central Blends

203–19 Street NW, 670 •5665

RASPBERRY-OAT muffins. With fresh raspberries. Sounds simple, doesn't it? And sublime? So why is Central Blends the only place in town where I can find decent oat muffins? There's good baking here, from cinnamon buns to pies and numerous squares. (I mean, where can you get a good square these days?) Combine all these tasty things with a funky hippie-era decor and some of the best coffee in the city, and you have a gem.

Central Blends is large and comfy and always has loads of classy reading material too. Sugar, caffeine, fibre, fresh fruit, and literature, the drugs of the new millennium. Let's get mellow, man.

Chocolaterie Bernard Callebaut

1313–1 Street SE, 266•4300

O VER a quarter-century ago, a tall, lean Belgian blew into Calgary with plans to make Cowtown the headquarters for a major chocolate business. Some thought the idea a little odd.

Since then, the name Bernard Callebaut has become synonymous with the best in chocolate. The main office/showroom/factory on 1st Street SE is filled with thousands of shapes, sizes, and flavours of filled, formed, and decorated sweets. Changing with the seasons, there is always new product on display, ready for consumption. You can even do a short tour of the factory, albeit from behind glass.

And true to Callebaut's plan, there are constant shipments to his thirty-four outlets across North America, including to the Calgary and Banff shops.

www.bernardcallebaut.com

The Cookbook Co. Cooks

Upstairs, 722–11 Avenue SW, 265•6066 or 1•800•663•8532

W ITH its extensive collection of cookbooks, its coolers filled with exotic cheeses and herbs, its expanded cooking school, and its knowledgeable staff, The Cookbook Co. is the epicentre of Calgary's food community. It's the place to go for those hard-to-find ingredients and recipes, plus instructions on how to use them. If there is a new food product on the market, it is likely to arrive here first.

The open, warehousey space is often filled with the aromas of fine cooking from the kitchen classroom where local and international chefs ply their skills for avid food fans. They've added classes in France, Spain, and Italy for those who like to travel and learn about food at the same time.

www.cookbookcooks.com

Dairy Lane

319–19 Street NW, 283•2497

I staunched more than a few hangovers at Dairy Lane in the early 1970s. The coffee was always hot and the grill was always smoking. The bacon and egg breakfasts had just the right balance of fat and protein to take the edge off a big headache.

Although my days of excess are (mostly) passed, I still enjoy a visit to this West Hillhurst landmark. It's been upgraded, gentrified, and generally cleaned up, but it still does an all-day breakfast and one of the best burgers in the city. And the fries are first rate. There's even a small patio now. (But it's awfully bright out there if you're—shall we say—under the weather.)

Decadent Desserts

831–10 Avenue SW, 245•5535

DECADENT Desserts, owned by Pam Fortier, is one of Calgary's finer custom bakeries. It is not a drop-in-for-a-piece-of-cake spot. It's a place to pick up dessert orders of whole cakes or pies or cookies by the dozen. A new location in 2006 plants them across the street from Mountain Equipment Co-op.

Fortier's repertoire includes a Lemon-Hazelnut Crunch Cake and a strawberry-rhubarb pie as well as oatmeal-raisin cookies and biscotti. There is big chocolate here, from the Chocolate Overdose Cake with over a pound of Callebaut chocolate to the Fantasy Fudge Cake accented with chocolate leaves. And if nuptials are in your future, ask about the elegant wedding cakes. Quality and execution are exceptional and creativity is stellar.

www.decadentdesserts.ca

DinoRosa's Italian Market

9140 Macleod Trail S (Newport Village), 255•6011

VIVA Italia! I've never seen a bigger smile on Dean Petrillo's face than the day after Italy won the 2006 World Cup. He looked a little shopworn from the celebration, but was ecstatic nonetheless.

That Italian spirit pervades DinoRosa's, a little deli-café-coffee shop in Newport Village. It's jam-packed with Italian pastas, coffees, olive oils, cheeses, cold cuts, freshly made sausages, and desserts. At Christmas it's loaded to the roof with panettone, those large boxed cakes from Italy. On one side is a small café where you can scarf back an espresso or a meatball sandwich and watch a soccer game on the television. DinoRosa's is a little bit of Italy in an unusual location.

Fairmount Spiceland

7640 Fairmount Drive SE (Astral Centre), 255•7295

IN the fall of 2005, Spiceland moved into the Astral Centre on Fairmount Drive. No matter where they've been located, the Kotadia and Muhamad families have been bringing Calgarians a broad selection of Asian foodstuffs for over thirty years now. Spiceland is the place to go for Indian spices, basmati rice in bulk, and fresh vegetables like guvar, karela, and torai.

This crowded shop includes everything from chapati presses and Bollywood videos to Caribbean herbs and buckets of lentils. We've even bought some tasty and extremely cheap (but good), prepackaged Indian meals here. Even if you're not in need of anything, Spiceland makes a fascinating visit. We never leave empty-handed.

Gourmet Croissant

1205 Bow Valley Trail (Rocky Mountain Professional Centre), Canmore, 609•4410

IFEL and Yasmina Costa have brought their baking skills from Paris and taken over the former Infuso coffee spot in Canmore. They produce some of the best croissants, pains au chocolat, and Viennoise pastries for miles around. They also serve fruit-stuffed crepes, ham- and cheese-filled galettes (the savoury version of crepes), quiches, and sandwiches made with their mini-loaves. This is quality food throughout, and the coffee is pretty good too.

Catherine's favourite is the financier, a small afternoon cake that they will make-to-order if you call a day or so ahead. It is superb with espresso. So she says. She doesn't share.

The Griesser Spoon

104B Elk Run Boulevard, Canmore, 678•3637

MANY Calgarians weekend on the woody slopes surrounding Canmore, escaping the hassles of city life. Caught between wanting to cocoon but not wanting to cook a lot, they are likely to SUV over to The Griesser Spoon for a curried vegetable pie or a breaded, pan-ready schnitzel or some smoked Valbella meats. They return in the morning for fresh croissants and cakes.

Formerly the Valbella Deli (Valbella just does wholesale now), The Griesser Spoon is run by Austrian chefs and brothers Roland and Harry Griesser. Their selection of ready-to-eat and ready-to-cook foods is perfect for the Canmore market. If only we had more of this sort of fare in Calgary.

www.griesserspoon.com

Heartland Cafe

940–2 Avenue NW, 270•4541
116–7A Street NE, 263•4567

THE original Heartland is a funky brick-and-wood Sunnyside café with creaky floors, tall ceilings, and good muffins and soups. Nice place, but a little out of the way for Catherine and me.

The new Heartland works perfectly for us though. One or the other of us has had many a social or business get-together here. (In fact, it is the place-of-choice to meet our designer Jeremy for a few espressos and a confab about this book.) This location is part of the huge Bridges development on the former General Hospital site and is in a "green" building. Even the H_2O in the toilets is rain water that has been fed into the system. Gotta mention the staff too—they're great.

The Holy Grill

827–10 Avenue SW, 261•9759

THE art of the hamburger is not dead. It's just in hiding at independent places like The Holy Grill. Good patties, good cheese, good buns, a little avocado or red onion or bacon, and you're set. And don't forget the fries—regular or sweet potato or beet. You can't beat beet fries. (I do not jest!) The Holy Grill also does killer paninis with grilled zucchini, yams, marinated eggplant, and provolone or with spinach cream cheese, artichokes, and smoked salmon, just to name two.

This is one busy place, and it's easy to see why. Give people what they want, price it right (everything is under $7.50), and they'll beat a path to your door.

Il Centro

6036–3 Street SW, 258•2294

FEDELE knows pizza. Fedele Ricioppo, that is. Ask any long-time member of the local Italian community about pizza and the conversation will inevitably come around to Fedele. He's made great, thin-crust pizzas in local restaurants for years and now has his own place in the understated Il Centro. Here you'll find the Siciliana with capers, anchovies, and olives; the capricciosa with salami, anchovies, and mushrooms; and the Calabrese with sausage, roasted peppers, and mushrooms, along with other Italian choices. If pizza is not your thing, you can also have salad, panini, or pasta.

Eat in or take out. Or just chat with Fedele. He knows pizza.

James Joyce

114 Stephen Avenue Walk SW, 262•0708

WHEN the lust for a lager calls, my thirst-quenching stop of choice is the James Joyce downtown. The historic Toronto Bank Building provides the perfect backdrop for a round of Guinness—served at three temperatures—or the local favourite, Big Rock. The food at the Joyce follows the Irish theme with a good ploughman's lunch always available, plus decent meat pies and fries.

The Joyce on 4th (*506–24 Avenue SW, 541•9168*) follows the downtown location's tone and taste. Both have fine service and an upscale Irish pub tone that is welcoming and lively. I can't wait for them both to go non-smoking.

www.jamesjoycepub.com

Janice Beaton Fine Cheese

1708–8 Street SW, 229•0900
1249 Kensington Road NW, 283•0999

CHEESE, glorious cheese! Epoisses, piconero, ossau, bouq' emmissaire. Such words are enough to inspire and intimidate. So ask for a taste, and Janice Beaton's staff will be happy to slice off a sample (unless you've come for lunch, that is).

These are the best cheese shops in town, bar none. When a certain cheese is called for, these are the places to go. (Unless it's Velveeta. Then you're on your own.) Always fresh, always changing, always interesting, the cheese selections span local gems like Sylvan Star's gouda to international, small-dairy, unpasteurized beauties.

Other culinary and cheese-related items are available too. Not cheap, but so good. Say cheese!

www.jbfinecheese.com

Java Jamboree

#9, 312–5 Avenue W (Cochrane Towne Square), Cochrane, 932•6240

THE current title-holder for "Best Espresso Outside Calgary," Java Jamboree takes its java seriously. Using their Synesso machine, they pull Malabar Gold from India (via San Francisco) or Vivace from Seattle. (Theirs was only the second Synesso machine in Canada.) This is serious espresso with thick, chocolatey, licoricey undertones hiding beneath a rich crema. Sometimes we'll pop in for a quick one on the way to Banff, and the taste lingers all the way to the park gates.

Java Jamboree is also into latte art, creating designs in your milk foam. That's fine, but personally, I'm there for the buzz. And maybe a brownie.

JK Bakery

1514 Railway Avenue, Canmore, 678•4232

I can never decide what to have at JK Bakery. The big loaves of crusty bread and the huge rolls are fine, but that's stuff for home and the freezer. When I'm stocking up at a good bakery like JK, it's required that I eat something right then. (It's a bylaw or something.)

JK's fresh cakes and squares are always tempting, and the sausage rolls can add a meaty-pastry buzz to my day. Then there are the sugar-dusted pastries and the chocolate-dipped cookies. If I'm lucky to be there at the right time, it's the glazed cinnamon buns that call out to me. (I quickly silence their voices.)

Ladybug Pastries

510–42 Avenue SE, 287•1137
4421 Quesnay Wood Drive SW (Calgary Farmers' Market)

I love baking my own chocolate croissants. The scent of butter- and chocolate-laced dough slowly browning in my oven is satisfying to a home baker such as I.

All right, I'll fess up. I'm more of a home defroster than a baker. I pick up Ladybug Pastries' frozen croissants or cinnamon buns in dough form at the Farmers' Market, let them thaw and rise overnight, and bake them in the morning. Or if I'm really lazy, I'll just visit her shop on 42nd Avenue SE and load up on organic loaves and maybe a raspberry and white-chocolate merveilleux. (And have a soup and sandwich while I'm there.)

Frozen-to-go or fresh from Ladybug's oven, these are fine, fine Belgian pastries. And the crepes they serve at the Calgary Farmers' Market are super too.

Lazy Loaf & Kettle

8 Parkdale Crescent NW, 270•7810
130–9 Avenue SE (Glenbow Museum), 266•1002

IT's a toss up which is trickier to negotiate—the lineup at the Lazy Loaf's Parkdale location or the diagonal street parking outside. Jockeying with caffeine-deprived Calgarians can be touchy at the best of times, but when they get within nostril-distance of the Lazy Loaf, it's best to stay out of the way.

Whichever location you visit, the coffee is revitalizing, and the fresh muffins, banana loaf, and cinnamon buns are a treat. For those even hungrier, a list of sandwiches and soups is also available. And my holiday turkey is always stuffed with the Lazy Loaf's Kettle Bread. It's the perfect texture and density for stuffing.

www.lazyloafandkettle.com

Les Truffes

315 Stephen Avenue SW (+15 Level, Bankers Hall), 269•1010
10816 Macleod Trail S (Willow Park Village), 225•9399
11979–40 Street SE, 241•1427

IN a town where Belgian chocolate rules, Les Truffes goes against the grain by making truffles with fine Swiss couverture chocolate. Ralph Buchmuller brings decades of experience to his work, creating amaretto, maple-whisky, peanut butter, chai, cognac, and thirty-two more varieties of the decadent round chocolates. He rolls, dips, shapes, and adds flavours at whim. They are divine. Chocolate bars, chunks, and shavings are also available.

The packaging for Les Truffes is almost as gorgeous as the truffles themselves. Unfortunately, it isn't edible.

www.lestruffes.com

Lina's Italian Market

2202 Centre Street N, 277•9166

LINA'S has become the Italian market of choice for many over the past decade. Lina and Tom Castle have a great shop: a terrific selection of fresh meats and cold cuts, a top-notch array of Italian cheeses, an in-house pastry shop, a respectable collection of fresh produce, and a huge amount of Italian kitchen wares. All this surrounds the dry-goods market featuring Calgary's largest assembly of olive oils, pastas, rice for risotto, and sauces.

When you tucker out from all the shopping, you can grab a seat in Lina's café and have a nice lunch prepared by the dedicated staff. Or you can slip next door to **Boccavino** (*276•2030*), Lina's smoker-friendly lounge, for a decent pizza and little kebabs of grilled lamb.

The Main Dish

903 General Avenue NE, 999•8818

ANOTHER entry into the burgeoning Bridgeland food scene, The Main Dish focuses mostly on the young, upwardly mobile folks who are moving into the wealth of new condos surrounding it. The Main Dish offers food to eat on-site, food to take home and eat, and food to take home and cook. There are sandwiches, hot dishes, meatballs to reheat, salads by the bowlful, and rich desserts. It's predominantly contemporary cuisine with a Mediterranean tone. And with a nod to the Italian heritage of the neighbourhood, The Main Dish pumps out a good espresso. Many of the older neighbourhood residents drop in too.

www.tmdish.com

Manie's

819–17 Avenue SW, 228•9207

FIRST Manie's was here. Then it was there. Then over yonder. Now, finally, Manie's has a good, hopefully permanent, home for their souvlaki and pizza. And it's almost back where it started. The new place is sleekly renovated and has a patio out front where you can watch the construction next door.

Manie's pizzas are as popular as ever. They're thick and heavily topped in the Greek style. There's lots of pepperoni and bacon and cheese. And there's a hearty rendition of many Greek dishes served here too. This is food you need to walk off. But it tastes so good.

Manuel Latruwe Belgian Patisserie

1333–1 Street SE, 261•1092

MANUEL and Lieve Latruwe, two skilled Belgian bakers, transform cream, butter, eggs, and flour into patisserie masterpieces here. A multi-layered caramel cake is a combination of seven separate recipes: there's a ganache, a caramel, a vanilla cream, a glaze, some caramelized pecans, the chocolate decorations, and the cake itself. Simply stunning flavours. And gorgeous too.

They make *the* best baguette in the city, lightly crusted on the outside and slightly chewy on the inside. They produce other elegant and more rustic breads too, such as their walnut-blue-cheese loaf. Their multi-grain bread has been a sandwich staple in our house for the last five years—we can't find one better.

And their ice cream is outstanding. So are their made-to-order waffles.

Marv's Classic Soda Shop

121 Centre Avenue W, Black Diamond, 933•7001

THE Foothills southwest of Calgary are filled with character and characters. Like Marv Garriott, chef/owner/entertainer at Marv's Classic Soda Shop in Black Diamond. Marv can mix a mean soda or malt, grill a hotdog or a house-made burger, sell you some vintage 1950s memorabilia, and sing and strum a few Elvis tunes. His soda shop is part kitschy, part trendy, and all fun. If it's from the 1950s and 1960s, you just might find it in Marv's eclectic collection.

And if a visit to Marv's isn't enough, he's got a new CD out featuring some of his favourite rock 'n' roll classics.

Mediterranean Grill

#108, 6008 Macleod Trail S, 255•0300

YOU don't see a lot of Israeli delis around town. Let's see, there's one—Itzhak Likver's Mediterranean Grill, located across Macleod Trail from Chinook Centre. It's a little place with great falafel and savoury shawarma. The chicken and lamb stacked on the shawarma rotisserie are marinated for two days, giving them a depth of flavour seldom seen in this meat-on-a-stick category. The hummus and pickled eggplant are equally well prepared and loaded heartily onto platters or takeout containers. The tabbouleh is great, and I even like the marinated onions.

Don't expect fancy here. Expect disposable plates, paper napkins, a reasonable price, and rich flavours.

North Sea Fish Market

10816 Macleod Trail S (Willow Park Village), 225•3460

NORTH Sea had been a seafood wholesaler for years, selling to restaurants and retail shops. But the opening of their retail store in Willow Park Village improved access to top-quality fish in the southern reaches of the city. Fresh salmon (wild or farmed), various kinds of tuna, scallops, swordfish, mussels, and whatever is in season are displayed here in all their oceanic glory.

Chef/Owner Brian Plunkett churns out chowders and thermidors and other dishes to take home. And now that he's added meats to the coolers, dry goods to the shelves, and breads to some display baskets, North Sea is almost one-stop shopping.

Pelican Pier

4404–14 Street NW, 289•6100

OH, I loves a good fish 'n' chips, I does.
And there aren't a whole lot of places to get a good batch of them around Calgary, by gar. But Pelican Pier, washed up on the shores of 14th Street just north of McKnight Boulevard, is one of the best. The fish is lightly breaded instead of heavily battered, allowing more of the seafood flavour to come through. They do it with a school of fish, from pollock to salmon, with cod, halibut, and haddock in between. And they serve it up with good, good fries. And a decent cole slaw.

And I likes the chowda here too, yes I does.

Pies Plus

12445 Lake Fraser Drive SE (Avenida Place), 271•6616

THE art of pie making has been in serious decline in recent years. Perhaps it's the challenge of the perfect pie crust or just the excessively sweet recipes that have been handed down for generations. So it's a pleasure to see that Pies Plus has not only a serious commitment to pies, but an ongoing one as well. Jeff Cousineau and his team have been at it for almost two decades now. They still make a great apple pie, the popular Dream Cream, and a host of fruit pies, using both fresh and frozen product. The summertime fresh peach pies are tart-ilicious, the Thanksgiving pumpkin pies are silky smooth, and the Christmas tourtières are a Quebec classic.

Pimento's

931 General Avenue NE, 515•0075

SPEAKING of pies (see page 152), it can be hard to find a good pizza. But the art of pizza has seen a bit of a resurgence lately. Pimento's, a takeout pizza parlour in the Bridges development, is one of the places that does it right.

Pimento's focuses on thin-crust, Neapolitan-style pies made with Italian pizza flour (a blend of soft- and hard-wheat flours), fresh basil, and organic tomatoes. Pimento's makes the Margherita (tomato sauce, basil, and mozzarella), the quattro formaggi (bocconcino, gorgonzola, parmesan, and provolone), the capricciosa (tomato sauce, bocconcino, ham, mushrooms, olives, and artichokes), and the rest of the traditional Italian pizzas.

Primal Grounds

3003–37 Street SW, 240•4185

2000–69 Street SW (Westside Recreation Centre), 663•0137

PRIMAL Grounds on 37th Street is a funky bakery-café and coffee house, a place with lots of character and decent food. And they have a second location too. They say that they sell happiness, that you can get food anywhere.

Primal Grounds makes sandwiches, soups, wraps, and hot entrees, many of which are gluten free. I'm particularly partial to their huge desserts. One piece of carrot cake, thick and moist with a lovely icing, is roughly the size of a small brick. The sandwiches follow suit. The roast turkey and cranberry is a three-hander. What's particularly nice is the amount of fresh greens in it—you get a salad along with the bread and meat. And all that happiness too.

www.primalgrounds.com

Purple Perk

2212–4 Street SW, 244•1300

WHEN The Planet disappeared, many of my caffeine-hyped brethren wept a big espresso tear. But from its grounds has risen a respectable replacement—the Purple Perk. The decor is much improved, the seats are softer, there are more of them, the lighting is agreeable, and the coffee is—well, it's not bad at all.

The Purple Perk uses beans from Fratello, a solid, local roaster. Many of the staff are holdovers from The Planet days, and they know how to make a decent coffee. I miss the old place, but I'm willing to convert to the new regime too.

Red Tree

2129–33 Avenue SW, 242•3246

I didn't think you could improve on banana bread. But layering it with peanut butter mousse is pure genius. Banana with peanut butter. How obvious! It's the kind of thinking I've come to expect from Red Tree and its owners, Aaron Creurer and Susan Hopkins. They are among the more creative—and popular—caterers in the city.

Red Tree also offers foods-to-go aside from the banana bread. Their showcase might be displaying Moroccan-spiced leg of lamb with Israeli couscous or citrus-chili-honey-glazed salmon, along with roasted-pepper dips and bowls of salads. You'll also find olives, vinegars, salts, and sauces to add zest to your cooking. And probably more brilliant food combinations.

www.redtreecatering.com

The Roasterie

314–10 Street NW, 270•3304

Most days, the sidewalks around 10th Street are filled with the aroma of roasting coffee emanating from The Roasterie. It's a small place where the roaster takes up almost half the room, pushing many coffee drinkers to the small plaza outside. The coffee is fresh and robust, from the ever-popular espresso through to the Danish Breakfast Blend and the Montana Grizzly. They'll make it as strong and dark and heavy as you want.

By now, coffee and tobacco smoke have permeated the walls, the stools, the staff, and everything about The Roasterie. It'll be interesting to see what happens after the smoke clears and Calgary's new smoking bylaw kicks in. (They've closed their second outlet across the street, the non-smoking one.)

Rocky Mountain Flatbread Company

838–10 Street, Canmore, 609•5508

If Rocky Mountain Flatbread was just about the food, that would be enough. Their pizzas are handcrafted from top-drawer, organic ingredients and are baked in a wood-fired oven. It's good pizza.

But Rocky Mountain also embodies the "green" spirit of Canmore. Recycling is big here, and rolling, overhead garage doors open the space to the great outdoors. They are committed to supporting local farmers and producers and are involved in many community projects.

There are special dishes for the kids and even a play area for them while you chow down. This is an eat-well, feel-good, help-the-planet place, perfect for Canmore.

www.rockymountainflatbread.ca

Rocky's Burgers

4645–12 Street SE, 243•0405

SETTLED hip deep in prairie grasses, the former Calgary Transit bus that is Rocky's looks as if it's there to stay until it dissolves into the landscape. But Owner Jim Rockwell says it's ready to roll if need be. Regulars would be devastated if it did though. They love Rocky's hand-formed, steamed-then-grilled Alberta beef burgers layered with cheese and mustard and such. And the sides of blistering hot fries. In fact, they love the food so much, they'll stand outside in blizzard conditions to place their orders.

The dine-in option is a couple of picnic tables set amongst the gopher holes out back. But most regulars eat in their vehicles, which range from beat-up pickups to detailed Beamers.

Second To None Meats

#3, 2100–4 Street SW, 245•6662

SECOND To None is about as pretty as a butcher shop gets. I almost feel guilty ordering a couple of rib-eyes here because it destroys the symmetry of the display. But Butcher/Owner Bob Choquette is happy to whip out his knives and add more product to his array. He's doubled the shop size in just a few years and added chicken, lamb, eggs, and produce to his cases. The place has become popular among Mission residents and a meaty destination for those who love quality—and mostly organic—foods.

But it's the naturally raised Galloway beef in all its glory that's king at Second To None. Like the name says …

www.second-to-none-meats.ca

Sherry's Caribbean Food

7640 Fairmount Drive SE (Astral Centre), 259•2527

I'D like to see more good Caribbean food in Calgary. I'm told the best is done in private homes around town. But not at my house, and no one invites me over for brown chicken and a drink of Ting at their place. So when I get the hankering for a goat hot pot or jerk chicken or just a good old Jamaican patty, it's off to Sherry's I go. The food is good, the atmosphere is Island-simple, and the taste is right. And a visit with Sherry always lifts my spirits. She's a lively gal who knows how to cook Island style.

Springbank Cheese

10816 Macleod Trail S (Willow Park Village), 225•6040

I like to step inside Springbank Cheese and take a big whiff. I try to pick out the blue cheeses (always the first to hit the nostrils) and then the fresh, goaty ones. There are always a few good sheep cheeses and some rich cow cheeses in the mix. There are aged and hard cheeses, soft and runny ones, fruit-flavoured fromages, pasteurized and unpasteurized, all creating a heady aroma.

Springbank Cheese usually carries over 350 kinds of cheese, backed up by friendly, knowledgeable service. They slice, they dice, they cube, and they fondue. Springbank is a cheese-head's odiferous Valhalla.

Sweet Madeira

#109, 112 Kananaskis Way, Canmore, 609•9957

AROUND Canmore, Cecilia Lortscher is known as The Cookie Lady. Around our house, she's known as That Amazing Woman Who Makes Un-Bloody-Believable Cookies. I don't know how she does it. Her cookies look pretty regular, but they pack more flavour than any others. The chocolate-mint one fills the mouth with chocolate and washes the palate with mint. The Madeira Dip sublimely balances butter and chocolate, and the brownie (okay, I know it's not a cookie, but just try one) fudges-over the brain. Lortscher's banana bread, her coconut macaroons, and her cinnamon buns are extremely decent too.

Best to call ahead though—her hours can be variable.

Tazza Grill & Deli

1105–1 Avenue NE, 263•5922

THERE are still a few people who stumble into Tazza thinking it's an ice cream stand. It used to be the Milky Way, but has been a fine Lebanese café for a few years now. You'd think the scent of garlic and roasting chicken would give it away. Although the shishtawouk sandwiches are always drippy-good and the tabbouleh is tart with lemon, it's the fatayer that steals the show at this Bridgeland eatery. The great pastry wrapped around a creamy spinach filling makes a nice, light lunch. In spite of the small space, Tazza offers a broad range of Lebanese food served by pleasant staff.

Tiffin Curry

188–28 Street SE, 273•2420

Iᴛ's almost as much fun to watch the Plexiglas machine rolling out fresh, hot rotis as it is to eat at Tiffin. The food is the pungently curried cuisine of Mumbai where tiffin-walas (couriers) deliver tiffins (stacked, metal Indian lunch containers) daily to hungry office workers. You can buy a tiffin at Tiffin or bring in your own from home to be filled with foods-to-go (they have takeout containers too though). Or you can just sit and eat your curries off a plate and watch the roti machine spin round and round, pushing out the fresh, hot breads.

Tubby Dog

1022–17 Avenue SW, 244•0694

Cᴀʟɢᴀʀʏ's late-night doghouse of choice (it stays open until 4 a.m. on weekends), Tubby Dog is the place to go when you need the right mix of carbs and oils and spices to absorb the excess liquid in your innards.

Tubby Dog is also worth a daylight visit, though the menu remains unrepentantly hardcore. There's a Sumo Dog with Japanese mayonnaise, wasabi, pickled ginger, and sesame seeds. There's the trademark Tubby Dog with chili, bacon, cheese, and mustard. And there's Sherm's Ultimate Gripper: a bacon-wrapped and deep-fried wiener topped with ham, chili, more bacon, hot peppers, onions, and a fried egg. Sure that sounds gross now, but rethink it some night at 2 a.m. (You want it, you really want it.)

www.tubbydog.com

Wild Flour Artisan Bakery Café

#101, 211 Bear Street (The Bison Courtyard), Banff, 760•5074

Wɪʟᴅ Flour fills a huge gap in the mountain bakery scene. Italian bakers Magi and Gianni Bianchi bring three generations of baking experience to their shop, producing organic baguette, ciabatta, rye, and whole-grain breads along with arrays of pastries, sandwiches, and soups. They offer daily bread, soup, and savoury specials too. Wednesday, for example, is the day for olive-wheat levain bread, black-bean soup, and meat pies.

Wild Flour is good for a quick coffee (they make a pretty good biscotti) or breakfast or lunch, and everything is made to take away also.

www.wildflourbakery.ca

Note: The day before this book was due at the printers, we discovered the new **Village Pita Express** at *7204 Fairmount Drive SE* (*253•3017*) and were impressed with their shawarma, falafel, and baklava. It is an off-shoot of **Village Pita** at *255–28 Street SE* (*273•0330*) and should have had a larger (and alphabetic!) entry in this book. Oh well, next edition.

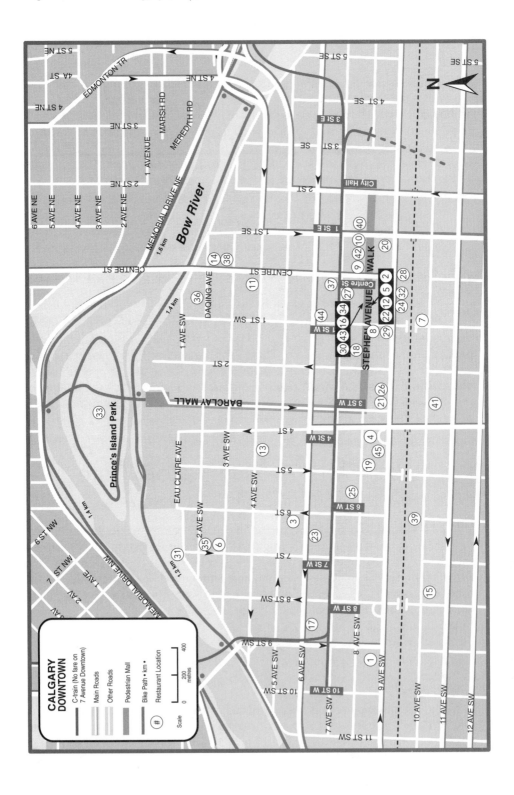

Dining in Downtown Calgary (Map)

1 Atlas
2 Avenue Diner
3 Bali
4 Belgo
5 The Belvedere
6 Buchanan's
7 Buzzards
8 Caffè Mauro (LE)
9 Catch
10 Centini
11 Chutney
12 Divino
13 Glory of India
14 Golden Inn
15 The Holy Grill (LE)

16 James Joyce (LE)
17 Jonas' Restaurant
18 Juan's
19 La Tavola (*see* Q in "Big Eats")
20 Lazy Loaf & Kettle (LE)
21 Les Truffes (LE)
22 Murrieta's
23 Mysore Palace
24 The Oak Room (*see* The Rimrock in "Big Eats")
25 Opus on 8th
26 Orchid Room
27 Palomino
28 Panorama
29 Piq Niq
30 Prairie Ink

31 Q
32 The Rimrock
33 River Café
34 Rose Garden
35 Sahara
36 Sakana Grill
37 Siding Café
38 Silver Dragon
39 Simone's Bistro
40 Teatro
41 Thai Sa-on
42 Thomsons
43 The Tribune
44 Velvet at The Grand
45 Yuzuki

(LE) Indicates entry is in "Little Eats" section.

Downtown Calgary offers over 20,000 public parking spots. Free parking is available at meters and along Stephen Avenue Walk after 6:00 p.m. daily and at meters on Sundays. Selected parkades provide $2 parking in the evenings and on weekends. Visit **www.downtowncalgary.com** for a detailed parking map.

The Lists

THESE lists will guide you to various food styles and geographic areas. Entries are in alphabetical order in the "Big Eats" section of the book unless an "LE" notation follows the name of the establishment. LE means an entry is in alphabetical order in the "Little Eats" section. All establishments are in Calgary unless noted otherwise.

The first list below is a category I call "Add Ons." Add Ons are establishments that do not have their own alphabetical entries in either Big or Little Eats. In the parentheses following the name of each Add On is the entry under which information on these places will be found.

Add Ons

Banffshire Club (Banff,
    see Bow Valley Grill)
Belmont Diner (see Palace of Eats)
Boccavino (see Lina's Italian Market, LE)
Bonterra (see Wildwood)
Charlie's Bakery (see Muse)
Cilantro (see Velvet at The Grand)
Cilantro Mountain Café (Banff,
    see Buffalo Mountain Lodge)
Cilantro on the Lake (Lake Louise,
    see Buffalo Mountain Lodge)
Deer Lodge (Lake Louise,
    see Buffalo Mountain Lodge)
Emerald Lake Lodge (Lake Louise,
    see Buffalo Mountain Lodge)
Galaxie Diner (see Palace of Eats)
Joyce on 4th, The (see James Joyce, LE)
La Tavola (see Q)
Mediterranea (see A & A, LE)
Namskar (see Chutney)
Oak Room, The (see The Rimrock)
Open Range (see Big Fish)
Ranche, The (see Divino)
Redwater Rustic Grille (see Vintage)
Siding Café (see The Tribune)
Typhoon (Banff, see Café Soleil)
Urban Baker (see Diner Deluxe)
Victoria's (see Reader's Garden Café)
Vue Cafe (see Diner Deluxe)
Waldhaus (Banff, see Bow Valley Grill)

Baked Goods/Sweets

Brûlée Patisserie (LE)
Bumpy's Cafe (LE)
Cadence Coffee (LE)
Caffè Beano (LE)
Calgary Farmers' Market (LE)
Central Blends (LE)
Charlie's Bakery (see Muse)
Chocolaterie Bernard Callebaut
    (Calgary & Banff, LE)
Decadent Desserts (LE)
Gourmet Croissant (Canmore, LE)
Heartland Cafe (LE)
Java Jamboree (Cochrane, LE)
JK Bakery (Canmore, LE)
Ladybug Pastries (LE)
Lazy Loaf & Kettle (LE)
Les Truffes (LE)
Manuel Latruwe Belgian Patisserie (LE)
Pies Plus (LE)
Prairie Ink
Primal Grounds (LE)
Saint Germain
Sweet Madeira (Canmore, LE)
Urban Baker (see Diner Deluxe)
Village Pita (LE)
Wild Flour Artisan Bakery Café (Banff, LE)

Banff/Lake Louise

Baker Creek Bistro (Banff)
Banffshire Club (Banff,
    see Bow Valley Grill)

Barpa Bill's Souvlaki (Banff, LE)
Bison General Store, The (Banff, LE)
Bison Mountain Bistro, The (Banff)
Bow Valley Grill (Banff)
Buffalo Mountain Lodge (Banff)
Café Soleil (Banff)
Chocolaterie Bernard Callebaut
    (Banff, LE)
Cilantro Mountain Café (Banff, see
    Buffalo Mountain Lodge)
Cilantro on the Lake (Lake Louise,
    see Buffalo Mountain Lodge)
Coyotes (Banff)
Deer Lodge (Lake Louise, see Buffalo
    Mountain Lodge)
Eden (Banff)
Emerald Lake Lodge (Lake Louise,
    see Buffalo Mountain Lodge)
Fuze Finer Dining (Banff)
Le Beaujolais (Banff)
Muk-a-Muk (Banff)
Pad Thai (Banff, see Thai Pagoda)
Post Hotel (Lake Louise)
Ticino (Banff)
Typhoon (Banff, see Café Soleil)
Waldhaus (Banff, see Bow Valley Grill)
Wild Flour Artisan Bakery Café
    (Banff, LE)

Breakfast/Brunch

Avenue Diner
Baker Creek Bistro (Banff)
Belmont Diner (see Palace of Eats)
Bow Valley Grill (Banff)
Buffalo Mountain Lodge (Banff)
Chez François (Canmore)
Coyotes (Banff)
Danube Creperie
Diner Deluxe
Galaxie Diner (see Palace of Eats)
Priddis Greens (Priddis)
Reader's Garden Café
Sage Bistro (Canmore)
Silver Dragon
Thomsons

Canadian

Boyd's
Buffalo Mountain Lodge (Banff)
Café Metro (LE)
Catch
Deer Lodge (Lake Louise,
    see Buffalo Mountain Lodge)
Diner Deluxe
Emerald Lake Lodge (Lake Louise,
    see Buffalo Mountain Lodge)
Fireside Place (Carstairs)
Isabella's by Infuse
Laurier Lounge
Muk-a-Muk (Banff)
Murrieta's (Calgary & Canmore)
Oak Room, The (see The Rimrock)
Opus on 8th
Palace of Eats
Panorama
Prairie Ink
Quarry (Canmore)
Ranche, The (see Divino)
Reader's Garden Café
Rimrock, The
River Café
Rouge
Route 40 Soup Company
    (Turner Valley)
Sage Bistro (Canmore)
Saint Germain
Thomsons
Treo (Canmore)
Wild Horse Bistro (Black Diamond)
Wildwood

Canmore

Beamer's Coffee Bar (LE)
Chef's Studio
Chez François
Crazyweed Kitchen
Gourmet Croissant (LE)
Griesser Spoon, The (LE)
JK Bakery (LE)
Murrieta's
Quarry

Rocky Mountain Flatbread
   Company (LE)
Sage Bistro
Sweet Madeira (LE)
Thai Pagoda
Treo

Chinese

Golden Inn
Leo Fu's
Pavilion, The
Shan Tung
Silver Dragon
Silver Inn

Coffee Bars

Beamer's Coffee Bar (Canmore, LE)
Bumpy's Cafe (LE)
Cadence Coffee (LE)
Caffè Beano (LE)
Caffè Mauro (LE)
Central Blends (LE)
Gourmet Croissant (Canmore, LE)
Heartland Cafe (LE)
Java Jamboree (Cochrane, LE)
Main Dish, The (LE)
Primal Grounds (LE)
Purple Perk (LE)
Roasterie, The (LE)

Contemporary

Banffshire Club (Banff,
   see Bow Valley Grill)
Belvedere, The
Bistro Twenty Two Ten
Brava Bistro
Buffalo Mountain Lodge (Banff)
Catch
Cilantro (see Velvet at The Grand)
Coyotes (Banff)
Crazyweed Kitchen (Canmore)
Divine (Okotoks)
Divino
Eden (Banff)

Il Sogno
Koi
Living Room, The
Murrieta's (Calgary & Canmore)
Muse
Orchid Room
Q
Quarry (Canmore)
Ranche, The (see Divino)
Raw Bar
Redwater Rustic Grille (see Vintage)
River Café
Rouge
Route 40 Soup Company
   (Turner Valley)
Simone's Bistro
Teatro
Thomsons
Wildwood

Diners

Avenue Diner
Belmont Diner (see Palace of Eats)
Boogie's Burgers (LE)
Dairy Lane (LE)
Diner Deluxe
Galaxie Diner (see Palace of Eats)
Marv's Classic Soda Shop
   (Black Diamond, LE)
Palace of Eats
Spolumbo's

Drinks

Belgo
Big Rock Grill
Buzzards
Fuze Finer Dining (Banff)
James Joyce (LE)
Joyce on 4th, The (see James Joyce, LE)
Laurier Lounge
Opus on 8th
Red Door
Vintage
Wildwood

Food Markets

A & A (LE)
Atlas
Better Butcher, The (LE)
Bison General Store, The (Banff, LE)
Boca Loca (LE)
Calgary Farmers' Market (LE)
Cookbook Co. Cooks, The (LE)
DinoRosa's Italian Market (LE)
Fairmount Spiceland (LE)
Griesser Spoon, The (Canmore, LE)
Janice Beaton Fine Cheese (LE)
Lina's Italian Market (LE)
Main Dish, The (LE)
Mercato
North Sea Fish Market (LE)
Red Tree (LE)
Second To None Meats (LE)
Springbank Cheese (LE)

French/Continental

Alexis Bistro
Bistro Provence (Okotoks)
Chez François (Canmore)
Eden (Banff)
Fleur de Sel
JoJo Bistro
La Chaumière
Le Beaujolais (Banff)
Piq Niq
Post Hotel (Lake Louise)
Priddis Greens (Priddis)
Rouge
Saint Germain

German/Austrian

Bavarian Inn, The (Bragg Creek)
New Berliner
Waldhaus (Banff, *see* Bow Valley Grill)

Greek

Barpa Bill's Souvlaki (Banff, LE)
Manie's
Ouzo
Parthenon
Santorini

Hamburgers/Hot Dogs

Boogie's Burgers (LE)
Buchanan's
Dairy Lane (LE)
Holy Grill, The (LE)
Opus on 8th
Rocky's Burgers (LE)
Tubby Dog (LE)
Vintage
Wild Horse Bistro (Black Diamond)

High Tone

Banffshire Club (Banff,
    see Bow Valley Grill)
Belvedere, The
Capo
Carver's
Catch
Da Guido
Eden (Banff)
Il Sogno
La Chaumière
Le Beaujolais (Banff)
Post Hotel (Lake Louise)
Q
Rimrock, The
Teatro

Historic Setting

Avenue Diner
Belmont Diner (*see* Palace of Eats)
Belvedere, The
Bonterra (*see* Wildwood)
Bow Valley Grill (Banff)
Buzzards
Catch
Cilantro (*see* Velvet at The Grand)
Deer Lodge (Lake Louise,
    see Buffalo Mountain Lodge)
Divino
Fireside Place (Carstairs)
Heartland Cafe
    (2nd Avenue NW location, LE)

163

Il Sogno
Isabella's by Infuse
James Joyce (LE)
Murrieta's (Calgary location)
Piq Niq
Post Hotel (Lake Louise)
Prairie Ink
Ranche, The (*see* Divino)
Reader's Garden Café
Rimrock, The
Rouge
Teatro
Thomsons
Tribune, The
Velvet at The Grand

Indian

Anpurna
Chutney
Clay Oven
Fairmount Spiceland (LE)
Glory of India
Kashmir
Mysore Palace
Namskar (*see* Chutney)
Puspa
Tiffin Curry (LE)
Village Restaurant (Pakistani)

Interesting Ambience

Baker Creek Bistro (Banff)
Bangkoknoi
Bella Italia (Airdrie)
Big Fish
Bistro Twenty Two Ten
Buzzards
Café Metro (LE)
Capo
Casbah, The
Crazyweed Kitchen (Canmore)
Diner Deluxe
Fleur de Sel
Jonas' Restaurant
Kinjo
La Brezza
LeVilla

Living Room, The
Mercato
Moroccan Castle
Muse
Palomino
Pulcinella
Raw Bar
Red Door
Redwater Rustic Grille (*see* Vintage)
River Café
Saint Germain
Sakana Grill
Sandro
Santorini
Thai Place East & West
Thai Sa-on
Victoria's (*see* Reader's Garden Café)

Italian/Pizza

Bella Italia (Airdrie)
Boccavino (*see* Lina's Italian Market, LE)
Bonterra (*see* Wildwood)
Caffè Mauro (LE)
Capo
Centini
Da Guido
DinoRosa's Italian Market (LE)
Il Centro (LE)
Il Sogno
La Brezza
La Tavola (see Q)
Lina's Italian Market (LE)
Mercato
Pimento's (LE)
Pulcinella
Rocky Mountain Flatbread Company
    (Canmore, LE)
Sandro
Spolumbo's
Teatro

Japanese

Chef's Studio (Canmore)
Globefish
Kinjo
Sakana Grill

Shikiji
Sobaten
Sushi Club
Towa Sushi
Wa's
Yuzuki

Latin American

Boca Loca (LE)
Juan's
Las Palmeras (Red Deer)

Middle Eastern

A & A (Lebanese, LE)
Aida's (Lebanese)
Atlas (Persian)
Mediterranea
   (*see* A & A, LE)
Mediterranean Grill (Israeli, LE)
Sahara (Lebanese)
Tazza Grill & Deli (Lebanese, LE)
Village Pita (Lebanese, LE)

Most Obscure

Alexis Bistro
Anpurna
Atlas
Bangkoknoi
Casbah, The
Chef's Studio (Canmore)
Clay Oven
Danube Creperie
Il Centro (LE)
Jonas' Restaurant
Juan's
Koi
Leo Fu's
Mimo
Parthenon
Pavilion, The
Puspa
Rose Garden
Sherry's Caribbean Food (LE)
Thai Nongkhai
Tibet on 10th

Velvet at The Grand
Village Restaurant

Okotoks/Foothills

Bistro Provence (Okotoks)
Divine (Okotoks)
Marv's Classic Soda Shop
   (Black Diamond, LE)
Priddis Greens (Priddis)
Route 40 Soup Company
   (Turner Valley)
Wild Horse Bistro (Black Diamond)

One of a Kind (Almost)

Atlas (Persian)
Bali (Indonesian)
Café Soleil (Banff, Tapas)
Danube Creperie (Serbian)
Jonas' Restaurant (Hungarian)
Little Chef (Family)
Marathon (Ethiopian)
Mimo (Portuguese)
Mt. Everest's Kitchen (Nepalese)
Pfanntastic Pannenkoek Haus (Dutch)
Sherry's Caribbean Food
   (Caribbean, LE)
Tibet on 10th (Tibetan)
Ticino (Banff, Swiss-Italian)
Typhoon (Banff, Eclectic Asian,
   see Café Soleil)

Red Meat

Bavarian Inn, The (Bragg Creek)
Better Butcher, The (LE)
Big T's
Bison Mountain Bistro, The (Banff)
Buchanan's
Buzzards
Café Metro (LE)
Carver's
Fireside Place (Carstairs)
Griesser Spoon, The (Canmore, LE)
LeVilla
Little Chef
New Berliner

Open Range (*see* Big Fish)
Palace of Eats
Palomino
Rimrock, The
Second To None Meats (LE)
Silver Inn
Spolumbo's
Tribune, The
Vintage
Wildwood

Romantic

Casbah, The
Le Beaujolais (Banff)
Living Room, The
Moroccan Castle
Muse
Panorama
Q
Ranche, The (*see* Divino)
Rouge
Simone's Bistro
Teatro

Seafood/Sushi

Big Fish
Boyd's
Catch
Chef's Studio (Canmore)
Globefish
Kinjo
Mimo
Murrieta's (Calgary & Canmore)
North Sea Fish Market (LE)
Pelican Pier (LE)
Raw Bar
River Café
Sakana Grill
Shikiji
Sobaten
Sushi Club
Towa Sushi
Wa's
Yuzuki

Thai

Bangkoknoi
Chili Club
Pad Thai (Banff, *see* Thai Pagoda)
Rose Garden
Thai Boat
Thai Nongkhai
Thai Pagoda (Canmore)
Thai Place East & West
Thai Sa-on

Vegetarian

A & A (LE)
Aida's
Anpurna
Bali
Calgary Farmers' Market (LE)
Casbah, The
Chutney
Clay Oven
Coup, The
Glory of India
Isabella's by Infuse
Kashmir
Koi
Marathon
Mediterranean Grill (LE)
Moroccan Castle
Mt. Everest's Kitchen
Mysore Palace
Namskar (*see* Chutney)
Prairie Ink
Puspa
Shan Tung
Tazza Grill & Deli (LE)
Tibet on 10th
Village Pita (LE)
Village Restaurant

Vietnamese

Mekong
Orchid Room (Vietnamese Fusion)
Saigon
Trong-Khanh

The Best of the Best

THE following will guide you to the best of the best. Entries are in alphabetical order in the "Big Eats" section of the book unless an "LE" notation follows the name of an establishment. LE means the entry is in alphabetical order in the "Little Eats" section. All establishments are in Calgary unless noted otherwise.

Best Bang for the Buck

A & A (LE)
Aida's
Anpurna
Avenue Diner
Barpa Bill's Souvlaki (Banff, LE)
Big T's
Boogie's Burgers (LE)
Coyotes (Banff)
Diner Deluxe
Jonas' Restaurant
La Brezza
La Chaumière
Le Beaujolais (Banff)
Little Chef
Mekong
Pelican Pier (LE)
Prairie Ink
Saigon
Sobaten
Trong-Khanh
Village Restaurant
Wild Horse Bistro (Black Diamond)
Yuzuki

Best Business Lunch

If someone else is paying:
Belgo
Belvedere, The
Buchanan's
Catch
Centini
Il Sogno
La Tavola (*see* Q)
Murrieta's (Calgary & Canmore)
Rimrock, The

Teatro
Thomsons
Tribune, The
Wildwood

If you are paying:
Avenue Diner
Boyd's
Café Metro (LE)
Caffè Mauro (LE)
Chutney
Jonas' Restaurant
Juan's
Lazy Loaf & Kettle (LE)
Piq Niq
Prairie Ink
Rose Garden
Sahara
Saigon
Siding Café (*see* Tribune, The)
Spolumbo's
Vue Cafe (*see* Diner Deluxe)
Yuzuki

Best Patios/Decks

Baker Creek Bistro (Banff)
Bavarian Inn, The (Bragg Creek)
Big Rock Grill
Bistro Provence (Okotoks)
Bonterra (*see* Wildwood)
Buchanan's
Buzzards
Cilantro (*see* Velvet at The Grand)
Cilantro Mountain Café (Banff,
    see Buffalo Mountain Lodge)
Deer Lodge (Lake Louise,
    see Buffalo Mountain Lodge)

La Chaumière
Living Room, The
Muk-a-Muk (Banff)
Prairie Ink
Priddis Greens (Priddis)
Ranche, The (*see* Divino)
River Café
Rouge
Sage Bistro (Canmore)
Teatro
Wildwood

Best People Watching

Belvedere, The
Brava Bistro
Cilantro (*see* Velvet at The Grand)
Coup, The
Divino
Fleur de Sel
Golden Inn
James Joyce (LE)
Lina's Italian Market (LE)
Quarry (Canmore)
Velvet at The Grand

Best Service

Banffshire Club (Banff,
    see Bow Valley Grill)
Belvedere, The
Capo
Centini
Da Guido
Eden (Banff)
Fleur de Sel
Jonas' Restaurant
La Chaumière
Le Beaujolais (Banff)
Leo Fu's

LeVilla
Mt. Everest's Kitchen
Ouzo
Pfanntastic Pannenkoek Haus
Post Hotel (Lake Louise)
Priddis Greens (Priddis)
Q
Rouge
Santorini
Simone's Bistro
Teatro
Thai Boat
Thai Nongkhai
Thai Place East & West
Thai Sa-on
Ticino (Banff)
Tribune, The
Vintage

Best View

Baker Creek Bistro (Banff)
Bow Valley Grill (Banff)
Buffalo Mountain Lodge (Banff)
Cilantro Mountain Café (Banff,
    see Buffalo Mountain Lodge)
Eden (Banff)
Le Beaujolais (Banff)
Muk-a-Muk (Banff)
Murrieta's (Canmore location)
Panorama
Post Hotel (Lake Louise)
Priddis Greens (Priddis)
Q
Quarry (Canmore)
Ranche, The (*see* Divino)
Reader's Garden Café
River Café
Sage Bistro (Canmore)
Waldhaus (Banff,
    see Bow Valley Grill)